INSTRUCTOR'S RESOURCE MANUAL

to accompany

Ramage/Bean/Johnson

The Allyn & Bacon Guide to Writing

Fifth Edition,

Brief Edition,

and

Concise Edition

with

The WPA Outcomes Statement for First-Year Composition

Susanmarie Harrington
Indiana University Purdue University Indianapolis

PEARSON
Longman

New York Boston San Francisco
London Toronto Sydney Tokyo Singapore Madrid
Mexico City Munich Paris Cape Town Hong Kong Montreal

Instructor's Resource Manual to accompany Ramage/Bean/Johnson, *The Allyn & Bacon Guide to Writing, Fifth Edition, Brief Edition and Concise Edition, with The WPA Outcomes Statements for First-Year Composition*

Copyright ©2009 Pearson Education, Inc.

Credit:

"WPA Outcomes Statement for First-Year Composition." © WPA: Writing Program Administration Volume 23.1/2 (Fall/Winter 1999): 59-63, and http://www.wpacouncil.org Used by permission.

ISBN: 0-205-59894-3

1 2 3 4 5 6 7 8 9 10–BIR–11 10 09 08

Table of Contents

Preface

Getting Started

Chapter Guides

Specialized Instruction

Preface

The earlier editions of this instructor's resource manual were enthusiastically received by both experienced and novice teachers, who praised the manual's thoroughness and helpful advice. In this edition, the strengths of the earlier editions have been retained, while the contents have been revised and updated in accordance with the changes and improvements made in the fifth edition of *The Allyn & Bacon Guide to Writing*. Most notably, discussions are included for all new readings, material has been added to support the text's new emphasis on analyzing visual rhetoric, all chapters are expanded in keeping with similar revisions in the textbook, and new chapters are included to accompany the text's new chapters on rhetorical theory and writing about field research data. In addition, the manual's early chapters have changed in light of the significant reorganization of material in Part 1 of the textbook. If you are familiar with the earlier edition of this instructor's resource manual, you will also note that even in places where the textbook remained unchanged, the manual has been revised for improved clarity and direction.

The manual begins with "General Teaching Strategies," a review of practical suggestions presented in a question-and-answer format. If you would like even more supplementary guidance of this nature, the following texts are suggested: *The Allyn & Bacon Sourcebook for College Writing Teachers* by James C. McDonald (a collection of scholarship on composition theory and pedagogy), *Teaching College Writing* by Maggy Smith (practical tips especially helpful for new writing teachers), *An Introduction to Teaching Composition in an Electronic Environment* by Eric Hoffman and Carol Scheidenhelm, and *In Our Own Voice: Graduate Students Teach Writing* by Tina Lavonne Good and Leanne B. Warshauer.

Other major sections of the manual you may want to read carefully offer advice for planning a syllabus based on *The Allyn & Bacon Guide to Writing* and using the textbook with non-native speakers and/or in an electronic classroom. The manual also contains answers to the handbook exercises found in the full edition.

The last chapter in this manual highlights the ways in which *The Allyn & Bacon Guide to Writing*'s approach offers many opportunities for students to work in each of the four domains outlined in *The Council of Writing Program Administrators Outcomes Statement*.

Each remaining chapter in this manual, numbered to correspond with the chapters in *The Allyn & Bacon Guide to Writing*, contains these sections: "Understanding the Chapter's Goals"; "Reinforcing the Chapter's Rhetorical Principles"; "Using the 'For Writing and Discussion' Activities"; and "Guiding Students through the Writing Project." Chapters 5 through 16, devoted to the writing projects, also include "Discussing the Readings." You will find the manual most helpful if you at least skim the chapter in the textbook first. Together, the textbook and the manual will give you ample methods to engage your students in the vital study of writing.

Acknowledgments

I am greatly indebted to my colleagues at Indiana University Purdue University Indianapolis, whose ingenuity and creativity show me new approaches to teaching writing with every hallway conversation and formal workshop or meeting. In addition, I am grateful to students I have taught at IUPUI. Their work helps me see new ways to apply the framework of *The Allyn & Bacon Guide to Writing* with each new class period. Any errors or infelicities here are of my own creation.

I am also grateful to Vicki Byard of Northeastern Illinois University. She wrote the first two editions of this resource manual. Her excellent work forms the foundation of this edition.

General Teaching Strategies

Overview

In this opening section of the instructor's manual, you will find many practical suggestions to help you accomplish your responsibilities as a writing teacher. If you are a teaching assistant or beginning instructor, you may want to read this section now and review it again as the course progresses. Even if you are a more experienced teacher, you are still likely to find ideas in this section that can enhance your expertise. Scan the headings for concerns that especially interest you. The teaching concerns addressed are these:

- Preparing for the First Day of Class
- Designing Lesson Plans
- Fostering Student Participation
- Asking Questions
- Discussing Readings
- Explaining In-Class Activities
- Assigning Homework
- Facilitating Peer Review Workshops on Drafts
- Conferencing with Students
- Managing Journals and Portfolios
- Grading
- Keeping Records
- Handling Difficult Situations and Students
- Seeking Feedback to Improve Your Teaching
- Reading More about Teaching Strategies

Beneath each heading, the teaching strategies are presented in a question-answer format to help you quickly identify your concerns and find workable solutions.

Recommended are four additional texts to supplement this discussion of general teaching strategies: *The Allyn & Bacon Sourcebook for College Writing Teachers* by James C. McDonald; *Teaching College Writing* by Maggy Smith; *An Introduction to Teaching Composition in an Electronic Environment* by Eric Hoffman and Carol Scheidenhelm; and *In Our Own Voice: Graduate Students Teach Writing* by Tina Lavonne Good and Leanne B. Warshauer (all are described in the annotated bibliography that appears at the end of this chapter). Contact your Pearson representative if you would like complimentary copies of any of these texts. You may also wish to access MyCompLab for additional resources at www.mycomplab.com.

Preparing for the First Day of Class

What handouts should I prepare for the first class?

The most important document is the syllabus. It's the first formal presentation of the course, and it gives students an idea of your goals and teaching style as well as key course policies. Later in this chapter of this instructor's manual there are suggestions for designing syllabi for quarter-length and semester-length writing courses that use *The Allyn & Bacon Guide to Writing*. In addition to a description of the course goals, an overview of major assignments, grading policies, and a review of any prerequisites, the syllabus should offer a daily or weekly schedule of requirements and activities. Even if you plan to distribute a more detailed schedule as the course moves ahead, use the initial syllabus to show students major deadlines, approximate reading and writing homework expectations, and examples of regular in-class activities. The syllabus should also provide contact information: when and where students can reach you (your office location and hours, your office phone number, fax number if you use it, and your e-mail address). The syllabus should also communicate your expectations for students' behavior (what kinds of participation you expect, what penalties may be imposed for absence or late work, for example), as well as what students may expect from you (how quickly do you respond to essays, for example). If you have firm preferences for the format of assignments, outline those on the syllabus, even if they will be repeated on individual assignment sheets. Tell students up front whether you accept handwritten essays, require that planning work be turned in with the final version, prefer particular margin settings, or have opinions about the uses of staples, paper clips, or folders.

Another document many teachers like to distribute on the first day is a questionnaire that asks students information about themselves. You may want to know how you can contact them if necessary outside class time (address, home and work phone numbers, e-mail address), their year in school, their academic advisor, their major(s) and possible minor(s), their prior writing experience, other responsibilities at home or work that may limit the time they can devote to your course, and any special concerns they may have about this course. While some teachers ask students to write basic contact information on index cards or ask students to answer these questions on their own paper, others prefer a questionnaire so that students can complete the form at home and return it when the class next meets. Any students who miss the first day of class can simply be handed the questionnaire to complete, along with the syllabus and other course handouts they may have missed. A questionnaire also allows for a few open-ended questions that can acquaint you with students more quickly and can be used as a disguised (and therefore less anxiety-provoking) diagnostic of students' writing abilities. Some possible opening-day questions include:

- What are your tentative educational and career goals? What previous writing courses have you had? What types of papers did you write in these courses?
- Do you usually like or dislike writing? Why?
- What kinds of reading and writing do you do outside of school?
- What is your opinion of your writing ability? What are your strengths? Your weaknesses?
- What do you hope to accomplish in this writing course? Are there any particular aspects of your writing ability you want more help with?

What should I try to accomplish during the first few class sessions?

Certainly it's important that students learn the goals of the course and what work will be required of them. Using the first class period to begin working on the first writing assignment communicates to students that class time matters and will be used to help assignments move forward. Design a first-day, in-class writing assignment that functions as a lead-in to the first assignment. Collecting writing quickly from your students will allow you to begin a routine of reading and responding to student work, and it will allow you to get a feel for the writing styles in your class.

The first few class sessions are also vitally important for establishing the learning environment you want to create and for building rapport with your students. Try to learn your students' names as quickly as possible, asking them to correct your mispronunciations and to tell you if they prefer to be called by other names or shortened nicknames. It may help you to ask students to identify themselves before they speak in class for the first few sessions. Call students by name as often as possible so that students can learn each other's names as well.

Some teachers like to use an icebreaker during the first or second class to help students become acquainted. An icebreaker makes students more comfortable with the teacher and their classmates, which can make participating in subsequent class discussions and small group activities less intimidating. Because students may be self-conscious introducing themselves, a common icebreaker is for students to interview each other in pairs and then each introduce his or her partner to the class.

Another icebreaker that works well is to give students a list of tasks and ask them to circulate among the room until they have completed every task. The tasks are structured to promote information conversation and get students learning each other's names quickly. You can ask students, for example, to find someone who spends twice as much time as they do driving to campus, someone who has more siblings than they do, someone who has never read their own favorite book, someone who went to a similar-sized high school, etc. This icebreaker gets students moving around the room, starting conversations that identify similarities and differences in the group.

You may also want to address during the first few class sessions your students' attitudes about writing or school that could affect their work in your course. In small groups or as a class, ask students to discuss how their current attitudes toward writing developed. What did they like and dislike about their past writing courses, their past writing instructors, and their past writing assignments? Explaining ways this course is likely to be different from their past writing courses—such as the opportunity to write open-form texts explained in Chapter 1 of *The Allyn & Bacon Guide to Writing*—may increase their enthusiasm for the course. It is helpful for students to be aware of any attitudes they may have that may affect the way they approach working in college, and it is also helpful for students to set personal goals for the semester.

During the first few class sessions, try to use the full range of pedagogical formats you intend to use throughout the term (for example, lecture, class discussion with the chairs arranged traditionally, class discussion with the chairs arranged in a large circle, and small group work). When students are introduced to various seating arrangements and activities quite early in the term, they have more time to get used to the demands of each format.

Designing Lesson Plans

Why are lesson plans important?

While the syllabus provides the goals and schedule for the entire term, a lesson plan indicates the goals and agenda for one class session. To understand why both macroscopic and microscopic plans are important, consider the similarity between designing a writing course and designing a handmade quilt. For both, the maker needs to be concerned with the pattern of each smaller unit (each class meeting; each quilt square) as well as how the smaller units are artistically combined to contribute to the larger product (the course or quilt). Obviously, such complex planning is difficult to complete in one's head. Writing lesson plans helps you to prepare for each class more thoroughly. Planning for each session in writing also prompts you to reflect on how to connect one class to the next.

The lesson plan has two audiences: you and your students. For teachers, lesson plans provide an organization and a structure. For students, lesson plans help them recognize the structure within each unit. Once you set goals for each class period with the lesson plan, communicate them with students. This helps students learn more effectively.

What should a good lesson plan include?

Begin designing your lesson plan by deciding on the objectives for the class session (based on the syllabus), the chapter of *The Allyn & Bacon Guide to Writing* students are currently reading, and their upcoming writing project. Once you've articulated the goal for the day—and one main goal is plenty—decide how that objective can be practically achieved.

Think of the class session as several fifteen- or twenty-minute segments. Strive to cover just one main concept per time segment, using a variety of examples and in-class activities to illustrate the concept. According to composition scholar George Hillocks, who systematically compiled the results of over sixty research studies of different pedagogical approaches to writing courses, students learn writing most effectively through hands-on, inductive activities that allow them to grapple with the underlying principles at stake. The in-class activity may be done individually, in pairs or small groups, or as a full class. Afterward, the teacher facilitates a discussion of the concepts learned through the activity. Optimally, each class period will introduce a new skill or activity, will allow students the chance to practice that activity with others, and will then ask students to work on their own.

Thus, when you are developing lesson plans, try to think of activities that can introduce students experientially to the concepts you wish them to understand. There are many ideas for such activities in *The Allyn & Bacon Guide to Writing* textbook and this manual, but add your own as well. Rather than creating a lesson plan that focuses on the question "What will *I* be doing during class?" try planning the class by asking, "What will the *students* be doing during class?" and "What will students be able to do after class that they couldn't do before?" Answering these questions will help you create lesson plans that keep each assignment moving according to your schedule.

In addition to in-class activities, it is helpful to plan in advance some provocative questions for class discussion (see "Asking Questions" on page 9).

You may want to begin each class session by quickly outlining for students in a corner of the chalkboard the agenda for that day's class session. Both you and students can then keep the day's goals in mind and be less tempted to drift from the topic. Previewing the plans with students also helps them to better understand the relationships among that day's discussion topics. End every class by asking student volunteers to summarize the principles they learned during the period and the relationship of these principles to students' next writing project. Also announce any homework, remind students what, if anything, they need to hand in that day, and forecast the topic of the next class meeting.

How do I decide how much to cover in each class session?

The mistake that many beginning teachers make is trying to cover too much in a class session. As you gain teaching experience, you will be better able to judge how much material to cover. You will also learn that, even for the same course at the same college, each group of students learns at a different rate. Thus, you will need to make adjustments as you get to know each class each term.

As a guideline for starting out, limit your lesson plan to just two or three concepts for each class session; then decide what activities you will use to teach these. Reserve time to discuss the activities afterward. Until you become comfortable with managing class time, also plan a brief discussion topic or activity that can be done if students finish what you've planned much more quickly than you expected. If this additional idea isn't needed, you may use it at the beginning of the next class session or save it for another day when the discussion ends prematurely. If you always have a standby discussion topic or activity ready, you'll have no need to panic and dismiss students early, a detrimental precedent that can make students less attentive at the end of subsequent class sessions.

Fostering Student Participation

Why is student participation important?

Participation helps students learn better: they get to try out their ideas and, based on the response they receive from you and classmates, probe their own understanding further. Through student participation, the classroom becomes less teacher centered. Students can learn much from each other; encourage students to directly address and respond to each other in full-class discussions, rather than using you as an intermediary.

How can I encourage more student participation?

The most important thing you can do to encourage student participation is to show students that participation matters. If you organize class activities so that students who participate in them move forward on whatever writing project is underway, students will value their participation. If participation comes to mean joining in a conversation about an essay in the book that is not clearly connected to the next writing assignment, or joining a conversation about current events without a related writing project underway, students will not see participating in class as valuable. Strive to construct activities that get students working with their drafts, developing new material or evaluating old material. If the activities you plan make a difference in the evolution of formal writing projects, students will respond well.

A good principle for encouraging participation: assign homework before every class period that requires students to prepare something, even if it is an answer to a simple question, a short informal writing assignment, or some additions to a current draft. Have discussions and activities that enable students to work with others during the class period to build on that preparation, and then assign homework that allows students to practice alone what they did with others in class. This cycle will ensure that each class period follows well on the next, and it will get students into a consistent habit of participation and preparation.

Sometimes students don't participate in discussions because they don't feel they are an integral part of the class. If you frequently lecture for long periods, they may think their involvement is unimportant and remain passive even when you ask them for their input. Try to routinely structure class so that students have an opportunity to speak within the first ten minutes of the period. Students will then be likely to contribute to discussions more often and at more length.

The majority of students in the class may also be quiet if they feel that a few vocal people are willing and able to carry the class discussion. Acknowledge frequent contributors but don't let any one student monopolize the discussion (e.g., "Thanks, David. I see your hand, but is there someone who hasn't spoken today who'd like to answer?"). You may have a student who regularly blurts out answers to your questions, while others wait to be called upon. Often a student who speaks out of turn sits in the front of the room and does not realize that students sitting further back want to participate. Simply ask this eager student to raise his or her hand so that you can include everyone in the discussion.

To encourage your students to participate more equally, direct questions to students sitting in different areas of the room. Make sure your eye contact is with all students, but particularly those in an area of the room where few people talk. If you tend to stand or sit in the front of the classroom, move from side to side rather than regularly positioning yourself in front of the same students. If you walk around in the front of the room, walk towards the desks of the students who are most quiet or inattentive; often your physical presence alone will be enough to regain their attention and invite them to speak.

Sometimes students need a "warm-up" to discussion. If you want the class to discuss material they read for homework, first ask someone to summarize that reading, to remind the class of its contents. Then ask remaining students to add any other details they remember as important that weren't yet mentioned. After focusing their minds on the reading in this manner, students will be better equipped to answer more challenging questions. If students are non-responsive when you ask a difficult, abstract question, give them a few minutes to first explore an answer in writing themselves or discuss their impressions with a classmate, and then ask several students to share their ideas with the class.

The examples you use to illustrate writing concepts also affect students' participation. Your examples should reflect the diversity of your students' backgrounds. For example, if some of your students are older than recent high school graduates, using activities or discussion topics that imply dependency on a parent will make these students feel they are not equal members of the class. Be alert to other possible biases in your examples too: gender, race, ethnicity, socioeconomic class, ablebodiedness, religion, etc. Use gender-neutral terms such as "significant other" or "partner" if you refer to romantic relationships to avoid assuming all students are heterosexual. If you show awareness of students' differences and accommodate the breadth of their identities in class discussion, students who might feel they are a minority within the class will feel more comfortable participating.

Students are also more likely to talk in class when they feel comfortable with the other students. You may want to hold discussions with the class sitting in a large circle so students can see one another. If so, vary the location of your own seat each time so that you become a more integral part of the circle and no one spot becomes viewed as the position of authority. Small group activities can also help students become acquainted and feel more comfortable sharing their thoughts.

When students do talk, listen. Nothing else you can do is more powerful in soliciting further student participation. Ask follow-up questions respectfully and encouragingly. Whenever possible, validate students' participation by using the students' exact wording in your response and when you write their ideas on the chalkboard.

When a student gives a wrong answer, how you respond will affect not only that student's future participation in class but also the participation of every student who considers it intimidating to talk in class. Never embarrass a student. First try to find the source of the person's misunderstanding by asking, "Why do you think that?" (ask this of students who give correct answers too) and, if possible, then ask questions about his or her explanation that will eventually lead to the correct answer. Instead of stepping in as the "answer giver," give that role to the class by asking, "Does anyone disagree? Why?" Even if the first person to disagree gives the correct answer, if you think other students will have different responses, ask for their views too, and lead the class to explore all the responses that are given.

Is it fair to require all students to talk in class?

Deciding whether or not to require all students to participate in class is difficult because the decision must be based on two quite significant yet disparate issues: what role you believe participation plays in the learning process, and how committed you are to respecting students' personal (and even cultural) differences.

A colleague tells a story about encountering a former student whom she had during his first semester of college. On the point of graduation, the student told my colleague how much he had enjoyed her course, even though he was aware she might not have realized this because he had never spoken in class. "In fact," he said, with obvious regret, "I've never spoken in any college class I've taken." He was a second-language student who feared other students might not understand his accent; the motives may differ for other silent students. This conversation illustrates that if teachers can do more to nurture into classroom discourse those students who almost never speak, particularly in first-year courses, their entire educational experience may change.

If you notice students who haven't spoken after the first several weeks of class, you may want to call on them at particularly non-threatening times (to answer a simple question or to read a brief passage from the textbook aloud). Another strategy to help excessively quiet students feel comfortable speaking is to gently tell them after class that you've noticed they haven't participated and then identify a specific question or topic you'll ask them about during the following class period so that they will have a chance to prepare. With a few such empathetic nudges, silent students may begin to participate more regularly.

If any portion of the course grade is determined by students' participation, clearly identify for students how you will evaluate this, and at several points during the term tell them their current participation grade

Asking Questions

What kinds of questions should I ask?

All questions are useful, but they serve different purposes. Some questions have a single correct answer and are helpful in assessing students' comprehension. Other questions have many possible answers and require higher-level thinking skills, such as synthesis, analysis, and evaluation. You may want to sequence questions so that what you ask becomes increasingly difficult as the discussion progresses. Also consider asking questions for which you don't have an answer in mind, such as questions that ask students to speculate about hypothetical situations. Use follow-up questions liberally to urge students to elaborate on their brief or general responses.

What are common mistakes when asking questions?

Teachers often do not pause long enough after asking a question to allow students to formulate an answer. If students don't answer after an *extended* pause, you may want to rephrase it or give them a few minutes to explore their responses in writing. Be sure that your question is specific enough to direct their thinking (not "Does anyone have any responses to chapter three?"). Also be careful not to ask several different questions at once, which can make students unsure of which question you want answered.

Discussing Readings

How should the essays in the textbook be discussed?

You may want to devote some time to discussing the content of essays included in the text, yet the readings are primarily intended to illustrate the rhetorical principles discussed in each chapter. Using the questions provided in both *The Allyn & Bacon Guide to Writing* and this instructor's manual, direct students to analyze the decisions the writer made in shaping the text.

You may also want to solicit students' impressions of the readings in order to make them more aware of readers' needs. If they complain that they disliked an essay or found it boring, can they explain why? Do they think most readers would have a similar reaction? Did their reactions to the piece change for the better or worse as they read? Why? How could the same topic be handled in a way that they would enjoy more? If they liked an essay, they should also be pressed to explain why. What from the reading is most memorable to them? Help students understand that it is not exclusively (or even primarily) the topic of the essay that determines its merit for readers. If they analyze their own responses as readers, they will discover techniques they may want to avoid or emulate.

Explaining In-Class Activities

How can I give instructions so that my students begin work quickly and stay on task

Students often are slow to start in-class activities because they don't know what's expected of them. Giving them five types of information can help them work more productively:

- What process they are to follow
- What product they should produce (including its length and state of completion)
- How much time they will have in which to work
- What will be done with the finished product: will it be turned in? shared with the class? graded? if graded, based on what criteria and what percentage of the course grade is this assignment worth?
- What the relationship is between the activity and the writing principles being discussed in class and/or the students' next major assignment.

If an in-class activity consists of several sequential tasks, explain only one at a time and let the students complete each part before you explain the next. If the activity is one that students will do in groups, have them move their chairs into groups before you explain the activity so that the groups will be ready to begin as soon as you finish giving the instructions.

What should be done after students finish an in-class activity?

Lead the class to discuss the lessons learned from each activity, particularly how those lessons apply to other writing that students will do. If the activity is done in small groups, structure the discussion so that the groups report their conclusions to the class through turn taking: ask the first group to tell one of its ideas; ask the next group to then share one different idea it generated; continue this turn taking with no group repeating what another has said. When one group has exhausted its ideas, simply pass over that group until all the ideas of every group have been voiced. This turn-taking method helps to keep the students in every group attentive throughout the discussion, rather than only when it is time for their group to speak. Turn taking also allows all groups to receive recognition for their ideas, rather than having the last group or two speak after most possible responses have already been given. Insisting on some product from each group activity—whether it is a report, or something turned in for participation points or a grade—keeps groups accountable for their work.

Assigning Homework

How much homework should I assign?

Many colleges have a published statement in their catalogue about the amount of time students should expect to spend on each course, usually three hours for each hour of class time (although national data suggests most students study about four hours a week for all their courses, making this commonly heard estimate of three hours of study time for each credit hour wildly unrealistic). Students write at vastly different paces, making it hard to judge how much homework to assign. You should also consider several traits of your student body when determining how much work to require outside class: the average course load of your students; the typical work and family responsibilities of your students; and students' skill in working independently. Based on these factors, you can judge what quantity and difficulty of homework will reasonably challenge your students. If you ask too much of them, they may feel that complete success is impossible and lose the incentive to even try. However, asking some amount of regular homework will keep students moving on their writing projects. Homework helps students prepare for class, so keep a regular homework schedule. If you assign journals, consider having the journals turned in according to a regular pattern (every Thursday, or the first class of every month). Patterns to homework make it easier for students to do their assignment.

Some brief tasks may be done during class time even more effectively than at home. If you want to discuss an essay in *The Allyn & Bacon Guide to Writing* that is only a page or two long, you may want to give students a few minutes to read it during class before discussing it, particularly if what you do during the first half of class time will prepare students well for the reading. Because their recall of the reading will be stronger, the discussion of the essay may be more enlivened and thorough than if students had read the essay for homework. Similarly, you may occasionally want to give students a few minutes to freewrite during class, where you can observe their behavior and urge those who stop for prolonged breaks to push themselves to keep writing. Of course, longer readings and writing exercises that require more extensive thought should be assigned for homework.

How should I evaluate homework?

Deciding how to evaluate written homework assignments requires you to weigh the management of your own workload against providing an incentive for students to complete the work conscientiously. A portion of students' course grades may be reserved for short homework and miscellaneous assignments (for example, some teachers give a grade to students' critiques of their peers' drafts) and if this is the case, the percentage should be identified on your syllabus. Then clearly explain to students how they can track their grade for these short assignments as the semester progresses (how much is a "check" or "check minus" worth?).

You can manage your own workload by having students receive more detailed responses to their short written assignments from the class. Use homework tasks as the basis for class discussion and call on students to share their ideas or even read what they wrote. You can also have students meet in small groups to provide one another with feedback on their assignments. When you then grade the work, your comments can be brief.

Facilitating Peer Review Workshops on Drafts

Why are peer review workshops important?

The most obvious benefit to peer review workshops is that the writers receive suggestions for revising their texts. But writers also benefit by having to make decisions about advice that may not be consistent among group members; such decision making prepares them for more independent life-long development of their writing skills. Peer review workshops can positively affect the identity of students too. When they know that their texts will be read by people other than the teacher, they may no longer compose texts as students completing assignments, but instead as writers who need to win their audience's interest.

Students also profit from critiquing others' work. By reading others' texts, students get to see a variety of ways that the same writing project can be approached, which in turn can increase their own creativity. When they cannot rely on the teacher to evaluate a text's merits, they can no longer dismiss writing as others' expertise and must try out their own critical abilities. As they listen to how other students in the group respond to the same draft, they learn what they overlooked in their own reading and become more critical readers.

Should I assign the students to groups or let them pick their own?

When students are given brief in-class activities, it may be easiest for them to work with students sitting near them; however, when students critique each other's drafts, I believe it is best to assign groups. Place students so that the groups are as evenly balanced as possible in gender, age, race, and ethnicity. Also make sure the groups all have at least one extroverted person who you think is likely to lead the group if others are withdrawn. It is also wise not to place friends in the same group: they are likely to read each other's drafts anyway, and it can offset the balance of a group if some members are far more familiar than others. It may similarly disrupt the balance of a group if students whose native language is not English are placed in groups in which some of the students speak their native language and others don't. A fringe benefit of assigning students who normally sit in different areas of the room to the same group is that as students get to know other members of the class better, students' participation in class discussions often improves.

You must also decide how students' levels of writing skills will affect how you group students. Some teachers like to diversify the skill levels in each group, on the premise that there will be at least one student in each group who can give quality feedback and the papers submitted for grades will thus be stronger. My own preference is to group students of equal abilities together. This way, the students with better skills receive helpful peer comments as well, rather than serving merely as tutors. Also, the students who are weaker writers are not tempted to simply let a peer "fix" their work. Of course, it is impossible to fully honor all of these criteria when forming groups—demographic diversity, outspokenness, native language, and writing ability—but do so as much as possible.

The size of peer groups should be based on how much time students will have to discuss the papers. Whenever possible, assign at least three students to each group to allow the chance for reviewers to disagree. When a group needs to resolve differences of opinion about a draft, all members of the group learn. Having more than five students makes a group unwieldy; the group members rarely participate equally. If the number of students in your class doesn't divide evenly, put the better students in a smaller group because they will still use the allotted time well. Also, if there are students who are regularly absent, assign them to larger groups or distribute them among all groups so that on the day of workshops, absences aren't likely to make any group too small.

The first time you assign groups, as you read off names and tell students which area of the room to convene in, locate the groups that you expect to have more difficulty in the front of the room, where you'll be able to eavesdrop more easily and can intervene if necessary. Groups with the strongest students can be positioned in more remote corners of the room.

Teachers differ on whether or not to change the assignment of groups throughout the term. Some teachers think it helps students to see how a wide range of students are completing the assignments. I prefer to keep the groups' membership consistent throughout the term for several reasons. First, if groups are assigned thoughtfully, as just described, it may be difficult for other arrangements to work as well. Second, the public exposure of one's work to a group of peers can at times be more intimidating than giving an assignment to the teacher. If students stay in the same group all term, they become more at ease with the other people in their group. However, you may want to rotate pairings for other kinds of activities to ensure that the whole class dynamic stays productive. If every group activity takes place in the same groups all semester long, cliques can form and sometimes disrupt whole class functioning.

The most helpful reason to keep the peer review groups consistent, I believe, is that students can then have the opportunity to observe and discuss the development of each other's writing abilities throughout the term, not just individual papers. A student who worked particularly hard on an assignment is more likely to be enthusiastically praised if his or her group members have read the student's prior assignments and notice the improvement. If a student's paper is noticeably weaker than earlier assignments, the group can recognize that too and help the student better diagnose the difficulty. Of course, if a group doesn't work well together, some substitutions should be made before the groups meet again. I recommend keeping the group membership the same, though, after any necessary adjustments early in the term.

What process will help students conduct peer reviews most effectively?

The three most common models of peer review workshops are described in Chapter 17 of *The Allyn & Bacon Guide to Writing*. Choose whichever of these models is likely to work best for your class. Students who work well independently can give more thoughtful responses if they prepare in advance, whereas less skilled students may need to interact with peers to thoroughly analyze a draft.

However you set up your groups, it is very helpful to have students prepare a writer's statement in advance of the peer review. A writer's statement is a type of single reflection (see Chapter 25 in *The Allyn & Bacon Guide to Writing*) that organizes the writer's thoughts about the work completed. At the start of the semester, give detailed instructions about the writer's statement; you may ask students to identify key portions of the assignment (where is the summary, where is the strong response, where is the thesis, for example), and you may ask students to report on the process they used to develop the draft. This gives the peer group valuable information about what has led up to the current draft. Perhaps the most important part of a writer's statement, however, is questions for reviewers. You will need to train students to ask good questions, which will help reviewers target their attention. Questions like "How can I make this draft better?" "What grade do you think this will get?" and "What did you think?" are not helpful, as they are vague and don't reflect anything about the writer's own thoughts. Questions like "Am I getting off topic in the introduction when I talk about walking my sister to the corner on her first day of school?" or "Does my tone on page 3 seem harsh? I'm trying to be fair to the people who disagree with the decision I'm describing" help readers understand the writer's purpose and will set up good conversations.

Whether the draft is initially critiqued at home or in class, the writer should provide a copy of the text for each member of the group so that others can refer to specific areas of the texts in their comments and can respond to concerns of organization and paragraphing more readily. If the group first encounters the draft in class, require the writer to read the draft aloud while their group members follow along on their own copies. Practically, this allows all readers to finish reading simultaneously and prevents the writer from waiting, nervous and unoccupied, while others read. The writer has a chance to correct errors or confusing details that may have gone unnoticed while proofreading, and the other group members may get a better sense of the writer's investment in the draft by his or her vocal expression, which can help shape how they present their responses. Because all the groups will be reading and/or talking, only the members of the writer's small group are likely to hear the contents of the paper. After the writer finishes reading, group members should be given a minute to look back through the text and gather their thoughts before speaking.

Whether students read the drafts in advance at home or in class, the discussion should always begin with the writer's request for help with one specific skill or section of the paper. This can be based in the writer's statement. In this way, the writer's chief concern is addressed and group members are cast in the positive role of aides, not judges, making both the writer and readers more likely to participate in the critique process comfortably.

After the group members address the writer's primary concern, they can share other ideas they have for revising the paper and identify what they view as the paper's strengths. While they may respond to the paper's subject matter—conveying content is, after all, why people write—they should spend the majority of their time discussing the paper's rhetorical strategies. To help students use their time productively, use (or adapt) the "Guidelines for Peer Reviewers" at the end of each chapter in Part Two of *The Allyn & Bacon Guide to Writing.* Direct students to spend most of their discussion time for each draft on difficulties that span more than one paragraph: if the thesis of the paper is unclear, the draft may need to be revised so extensively that the sentences now containing minor errors will no longer be included in the revision.

Instruct groups to discuss each draft collaboratively, rather than having each student provide individual feedback in turn. When groups are interactive, they challenge or confirm each other's opinions and reach consensus about a draft better. As students work, watch their interactions and intervene if they are not talking with one another.

What are common problems with peer review workshops and how can I minimize them?

One obstacle to small group work, whether responding to drafts or any other in-class activity, is that students are more accustomed to class sessions that focus on the teacher. Thus they may feel awkward or nervous when the traditional classroom format is altered. When you ask them to move into small groups, they may not fully face each other.

Someone may sit a bit outside the group or, if no one in the group assumes responsibility for initiating the activity, they may begin completing the assignment individually. You can correct such reticence to group work simply by noticing it, walking over to the group, and asking for the change you'd like (e.g., "Could you scoot your chairs so there's room for John to move into the group more?" or "I'd like you all to discuss each draft together, not just pass them around and write comments. Which paper do you want to discuss first?").

Often students who are asked to critique another student's draft will distrust their ability to do so. They may purposely undermine their comments by admitting that they have not done well in past writing courses, or they may state that only the teacher's opinion matters because that is the person assigning grades. Some students overemphasize proofreading as a way to resist critiquing others' work, confident only when they can offer objective corrections and convinced that any other suggestion they might make would be arbitrary.

You can increase students' confidence in their judgment by critiquing a sample draft with the class for each writing project. Role-play the writer of the draft and have the class role-play members of your small group. If they offer you general advice, such as "Add more examples," model how a writer should ask for more specific guidance: "Where?" If students disagree in their advice, don't succumb to their requests that you supply the answer, but ask them to resolve the conflict themselves as they would need to do in groups when the teacher is not present. I have also found it helpful to ask students to discuss what grade an essay might get. In my experience, classes are quite skilled at assigning letter grades on anonymously authored drafts. Asking them to explain their reasons for assigning that grade can help students to summarize the critique and remind them to devote their greatest attention to large concerns, not minor errors.

Even when group members willingly share specific suggestions, sometimes writers become defensive and monopolize the workshop time with justifications of their writing decisions. You can reduce this tendency by reminding students before the workshops begin that each writer has final authority in deciding what revisions to make in his or her text. Tell students that because there is limited time to discuss each paper, writers should restrict their own explanations of the paper and seek to discover how the writing is perceived by readers. If one person has a response they disagree with, they may want to disregard that suggestion, but if most of the group suggests a revision they dislike, it may be an indication that their text is coming across quite differently than they realize.

You may have groups that finish responding to the drafts well before the class session is finished and ask if they may leave early. Allowing early dismissal sets a detrimental precedent. If other groups see some students leaving, they may rush through the drafts they haven't yet discussed. Also, if students learn they can leave class when they finish their group work, they may not be as thorough in future class sessions when they participate in peer review workshops. The best remedy for this problem is prevention: before students meet in groups for the first time, tell them that they must stay for the entire class session so they should pace their discussion of the drafts equally.

Peer review activities need not take up a whole class period, and if you find that groups are consistently finishing early, you may want to rethink your timing. Particularly early in the semester, it is more effective to start with shorter review assignments that help students learn how review groups function. With tight time constraints students may stay on task better, and they will gradually move into spending longer on reviews. Structuring reviews so that the tasks get more complicated over the course of the semester is a good way to help students learn how to be effective peer reviewers. Responding to writing is difficult work, as any writing teacher knows, and students will need support and instruction in order to improve their own skills in this area.

You can help in this pacing by periodically announcing the time and saying how far along the groups should be (how many drafts done, how many to go). If a group still finishes early, you can prompt them to be more thorough by asking each member of the group what suggestions he or she received for revising the paper. If, for example, the student says, "They told me to include more examples," ask the student to tell you what places in the paper need additional examples and what those examples could be. If the student cannot be specific, you can then direct the group to help that writer further. In a group that finishes early, there is almost always at least one student who doesn't know how to apply the group's suggestions specifically, so redirecting the group in this way gives them more to work on. If all in the group are convinced they have nothing else to discuss, direct them to use the remaining class time to begin revising.

What should I be doing while my students are working?

If you join a group, students will view you as the authority and be less likely to assert their own opinions about a draft. Instead, be available as a resource person if any group has a question that no member of the group can answer. Even then, it is helpful not to sit down with the group, which could prompt you to stay longer. Rather, model your behavior after a Chinese juggler, who keeps several plates swirling on top of poles, returning to quickly spin whichever is beginning to wobble, but staying only long enough to give it the momentum it needs to keep moving.

When no group needs your help, watch the dynamics of the groups carefully from the front of the room. If any group is especially quiet, approach it and ask what's causing the difficulty. You can also use your time to check that each student has his or her draft completed and, if it does not excessively interfere with a group's progress, you might call a student who has been doing poorly in the class to confer with you in the front of the room about his or her work. Avoid interrupting groups that seem to be working productively without your assistance.

Conferencing with Students

Why is conferencing with students important?

Conferences constitute the safety net that ensures each student receives individual attention, that comments you make on papers are reinforced, and that students' needs get voiced. Some teachers use conferences to respond to every paper a student writes, while other teachers schedule only periodic conferences with students throughout the term or perhaps just a midterm conference to assess with each student his or her progress.

However frequently they are held, conferences allow you to individualize your instruction, much like mini-tutorials. You may want to use conference time to help each student identify the consistent strengths and weaknesses of his or her previous assignments and then set goals for their future work. Conferences also give you the chance to discuss problematic behavior with students, such as frequent absences, tardiness, or missed tutorial appointments.

How can I manage conferences most effectively?

Prepare a sign-up sheet to take to class so that students will have a precise time to see you. Impress upon students the importance of arriving on time or calling your office if an emergency requires that they reschedule the conference. Then explain to the class the format you will use when you meet with them each individually.

If you are using the conference to respond to the draft of a writing project or to grade its revision, you may either read it with the student during the conference or in advance. In either case, remember that the chief asset of conferencing with students is the teacher-student dialogue conferences permit, so be careful not to monopolize the discussion. Ask the student his or her own reactions to the paper and together devise a plan of action for revising the paper or, if this is a final graded version, applying what has been learned from this paper to the next writing project.

In my own experience, periodic conferences work best when students are told they will direct the discussion and are given an assignment to help them prepare. For example, you might tell students to look at your comments on their last several papers and list what writing skills they most need to improve. They can prepare to discuss with you their plans for improving this skill and how they intend to address it in their next writing project. In the conference, you can then confirm or redirect their plans. You might also assign students to come to the conference with one or two questions they have about what has been discussed in class or what they have been reading in *The Allyn & Bacon Guide to Writing*.

Managing Journals and Portfolios

Why and how might I assign journals?

Teachers have different objectives for assigning journals in writing courses. Some present journals as storehouses for writing ideas. Others want students to increase their self-awareness and self-expression through journal writing. Still others want students to write often, simply to improve their stylistic fluidity and gain a more individualized written voice. If you require students to keep journals, examine your own motives so that you can shape the requirement accordingly.

You will need to decide whether you will occasionally assign students certain subjects to write about in their journals or always let them write about whatever they wish. To encourage students to use their journal for personal reflection, many teachers give students the option of folding over and stapling shut any pages they don't wish the teacher to read. In my experience, however, journals work most effectively when they are clearly connected to other work. Make sure students understand why you are assigning journals, and what function you ascribe to them. Simply writing more will not make students write better. Be explicit about what role you hope journals will play. Also tell students how often you will collect journals. If you wait until the end of the term, some students undermine the purpose of the journal by writing a lot at the last minute as if it were written earlier. You might prevent students' procrastination by collecting journals periodically (to manage your own time, you might even divide the class into half or thirds and collect the journals from different groups at different times) or by asking them to bring their journals to scheduled conferences so that you can quickly browse their work.

Additionally, tell students how you will evaluate their journals. Some teachers use quantity as the only criterion for journal grades. If you require extensive journals, it may not be feasible for you to comment on them in detail; writing summative comments on a separate sheet of paper can help preserve the student's sense of ownership regarding the journal. Another possible approach to journals is to not require them of all students, but to make them a necessity for anyone wanting an "A" in the course.

Why and how might I assign portfolios?

The portfolio method entails grading each student's work cumulatively, rather than grading the writing projects individually. The chief benefit of portfolios is that they allow students more opportunity to revise their papers and to apply lessons learned at the end of the course to papers drafted early in the course. In this way, portfolios allow a teacher to more easily assess students' growth in writing skills, rather than evaluating students' papers as discrete texts.

Portfolios can vary greatly in their design. Some teachers require students to include all of their writing assignments in their portfolios with substantial revisions. Other teachers let students select which writing projects they revise to include in their portfolios, arguing that even professional writers do not submit every piece they write for evaluation. Whichever of these common approaches you prefer, make sure students understand the number of documents and revisions you expect their portfolios to include. If you do permit students to choose which texts to include, you may wish to still set some general parameters; for example, when you are using *The Allyn & Bacon Guide to Writing*, you might require students to include at least one open-form document.

Some teachers also assign students to include an analysis of their work in the course as a part of the portfolio. In this analysis, students might discuss the following: why they chose to include particular documents in the portfolio (if they are not required to include every assignment); a self-assessment of their strengths as writers, with particular references to texts in the portfolio that can support their claims; an analysis of the ways in which their writing skills still need improvement; and a plan for their continued development as writers after the completion of this course.

Most teachers grade portfolios holistically, assigning one summative grade for all the work contained in the portfolio. Thus, portfolio evaluation changes not just *when* papers are graded but also *how* they are graded. Do all you can to demystify portfolio grading. Provide clear, written criteria for how you will evaluate portfolios. If your program has grading rubrics, show them to students early in the semester, and note on your assignment sheet how each individual assignment is connected to your course goals and grading rubrics. Explain as specifically as possible the extent to which including a single text in the portfolio that is particularly strong or particularly weak will impact the grade of the entire portfolio. If possible, several weeks before portfolios are due, provide students with a sample portfolio that you can use to demonstrate how you will read and evaluate their work. You may want students to read the sample portfolio for homework, then discuss the portfolio in small groups until each group arrives at a consensus for the grade it would assign the portfolio. The groups can then explain their reasons for assigning that grade to the class until the entire class, along with you, comes to a consensus about the grade the portfolio should receive. This exercise can help students better understand your expectations for their own portfolios.

You can also lessen students' anxieties about grades by giving them a tentative course grade at midterm and/or discussing their progress with them in detail during conferences. In some portfolio systems, midterm portfolios are graded, which can be a nice compromise between students' desire for clear direction about grades and teachers' desire for students to have time to revise.

Grading

What should my comments on papers include?

Your comments on students' writing projects should accomplish three goals: they should develop students' sense of an audience by reacting to the paper's content; they should explain and justify the grade or other evaluation; and they should provide guidance for students on how they can improve their future writing. Terminal (end-of-paper) comments are best if they adhere to this sequence.

In evaluating writing projects, direct your greatest concern to major rhetorical principles. Make sure the project has a thesis or focus, that the ideas are well developed and are suitable for the intended readership, and that the paper is well organized. Most writing specialists agree that deficiencies in sentence style, grammar, punctuation, and spelling are of secondary concern, unless they are so pervasive that they affect the intelligibility of the text. Early in the semester, you may want to focus on identifying repeated patterns of error rather than marking every mistake. This will help students set reasonable personal goals for editing the mechanics of their writing. It also helps students understand that their grade is primarily the result of rhetorical issues, that every error has not necessarily lowered their grade.

Including positive comments can be as important as making corrective remarks, even (perhaps especially) when the paper receives a low grade. If there are few strengths in the paper, marginal comments that praise a single sentence or paragraph—"Great description here!" or "Good insight!" —can motivate the student to continue improving.

It is important to help students see specific places in their work where they have achieved strengths. Simply telling a student "wonderful analysis here" may not help the student understand where that analysis was achieved. Similarly, help students see where the specific weaknesses in their text are located. Your comments should help students see their essay in a new light, and that will only happen if your comments are specific.

How should grades be communicated?

Students have a right to receive grades on their papers in a timely manner, and always before they are assigned to draft the next essay so that they can apply your advice from their previous work. If it is possible to have a schedule for returning papers, such as one week after they are submitted, announce that in class so that students will know what they can regularly expect.

As you grade, some minor alterations in your practice can help to make students feel less alienated from their own work. After years of having their schoolwork graded by teachers who use red pens, many students associate this ink color with authoritarian instruction and their own errors. Simply changing writing implements—for example, to a green fine-point marker, which stands out well from type and students' own ink colors—can affect students' reception of your comments. Make comments personable by beginning the terminal comments with the student's name. Also, marginal comments and some terminal comments can be stated quite effectively as questions: "How could you divide this long paragraph?" or "What about the counter argument that . . . ?" Using a question format prompts students to consider other possibilities without becoming overly defensive.

Don't use unfamiliar grammatical terms or obscure abbreviations. You may want to try using a highlighting pen to identify students' errors, without labeling or correcting them, and then assign students to turn in corrections. When you return essays, you can organize students into groups to compare highlighted errors and try to correct them. Any errors that stump the group can be turned over to the whole class for discussion. When you think the student needs a fuller explanation, list the page numbers that the student should read in the handbook portion of the textbook.

If a grade was lowered as a penalty for lateness or some other policy, clearly indicate that on the paper, or return the paper with a copy of the relevant portion of the syllabus attached and the policy highlighted.

At key points during the semester—certainly at midterm and just prior to students' final writing project—tell each student his or her current grade in the course.

What additional techniques can make the grading process more educational for students?

Different students will react differently to the *quantity* of your comments. Some students will study every comment carefully and attempt to learn from each. Other students will have difficulty distinguishing between major and minor comments and may feel so overwhelmed by extensive comments that they are not able to concentrate on any of them. If you view comments as a teaching tool, not just a means of evaluation, it is important to adapt the quantity of comments to students' individual learning styles. I do this by asking students to tell me how extensive they want me to be in my comments: whether they want me to identify just the most major concerns; whether they'd like me to comment on every concern I notice; whether they want me to mark only the grammar and punctuation mistakes that become a repeated pattern or whether they want every error identified. Asking students to tell me how they interpret teachers' comments improves their learning and saves me time from writing comments students won't use. Students can best judge their own learning process. If you use writer's statements, as suggested above, students can communicate these sorts of preferences there.

One way to understand how students are using your comments is to ask them to write back to you after each essay. If you ask students to summarize, and then react, to your comments, you will quickly learn where interpretive differences arise. It will enable you to negotiate styles of responding that are appropriate for each individual. With this technique, students can raise questions about a comment or marking you've made they don't understand, an emotional reaction to their grade, an explanation of their intentions in writing something you found problematic. When you require students to respond briefly in writing to your assessment of their assignments, you are assured that students have read your remarks thoroughly, and you enable those who would be reticent to discuss their concerns with you to take that initiative.

The first time students write these responses, you can convey your appreciation by writing short notes in return to all students. Thereafter, you need only to thank students for their responses and write your own responses just to students who ask you questions. Such exchanges diffuse the authoritarian nature of the grading process. They bring students' voices into the evaluation process, the last bastion of the teacher-centered classroom. Without student-written responses, I would not have learned that one of my students thought clichés were desirable when used as transitions. I would not have known that, even though I had written a personal response to a student who wrote about the death of several family members in a car accident, the feedback she most wanted was to know whether reading her paper had made me cry. This told me she was successful in seeing me as an authentic audience, not a teacher reading her work out of compulsion.

To get students' most honest responses, give them a few minutes to write them in class after you've returned assignments. Immediate response has the added benefit of letting students express any strong emotional responses (delight or anger/frustration). It is often better to return work toward the end of a class period, so that responding to your comments can be the last activity of the day. If students respond to your work earlier in the class period, they may be distracted from the work of the day.

An alternative to writing comments is to provide audiotaped comments. Students can turn in a blank cassette tape with their paper, allowing you to discuss the paper more extensively than may be feasible in writing. I have done this by identifying the paper on tape before I begin reading it, then pausing the tape as I read but recording again whenever I have a comment or response. This technique works well with both weak and strong writers. Weaker writers respond better to the conversational tone of a tape than the commanding tone they imagine lurks in succinct, written comments. Strong writers appreciate the more thorough feedback that speech makes possible. You can often convey both praise and encouragement more enthusiastically on tape because the student hears your voice. When conferences may be unrealistic for every assignment because of schedule constraints on you and your students, audiotapes allow a similarly conversational response. Conferences give students the chance to participate in the discussion, but tapes have the advantage of greater permanency. A student may listen again to your comments before writing the next paper or may save the tape if the paper is one he or she especially likes. On the paper itself you need write only the grade and a brief sentence or two summarizing your taped remarks, to satisfy students' curiosity until they have an opportunity to hear the tape.

How can I feel less frustrated by the sheer volume of grading I must do?

Many teachers consider grading their least enjoyable duty. Certainly it is time consuming and often its chief reward is just that one finishes it. While grading may always be labor intensive, it may be less frustrating if you perceive it as not merely evaluative. Try viewing grading as integral to your instruction in the course. While during the class session you are able to address your students as a group, when you grade you are able to teach each student individually. Grading gives you the opportunity to know your students better and personalize your instruction through your comments.

Keeping track of the time you spend on each essay is important. Less experienced teachers often agonize over grading, and end up spending much more time on each essay than might be necessary. Grading can easily expand to fill the time available, and you can use an egg timer to help limit your own time. Set a reasonable standard (say, fifteen minutes per draft) and see what it would take for you to stick to that time. Even if you adjust the amount of time you spend per draft upward, you will become more conscious of what you are doing at what pace.

The techniques described above for making grading more educational for students can also make grading papers a more satisfying experience for teachers. If you use the technique of audiotaped comments, the greater variety of grading methods can make it less tedious and keep you engaged. Also, when students respond to your comments on their papers, you won't feel the disappointment that can come from hours of writing careful comments only to see students quickly shove their papers into backpacks and never look at them again (at least not in your presence). Their feedback can show you that your work is making a difference.

Keeping Records

What information should I record about each student and each completed assignment?

Obviously you need to keep a record of students' assignment grades. If you have an attendance policy, record absences. If participation in discussion is part of students' course grades, periodically assess and record that evaluation. You may want to note the dates of students' visits to your office hours or tutorial sessions in the writing center so that if a student's course grade is borderline, you can use such indications of extra effort to decide between grades. Record any lateness of students' work or failure to have completed drafts for small group critiques.

In addition to the grades on writing projects, you may want to note for your own reference the topic of each student's paper so that you can remember the paper more easily if you or the student refers to it later. This record of topics is also helpful if any students in future terms cannot think of topics for their papers. Also briefly jot, for your eyes only, your impressions of each paper, especially its major weaknesses and the suggestions you gave the writer for improving the next paper. You can then more easily track patterns in each writer's difficulties and improvements as the semester progresses.

What alternatives exist to grade books for keeping records?

One alternative to the traditional grade book is to keep all your records on large index cards. Use one card per student and on the front side, record all information with the exception of written work. This might include attendance and, if you'd like, reasons students give you for absences; reminders about excessive tardiness (so that you can speak to a student if this becomes a recurring problem); and dates of office hour visits and writing center tutorials. Reserve the back of the card for grades and notations about students' written assignments. Jot here too any reminders that drafts or papers were late so that you will see that note as you assign the grade.

Index cards allow more room for notes than grade books so you are able to guide students' progress better, rather than responding to each assignment in isolation. They are also less messy: rather than marking students absent and then needing to cross those marks out when students enter the room late, simply set to one side of your desk the cards of the students who are not there when you check attendance and as they come in, move their cards to the stack of those who are present. At the end of the period, record the absences on the remaining cards.

You may also wish to explore any of several electronic programs for keeping records. If you still prefer using a grade book, wait until the class enrollment stabilizes (at least the second week of classes) before recording students' names in the book. To minimize errors, skip lines between names and between vertical entries.

Handling Difficult Situations and Students

How should I handle student absences and tardiness?

Stating an attendance policy on your syllabus and consistently enforcing it clarifies your expectations for students and tells them what behavior will allow them to succeed in the course.

An attendance policy also benefits you. You don't need to repeat lessons for those who have missed class. If students have attended class regularly, they will know the strategies specific to each assignment and your grading is likely to be quicker. Regular attendance also helps the students in the class to be better acquainted, which improves the dynamics of class discussion and small group work.

The attendance policy you set should be based on your college policy (if one exists), any special characteristics of your student body that could affect attendance (such as a high enrollment of students with children and full-time jobs), and the number of times per week the course meets. Also decide if you will distinguish between excused and unexcused absences and adjust the number of permitted absences accordingly. Finally, word the policy so that the penalty is clearly understood. If the penalty is a drop in the course grade for three unexcused absences, how great is the grade reduction? Does the grade change take effect on the third absence or the fourth? Will the reduction occur for *every* three absences or only the first three, no matter how many absences follow?

If you have an attendance policy, make sure students see you recording absences even after you have learned their names and no longer need to call roll. Otherwise, they may think you won't enforce absence penalties.

If you have a policy that involves distinguishing excused and unexcused absences, be clear to students about how you will make those distinctions and what information you will need to make the determination. If you require documentation, explain that on your syllabus.

The key element to successful attendance policies is keeping an emphasis on the positive value of class activities and student participation. Assure students that class time matters, and make your daily lesson plans reflect your belief that students can get things done in class that advance their writing projects. If class time is used well, students will be more inclined to come to class. Even if students miss class, a healthy emphasis on well-chosen activities enables you to have conversations with students about how they are planning to make up the work they missed, rather than conversations about the reasons behind their absences. Keep your focus on the work you want students to do, and attendance issues will not be a burden.

How should I respond to students who are disruptive or inattentive?

It can be difficult to concentrate on your lesson when you notice a student who is talking, eating, or even sleeping. Because students may simultaneously be enrolled in large lecture classes where such behavior goes unnoticed, don't assume that students are knowingly being disrespectful. A student may be talking to her neighbor because she is asking a question about the discussion topic, or a student's eyes may unintentionally drift closed because he was awake all night studying for an exam or has arrived at a morning class after working a night shift. Rather than interpreting such behavior as a deliberate offense and becoming angry, a brief comment such as "Karen, I need your attention" is usually sufficient. Often students are naive about the effect their behavior has on you and their classmates.

If a problem persists, discuss it with a student after class, stating firmly but calmly what behavior must be changed. Only if the inappropriate behavior still continues should you address the student more stridently during class: "Brian, I've discussed with you now several times how disruptive it is when your beeper goes off during every class. You *must* turn it off before class starts."

In all situations, it is both cruel and counterproductive to humiliate students. Remember that your response to one student may affect your rapport with the entire class.

How should I handle student complaints?

If a student comes to you with a complaint—whether it be about a course policy, their small group, or a grade—listen with an open mind. Try to resolve any difficulty with the student as fairly as you can. If you are unsure whether to grant the student's requested change, tell the student that you will reconsider the matter and let him or her know your decision the next time class meets. Don't feel pressured into making a quick decision simply because a student has a complaint; your only obligation at the time is to listen respectfully. Whenever you do not fully grant the student's request, inform him or her of the college's grievance procedure so that the student can decide whether to pursue the matter further. Such information ensures that students' rights are not violated and can also diffuse a student's anger.

If a student becomes confrontational, begin keeping a detailed log of your encounters with that student to defend yourself from any charges the student may eventually make. Immediately after each troublesome incident with the student, record in detail what was said by both you and the student and, if there were any witnesses, their names. Date each entry. If you anticipate the student making a formal complaint, don't wait until that happens to discuss the situation with your program coordinator or department chair. If you are ever physically or verbally threatened by a student, alert campus security immediately.

How should I respond to students' personal problems?

The first year of college is an emotionally difficult time for many students. Students may write about personal difficulties they are currently facing in their journals or writing projects, or they may come to your office to ask for advice directly. Your best course of action is to express appreciation for the students' trust and then inform them of campus resources where staff are professionally trained to help them. If you sense a student is in grave danger—perhaps suicidal or at risk of being physically harmed by someone else—request permission to call the proper support services while the student is there in your office. On the phone, you can discreetly indicate that you have a student in your office who needs to speak to a counselor on an emergency basis. If possible, then walk the student to that office and wait together until the counselor is available.

Seeking Feedback to Improve Your Teaching

What techniques might I use to personally reflect on ways to improve my teaching ability?

In addition to using outside resources to improve your teaching—students, colleagues, and publications, all discussed in more detail below—you can regularly evaluate your own teaching performance. After each class meeting, make notes on your lesson plans about which activities, questions, and discussion topics worked well and which didn't. Although a different group of students might not respond identically, over time this type of analysis will help you develop a larger repertoire of teaching ideas and better judge the effectiveness of new techniques.

Keeping a journal solely devoted to your teaching is also a way to improve your teaching ability. Explore your goals for your classroom persona, your relationship with students, what your mission is in teaching writing, and how you see your identity developing as a teacher. Whenever an observation or experience that affects you outside school seems relevant to your teaching, jot it in your teaching journal. If anything disturbing happens in class—for instance, if a student makes a prejudiced remark—write about how you handled the situation, how you felt about that action, and how you might want to respond the next time a similar incident occurs. Use the journal to record insights about teaching you have gained from particular students or from interactions that have taken place in class.

How can I learn from students to improve my teaching ability?

Typically, students' anonymous evaluations are solicited at the end of the course. If your college or department uses standardized forms with closed-ended (multiple choice) prompts, you may want to supplement the required evaluation with your own form to obtain a more thorough assessment from your students. Some helpful questions to consider are:

- What do you think are the strengths of the course material?
- What suggestions do you have for improving the course material?
- What do you think are my strengths as a teacher?
- What suggestions do you have for improving my teaching ability?
- What is your overall evaluation of this course?

If you ask about the course and your instruction so generally, without prompting students to discuss specific components of the course (such as small group critiques of drafts), you will learn what components of the course students found most significant.

Final course evaluations help you improve your teaching in future academic terms. To make improvements for your present students, you may want to also have students complete midterm evaluations of the course. This is particularly helpful if you sense the course is not going well but are not sure why. At midterm, it can be helpful to ask students four questions:

- What should I continue to do in order to make this class successful for the rest of the semester?
- What could I change from this point forward in order to make this class more successful for the rest of the semester?
- What should you continue to do in order to make this class successful for the rest of the semester?
- What could you change from this point forward in order to make this class more successful for the rest of the semester?

These questions encourage students to reflect on their own role in the successes and failures of each class period, and they usually result in quite practical suggestions for manageable changes (for example, students sometimes ask me to adjust the schedule by which I post information to our course Web site). To increase students' assurance that their evaluations will not affect their grades, you could require anonymous, typed evaluations as a homework assignment. If you cannot grant students' requests for change, explain why. The student-teacher discussion generated by midterm evaluations can correct misunderstandings of both parties.

Another strategy for midterm evaluations is for you to leave the room while students arrive at a consensus about their evaluation of the course. To do this, students first meet in small groups and generate a list of what everyone in the group agrees are the strengths of the course and the areas that need improvement. The only ideas that should be recorded on the group's list are those agreed upon by every group member. A spokesperson for each group then reads the list and if most other students agree, the idea gets recorded by a student volunteer on one master evaluation that will be given to you. Once the master list is generated, the class should discuss specific ways you might implement the suggested improvements. These recommended actions should also be included on the evaluation. It is useful to allot the second half of a class meeting for this activity and have one student deliver the evaluation to your office or mailbox at the end of class. That way, you have time to carefully consider their evaluations before responding. On some campuses, facilitators are available who can come into your class and conduct such conversations with students, which can help manage high feelings.

Apart from explicit evaluations, students reveal your effectiveness through their course work and comments. If most are having a similar difficulty, you may not have caused it (it may be a weakness typical of first-year writers), but it can indicate how you can better help your students. When students ask questions or make comments in class that show misunderstandings, thoughtfully consider whether you have unintentionally caused that confusion. By not becoming defensive, you are able to learn from your students how you can best teach them.

How can I learn from colleagues to improve my teaching ability?

If you are fortunate, you have colleagues who would also like to discuss teaching and improve their instructional skills. You might urge the department to announce a regular meeting time for teachers interested in exchanging instructional ideas, perhaps over lunch in the campus cafeteria. Or, you can discuss your courses with a few colleagues to identify who is eager for such interaction and then form a professional support group. In addition to discussing together what you have done in class and what you plan to try, you might also observe one another teach.

Many campuses also provide services to enhance teachers' instruction. Check to see if your college offers workshops or employs teaching consultants. Most colleges have services for videotaping the teacher for a class session, which is an invaluable means for you to assess your delivery style.

Reading More about Teaching Strategies

Where might I find more ideas about teaching techniques?

This selected annotated bibliography lists especially helpful books that discuss techniques for teaching college-level writing courses. The books themselves include more extensive bibliographies.

Anson, Chris M., Joan Graham, David A. Jolliffe, Nancy S. Shapiro, and Carolyn H. Smith. *Scenarios for Teaching Writing: Contexts for Discussion and Reflective Practice.* Urbana, IL: NCTE, 1993.

This text—designed for use by teaching assistants, new faculty members, and adjunct instructors—offers practical advice on many components of writing pedagogy: creating assignments; using readings; responding to student writing; teaching grammar; managing class discussion, conferences, and small groups; and designing courses. Each chapter includes scenarios and "ideas for discussion" to facilitate novice teachers' comprehension of the topics discussed.

Belanoff, Pat and Marcia Dickson, eds. *Portfolios: Process and Product*. Portsmouth, NH: Boynton/Cook, 1991.

Seven of the twenty-three essays in this collection discuss how to use portfolios in writing courses, including their use in secondary classrooms, a basic writing course, first-year composition courses, a writing-across-the-curriculum course, and training programs for new college writing teachers. The text also includes essays discussing the use of portfolios for proficiency testing and for program assessment, essays addressing the political ramifications of portfolios, and a selected bibliography.

Good, Tina LaVonne and Leanne B. Warshauer. *In Our Own Voice: Graduate Students Teach Writing*. Boston: Allyn & Bacon, 2001.

This text offers a variety of views from graduate student teachers of writing, some new, some more experienced. It offers a balance of theory and practice, offering practical support for new teachers while encouraging them to problematize and theorize their teaching situations. The collection is arranged thematically.

Harris, Joseph. *Rewriting: How to Do Things with Texts*. Logan, UT: Utah State UP, 2006.

This text models activities for teaching academic writing moves, emphasizing the ways writers connect with their sources. It's an inspiring short read.

Harris, Muriel. *Teaching One-to-One: The Writing Conference*. Urbana, IL: NCTE, 1986.

After providing a rationale for writing conferences, the author discusses how to organize conferences, reviews possible conference activities, explains the role of diagnosis in conferences, and recommends strategies for teaching grammar. The book ends with a bibliography and appendices of conference excerpts and practice activities.

Hoffman, Eric and Carol Scheidenhelm. *An Introduction to Teaching Composition in an Electronic Environment*. Boston: Allyn & Bacon, 2000.

This text provides detailed guidance for both experienced and inexperienced teachers who wish to make creative use of technology in a composition environment. Topics covered include the use of word processing, e-mail, and the Web in composition classrooms; course preparation and lesson plans for teaching a computer-assisted writing course; strategies for finding and evaluating resources electronically; netiquette; sample Web pages; a troubleshooting guide; and a glossary. This text is available as a complimentary supplement for adopters of *The Allyn & Bacon Guide to Writing*.

32

Lindemann, Erika. *A Rhetoric for Writing Teachers*. 3rd ed. New York: Oxford UP, 1995.

This volume offers a scholarly introduction to the teaching of writing, including concise synopses of related fields: the history of rhetorical theory, linguistics, and cognition. The text provides advice for instruction about words, sentences, and paragraphs, as well as prewriting, drafting, and rewriting. Suggestions for designing courses, developing assignments, and responding to student writing are also included.

McDonald, James C., ed. *The Allyn & Bacon Sourcebook for College Writing Teachers*, 2nd ed. Boston: Allyn & Bacon, 2000.

In this collection of previously published essays, leading rhetoricians offer essential discussions of composition theory and pedagogy. The issues treated most thoroughly are composing processes, organization, style, critical thinking, argumentation, and evaluation. Selected bibliographies are also included. This text is available as a complimentary supplement for adopters of *The Allyn & Bacon Guide to Writing*.

Neman, Beth S. *Teaching Students to Write*. 2nd ed. New York: Oxford UP, 1995.

Most of this text is devoted to an explanation of how to teach expository writing, particularly its structure and style. Specific guidance is offered for teaching the research paper and the rhetorical analysis, as well as narrative writing and poetry writing. Additional chapters discuss the roles of students and teachers.

Rankin, Elizabeth. *Seeing Yourself as a Teacher: Conversations with Five New Teachers in a University Writing Program*. Urbana, IL: NCTE, 1994.

This book is the result of the author's weekly interviews with five graduate students who were second-year teachers of writing. Through extensive interview excerpts, the author explores the formation of teachers' professional identities. Some of the issues discussed include some new teachers' resistance to theory, the impact of past teachers on new teachers' performance, the relationships of new teachers with their students, and the difficulties some new teachers face in considering themselves teachers.

Roen, Duane, Veronica Pantoja, Lauren Yena, Susan K. Miller and Eric Waggoner, eds. *Strategies for Teaching Writing*. Urbana, IL: NCTE, 2002.

Designed for new teachers of writing, this text collects a range of practical advice on everything from designing a syllabus to preparing a teaching portfolio. The book's fourteen sections each contain examples of experienced teachers' practice, plus excellent advice on how to reflect on and develop additional materials.

Smith, Maggy. *Teaching College Writing*. Boston: Allyn & Bacon, 1995.

This text is written for first-time college writing teachers. It explains how to prepare for the course before it begins (including designing a syllabus) and how to teach the first four class sessions of the term. The largest section of the book discusses techniques teachers can present to help students with their prewriting, drafting, revising, editing and proofreading. The final chapter offers advice about grading. This text is available as a complimentary supplement for adopters of *The Allyn & Bacon Guide to Writing*.

Vandenberg, Peter, Sue Hum, and Jennifer Clary-Lemon. *Relations, Locations, Positions: Composition Theory for Writing Teachers*. Urbana, IL: NCTE, 2006.

This anthology combines presentation of composition theory (particularly writers working in the post-process tradition) and pedagogical insights that close each section of the collection. The authors emphasize the social nature of writing and writing instruction.

Williams, James D. *Preparing to Teach Writing*. Belmont, CA: Wadsworth, 1989.

The first half of this book develops a theoretical framework for the teaching of writing, including, but not restricted to, college-level courses. In part two, concise, practical advice is given for facilitating classroom instruction, teaching "nonmainstream" students, designing writing assignments, and grading. The author uses the findings of empirical studies to support his recommendations.

Suggested Syllabi for
The Allyn & Bacon Guide to Writing

A major asset of *The Allyn & Bacon Guide to Writing* is its adaptability for widely divergent course objectives and schedules. The text offers a cornucopia of writing projects, enough to allow instructors to vary their assignment selections when they teach the same course and to make the text useful for consecutive courses. As you become more familiar with *The Allyn & Bacon Guide to Writing*, and more excited about its opportunities for instruction, your most difficult decision will be what chapters to exclude.

Most teachers allot one to two weeks for each major writing project, although a researched project may require up to three weeks for the development of a first draft. Many teachers allot additional time for revising workshops, particularly in a portfolio context. Possible adjustments to this schedule include the following: spending only a short time on the brief projects in the first four chapters; spending more time on longer papers that involve research; teaching chapters in Parts Three and Four of the textbook simultaneously with related chapters in Parts One and Two; and sequencing some of the writing projects in Part Two so that students can write on the same topic, making possible a quicker succession of assignments.

The discussion that follows can help you design a syllabus that is most appropriate for the objectives and length of your course. Rather than delineating a weekly syllabus, this advice allows you to decide the number and pace of writing projects your students will complete, and which additional chapters you would like to assign. The recommendations are divided into what you might want to cover during general time periods of the course (beginning, middle, and end), what chapters are best for courses with different emphases (sampling of genres; informative writing and research paper; computer-assisted writing), and what adjustments to make for courses that are shorter or longer than a semester (in a quarter system or two-semester system).

Beginning of the Course

The first four chapters of the textbook lay the foundation for students' understanding of writing as a process that involves problematizing and rhetorical assessments. Chapter 17, "Writing as a Problem-Solving Process," supplements this discussion by explaining writing as a process. The information presented in these chapters is crucial to students' successful understanding of writing, so try to include all five chapters in your syllabus. The writing projects they assign are brief, often completed in less than an hour (and Chapter 17 has no writing assignment). If you like, you may even assign the chapters for reading without requiring that students complete all of these short projects.

The class can also begin to read and work with Chapters 17–19 early in the course, although this section of the book is so comprehensive that it is best to work with particular skills (twenty in all across the three chapters), while working with a writing project. Simply get students started on a writing project from Part Two of the text and, when they are well underway, incorporate the skills from Part Three of the textbook.

Chapters 5 and 6, grouped under the heading "Writing to Learn," are not within the traditional repertoire of composition textbook assignments, yet they should not be overlooked. These chapters teach students that what they see and read is constructed, not fixed truth, and therefore open to interpretation and critique. The chapters can dramatically improve students' critical thinking abilities. Ideally, cover both, but if you don't have time, Chapter 6, "Reading Rhetorically: The Writer as Strong Reader," will be most applicable to the research-based projects students might be assigned in this course or other courses they will take.

Middle of the Course

Select from among the writing projects in Part Two to decide which chapters you would like to teach. The section below titled "Well-Paired Chapters" offers advice about which chapters work particularly well together. There are also suggestions below for courses that aim to introduce students to a wide range of genres, that emphasize informative and research writing, and that emphasize computer-assisted writing. Chapter 18, "Composing and Revising Closed-Form Prose," can be divided into its different lessons and taught throughout the middle section of the course, to help students improve in basic skills while they simultaneously work with other chapters devoted to major writing projects.

At midterm, you may want to schedule conferences with students (if you haven't held them already) to confer with them individually about their progress in the course and goals for the remaining weeks. Consider having students write a reflective self-evaluation of their writing midterm (based on Chapter 25) to both assess what they have learned and to plan goals for improving their skills in the remainder of the course. You may also want to have students review Chapter 25 so they can reassess and improve the dynamics of their group activities and peer reviews.

If your course will include a research paper, it need not be the last assignment. Students are often overburdened with work at the end of a term, so scheduling a research paper earlier can enable them to devote more time to it. Any of the chapters in Part Four, "A Rhetorical Guide to Research" can be combined with one or more assignment chapters to guide students throughout the process.

End of the Course

If you would like to include in your syllabus Chapter 12, "Analyzing a Short Story," or Chapter 24, "Essay Examinations: Writing Well Under Pressure," remember that these are good selections to reserve for the end of the term. Both address academic genres quite differently from the other writing projects in the textbook. Their novelty can help keep students engaged as the course ends, and their relevance to other college courses can serve as a transition into the next academic term. If you'd like, you could even assign an essay exam as the final for your course, asking students to respond to questions about key concepts you have taught, e.g., methods of exploratory writing and talking; the writing process; or the continuum of closed-form to open-form prose. The comprehensive reflection described in Chapter 25, when assigned at the end of the course, helps students synthesize what they have learned.

Well-Paired Chapters

Many of the chapters in *The Allyn & Bacon Guide to Writing* complement each other well. Often the chapters that don't assign writing projects can be taught simultaneously with related chapters that do, enabling you to fit more instruction into the course. Another way to accommodate more chapters into the course is to have students pursue a similar topic through sequential assignments. What follows are suggestions for links you may want to make as you plan your syllabus:

- Chapters 1, 2, 3, 4, and 17 can be taught in quick succession during the first few weeks of class (see "Beginning of the Course" above).
- Chapters 5, 6, 10, and 11 can serve as a powerful sequence of assignments. They expand students' notions of what constitutes "text"; help them see these texts as constructed, not fixed truths; and encourage students to interpret and critique in ways they may never have before.
- Chapters 7 and 19 can be taught simultaneously.
- Chapter 8 can be taught with Chapters 13, 20, 21, 22, and 25.
- Chapters 9, 10, 11, or 12 can be taught with Chapter 18.
- Chapter 10 can be taught with Chapters 20 and 21.
- A wide array of chapters can be linked in a research sequence (see "Course Emphasizing Informative Writing and the Research Paper" below).
- Chapters 14, 15, and 16 can be taught as a persuasive sequence

Course Emphasizing Range of Genres

If you want your course to introduce students to a wide spectrum of types of writing, you could, for instance, have them work with Chapters 1 through 4 to gain a basic understanding of the premises of college writing, then assign writing projects based on Chapters 7, 9, either 10 , 11 or 12, 14, and 25. You can coordinate these chapters with the chapters in Parts Three and Four of the textbook as suggested above.

Course Emphasizing Informative Writing and the Research Paper

If you want to devote a large portion of your course to informative writing supported by research, there are many chapters you can link to help students build their skills cumulatively. You might begin this section of the course with Chapter 6 to teach students to be critical readers. Chapters 8 and 13 taught together could then help them plan and initiate a research project they will carry out over the term. While students continue their research, teach Chapter 10 to help them understand how to write about data, or Chapters 20, 21, and 22 to help them find and analyze more sources. Then teach Chapter 9 as the basis of the research report, simultaneously covering Chapter 17 on composing and revising closed-form prose, and returning to Chapter 22 for support in using and citing sources.

An alternative to basing the research paper on Chapter 9 is to require that it be a proposal and to base it on Chapter 16. In either case, this chapter sequence need not be adopted in its entirety. You can decide how much time you have to devote to this project and how much you think it would profit students.

If you link multiple chapters, it is imperative that students choose a topic they will remain interested in for several projects. The benefit of sequencing assignments so that they can be done on the same topic is that students will not need to continually exert effort over new content, but can instead devote their energies to reading about new writing strategies and applying them to familiar material.

Course Emphasizing Computer-Assisted Writing

In a course emphasizing writing in electronic environments, teach Chapter 21 much earlier in the term than you otherwise might and focus attention on the evaluation of electronic sources. You might begin with this chapter, or teach it in conjunction with Chapter 2, which teaches non-electronic exploration. Chapter 8 contains the exploratory material from a student project on online social networks (the final version of which appears in Chapter 23), and Chapter 13 contains sample blog posts on immigration. These materials will help introduce students to debates about online environments and writing genres emerging online. Chapters 3 and 4 have sections emphasizing document design, and the graphics that appear at the start of each Part of *The Allyn & Bacon Guide to Writing* can help you introduce additional attention to visual literacy. Introducing computers as simply another tool for exploration might ease the minds of students who have little experience with computers.

Read "Using *The Allyn & Bacon Guide to Writing* in an Electronic Classroom" at the end of this instructor's manual for more advice. Also, ask your Pearson representative for a copy of *An Introduction to Teaching Composition in an Electronic Environment* by Eric Hoffman and Carol Scheidenhelm, a complementary supplement published by Allyn & Bacon in 2000.

Quarter-System Course

Despite its length, *The Allyn & Bacon Guide to Writing* is ideal for use in colleges that operate on a quarter system. The brief writing projects in Chapters 1, 2, 3, and 4 allow you to collect a number of assignments quickly in the term. The potential for linking assignments also enables you to use much of the textbook (see "Well-Paired Chapters" and "Course Emphasizing Informative Writing and the Research Paper" above). You can also vary your syllabus from one quarter to the next to give students a representative range, but gain more exposure yourself to chapters that especially interest you: you may alternate Chapters 5 and 6, Chapters 10 and 11, and Chapters 15 and 16.

Two-Semester Course

The Allyn & Bacon Guide to Writing contains ample material for a two-semester course. Rather than making difficult decisions about which chapters to exclude and which to overlap, you can teach all the chapters. One possible plan would be to teach Chapters 1, 2, 3, 4, 5, 6, 7, 10, and 12 in the first semester. This plan would require students to complete the four very brief writing projects and five major writing projects. Chapters 17, 18, 19, and 25 could also be integrated where appropriate, as suggested above.

The second semester could then be devoted to informative and research writing, in keeping with the chapters suggested above for this course emphasis. Chapter 13 makes an excellent start for a course encouraging an extended research project. Critical chapters like 17, 18, and 25 could be repeated.

Chapter 1
Thinking Rhetorically About Good Writing

Understanding the Chapter's Goals

This chapter lays out the philosophy of writing and rhetoric that guides the textbook and any course it supports. It invites students to consider what constitutes good writing, what kinds of questions motivate good writing, and what kinds of choices writers make as they work. This chapter will help students think about their previous school writing experiences as they form expectations about the semester or quarter to come.

Reinforcing the Chapter's Rhetorical Principles

The Rewards of Taking a Writing Course

For students to take their writing seriously, it is important for them to see themselves as writers. To motivate them to want to learn all they can about writing, emphasize that writing is a skill that can help them in all areas of their lives: in school, in the workplace, and always in their personal lives. This chapter emphasizes writing as a habit of mind that will help them explore the complexities of issues that matter. You will find that working with this principle helps set a tone of exploration and intellectual adventure. Some of the following activities can be used as icebreakers at the start of the term; they can set a friendly tone in your classroom, help students get to know others in the class, and provide incentive for working hard in the course.

If your students consider writing to be an activity that has little impact on their lives, you may want to ask them to list the types of writing they've done in the past few months or even in recent years—everything from grocery shopping lists to voter registration forms, birthday cards for friends and college applications. Alternatively, you may want to ask students to keep a running log until the next time your class meets of all the writing they do, indicating its page length or time commitment, audience, purpose, and genre. These activities should help students realize that they are already writers, that "writers" are not only those who publish. Ask students to discuss the lists in small groups, and then ask a spokesperson from each group to report to the class about the ways in which the group's lists were both alike and diverse. Similar conversations and records about the kinds of reading students do (signs, maps, directions, newspapers, billboards, magazines, etc.) can start conversations about the audience, purpose, and genre of what they have read.

To help students understand the role of writing in college, ask them to bring to class the syllabi they have been given for other courses they are taking this term. Create a cumulative list on the board of all the types of writing assignments students in your class will complete in just the next few months. If the syllabi specify page lengths for the assignments, you can ask students to add up the page lengths of all the assignments in all their courses. Then, simply because large numbers may add impressive credence to your claims about the importance of writing in college, you might even want to bring a calculator to class and take a minute to add together the total page requirements of all the students' papers in your class.

Although this activity will help students better understand the quantity of writing they'll be expected to do in college—and point out to them that upper-level courses usually require far more writing than the first-year courses they are currently taking—it does not yet help them to understand the role that writing quality plays in college grades. For this purpose, ask students to look again at the syllabi for all courses they are currently taking and to determine the percentage of the course grade that is based on writing assignments. If, for example, 85% of a course grade is based on written assignments, certainly a significant portion of that assessment will be based on their knowledge of the subject matter. But point out that their ability to convey that knowledge through exams and papers will affect their grade just as much. You may also want to note that whatever assignments students think do *not* pertain to writing—such as class participation and oral presentations—usually *do* require writing in order to be completed effectively. It is easier for a student to participate in class if he or she takes careful notes while reading and even jots down questions about the readings. Good oral presentations require careful note taking, outlining on paper or note cards, perhaps a fully scripted (and then memorized) introduction and conclusion, and even a handout for the audience.

To reinforce the importance of the role that writing plays in college, you may want to describe the tangible evidence of your college's institutional commitment to writing: writing courses required of all students; writing-intensive courses or WAC curricula; college-funded writing labs or tutoring centers; a writing exit exam for graduates. Finally, whereas most students in your course are probably in their first year, you may have a few who have already completed a year or two. If so, ask them to share with the class the types and amount of writing they have done while in college, as well as how important they believe writing skills are to the work required of students.

You may want to ask students to conduct their own informal research on the importance of writing in the workplace. For a homework assignment, they could interview employers, coworkers, teachers, relatives, or friends about the amount and types of writing they do for their jobs. Students should also ask these professionals about the importance of writing skills and whether they would value an opportunity to improve their writing capabilities. You could then either ask students to briefly summarize their findings in writing, and then grade this as a miscellaneous homework assignment, or ask a few volunteers to share their findings orally with the class. As an alternative activity, you could invite a few of your own colleagues and friends from various professions to speak to your class about the importance of good writing skills in their respective fields.

Although good writing skills will serve students well in college and on their jobs, it is also important for students to realize that writing is highly valuable apart from reasons imposed by others. Through self-initiated writing, they can gain deep satisfaction by expressing themselves more fully, forging more meaningful relationships with others, and even handling practical difficulties more efficiently. For example, they could use writing to advocate for themselves to a company or appeals committee. You may want to share with your class the role that writing has played in your own life: how you became particularly interested in writing yourself; what texts you've written that hold special meaning for you; your own views about how writing empowers an active citizenship in a democratic society.

Closed and Open Forms

Presenting writing structure on a continuum with closed (highly constrained) forms on one end and open (more free-form) forms on the other is one of the most innovative features of *The Allyn & Bacon Guide to Writing*. Many texts devote only one chapter or assignment, if any at all, to distinctively "open-form" texts. *The Allyn & Bacon Guide to Writing* is progressive in placing the textual forms on a continuum between closed and open, thus highlighting the rhetorical choices writers make in shaping their texts. You and your students may slip into referring to open and closed forms as a binary opposition, and it is important to remember that the relationship between closed and open forms is always one of degree (as the figure on page 10 makes clear).

Be sure to spend at least one class session working with the concepts of "closed" and "open" forms because this distinction will be referred to often throughout the textbook. You will find that these terms are so important throughout the text that you will return to them repeatedly. The "For Writing and Discussion" activity following the sample passages by David Rockwood and Thomas Merton is very useful for helping students articulate their own understanding of these forms, but if they have never tried to intentionally create a metaphor before, you can guide them through this task using the suggestions in the next section of this manual, "Using the 'For Writing and Discussion' Activities."

If your students are adept at creating metaphors and you want to probe their understanding further, you might bring to class other brief passages of text that are at less extreme ends of the open-closed continuum and ask students to decide where on the continuum those texts fall. You could either read the passages you bring aloud to the class and then facilitate their discussion, or pass out copies of the passages to small groups, have the groups discuss the texts' placement on the continuum, and then compare as a class the decisions of different small groups. You could also ask students to bring in short selections themselves for the class to analyze. If your students have a firm enough grasp of the continuum that some ambiguity would not unduly frustrate them, you could even ask them to bring to class a short passage that they would have trouble placing on the continuum. Such passages could provoke lively discussion in small groups. These activities can be repeated throughout the semester as students work with new writing projects. Whatever activity you choose, at whatever point in the course, make sure you ask students to support their analysis with evidence from the passage itself. Again, encourage students to view their disagreements as an opportunity for problematizing. Urge them to convince one another of their opinions, rather than appealing to you for the answer. As they discuss the passages, ask questions that help them consider textual practices more carefully, such as "How far into the text did you read before identifying its form? What were your earliest clues?" and "In what kinds of publications are we more likely to find open-form texts?"

Questions and Writing

Students often begin a composition course wrongly believing that writing entails merely recording what one already knows—one's own expertise. It is no wonder, then, that many students dislike writing courses: they may view writing as drudgery, a time-consuming exercise for scribes in which little new knowledge is gained (other than how to please an idiosyncratic teacher). Chapter 1 challenges this misperception by emphasizing writing as a means of learning. It helps students to understand that writers are not expected to be subject-matter experts, but rather experts at question posing and problem posing. Questions help writers connect with their audience, for the question that motivates a writing assignment should be one that also prompts readers to engage with the text. Questions identify what's most important; they show why the subject under discussion matters (to the writer, to the audience, to a larger community).

As a teacher, you can best support this goal by your own attitude toward questions and difficulties that surface throughout the course. Never dismiss your students' questions, even superficial ones such as when you'll be returning their graded assignments. When a problem presents itself about the course schedule or course material, offer it to your students as a chance for collective problem solving. You do not need to be the sole provider of answers for the class. Even when you know an answer, your students will often learn much more about problem posing when you act as a guide for their process of clarifying, investigating, and answering the question for themselves.

You might remind them of the natural curiosity of young children, who perpetually insist on knowing "why." Much has been written about the educational system's responsibility for stunting children's curiosity, as they are taught to avoid errors at all costs, so be patient if students seem unskilled at problematizing or distrust your request that they not offer readily available answers. Look for opportunities throughout the course to affirm your commitment to identifying questions that drive writing projects. It doesn't hurt, either, to share with your students relevant examples of your own problematizing and problem-solving processes as they arise during the term, particularly when writing is one of the tools you use to learn from or to manage a given situation.

It can be helpful to return to the class analysis of students' syllabi and examine the ways in which other course assignments invite students to examine shared problems. If students have a sense of the ways principles from their writing courses are active in other courses, they can more easily see the rhetorical principles at work. Class discussion can emphasize the ways in which writing assignments provide opportunities for students to learn more about ongoing problems in other fields. Similarly, you can ask students to interview one of their other professors about shared problems in their other classes, or to interview other students about the ways in which their courses have addressed inquiry and problematizing.

Purpose

First-year writing textbooks generally distinguish types of writing using two systems of classification. One system of classification is written texts' modes of organization. Textbooks using this system might have a chapter explaining how to write comparison-contrast essays, another explaining definition essays, and another on classification essays. These rhetoric textbooks teach students how to structure and organize a piece of writing but give little attention to rhetorical concerns, most notably purpose and audience.

The Allyn & Bacon Guide to Writing uses the other common system for classifying discourse types: by their purpose. Except in a writing course, students will rarely encounter writing tasks that ask them to generate texts in particular organizational modes (the chief exception may be essay exam questions in other courses, where students may be asked, for example, to compare and contrast two discipline-specific concepts). In non-academic writing tasks—and many academic ones too—students must instead decide how to develop their text by discerning what they hope to accomplish by writing. Thus, classifying discourse types by purpose reflects more accurately the hierarchy of decisions writers usually make when approaching a writing task. This classification serves students well long after they have completed their education. Whenever they write, they can decide their purpose and, based on the chapters in Part 2 of *The Allyn & Bacon Guide to Writing*, know how to begin, even if the text's genre is one they haven't attempted before.

This chapter challenges students to consider purpose from multiple perspectives: the rhetorical context (what Ramage, Bean, and Johnson call the "motivating occasion"), the connection to the reader (how the writer wants to affect readers), and the rhetorical aim. Although the rhetorical basis for writing forms the bulk of the chapter, it's important to consider the other elements of purpose as you work with your students. Students frequently consider only the motivating occasion for writing ("I'm writing because I have to") and it's important to consider ways in which you can move them toward a more rhetorical view. It's equally important to help students see how thinking rhetorically can help them achieve their motivational goals.

The classification of discourse types by rhetorical purpose is explained in more detail in James Kinneavy's *A Theory of Discourse*. Kinneavy explains that four elements are present in every act of communication, whether written or oral: the person initiating the communication (writer or speaker); the audience that receives the communication (readers or listeners; the audience can also be simply oneself); the subject matter that is being communicated; and the language that is used to convey the message. Although all four elements are present in every communication, determining which element is most important in shaping the text exposes its rhetorical purpose. If it is the writer who most defines the text, Kinneavy terms that discourse expressive. If the subject matter is of greatest importance, the text is referential. Persuasive texts stress audience and literary texts stress language, especially its aesthetic qualities.

Ramage, Bean, and Johnson's delineation of purposes is consistent with Kinneavy's schema. Their identification of the expressive purpose, persuasive purpose, and literary purpose align with Kinneavy's terms precisely. Ramage, Bean, and Johnson's identification of the exploratory purpose, informative purpose, and analytical purpose mirrors Kinneavy's subdivisions of the referential aim; all emphasize subject matter more than writer, audience, or language. You may want to discuss with your students as well that the purposes of writing often overlap. For example, an essay may be primarily informative yet have a persuasive conclusion. Or an informative essay may be developed through rich autobiographical details, giving it undertones of an expressive essay.

The purpose of a piece of writing is more abstract than its thesis. The purpose is what the writer hopes the text will accomplish, whereas the thesis states the writer's conclusions about the text's subject matter. Clarify this distinction for students by discussing with them the purpose statements on page 22 in the textbook. For each statement, ask them to identify which of the six writing purposes the statement illustrates. Then ask students to invent a possible thesis for that purpose and topic. For example, students should identify the first statement as being expressive in purpose. A possible thesis would be, "Through my struggle with Graves' disease, I learned that the human spirit is more powerful than human frailties."

Audience

If students write papers expecting them to be read only by the teacher, they may become adept at writing papers that please only teachers. The ability to adapt a text to its intended audience is a difficult skill; therefore, it is important for students to gain experience writing to audiences besides the teacher. Students still need to turn in work that meets the criteria for acceptable college-level writing (choosing an audience with low literacy is no excuse for them to make errors), but as the teacher you can serve as their secondary reader, evaluating their success in adapting the text for another audience.

As Ramage, Bean, and Johnson suggest in their discussion of audience, you may want to specify an audience for students' writing projects. Alternatively, you can ask students to choose an audience themselves, based on the topic and purpose of the paper. They might, for example, write an informative essay for high school seniors explaining how to survive the first semester of college life, then give it to an academic advisor at the high school they attended. They might want to persuade a friend not to make an important decision hastily and use the persuasive writing assignment to present their arguments as a letter to this friend.

Although some students may decide to actually give their papers to these audiences, it is not necessary that all do. Yet they should all use the list of questions in the chart on pages 22–23 to think about how their audience will affect the content, form, and style of their text.

You may want to ask students to turn in written responses to these questions prior to or along with each major writing project. Students could also use these questions to explore the impact of their audience and then write a brief paragraph as a cover sheet for each assignment, explaining who the audience is and how as writers they have met the needs of such readers.

Genre

Usually when students write, the genre is assigned. Writers, however, are frequently able to choose which genre best suits the purpose and audience of their desired communication. Therefore, in addition to letting students choose the audience for their writing projects, you may want to experiment with letting students also select the genre. For some purposes, audiences, and theses, letters are a more effective genre than essays. Decide any limits you might set on their selection. Would you accept a diary entry for the expressive paper? Could they develop a brochure for the informative assignment?

The table on page 24 outlines an array of genres you and your students can discuss during the semester.

Using the "For Writing and Discussion" Activities

The "For Writing and Discussion" activity on page 8 is designed to introduce students inductively to the concepts of closed and open forms, before they read the subsequent explanation. There are several ways you can preserve this activity as an inductive exercise: distribute Rockwood's and Pratt's pieces on handouts on the first day of class if students are not likely to have purchased their books yet; have students do this activity on the first day that they have their books but before you assign any reading; or ask students to read only to the middle of page 6 for their first reading assignment. The activity also works well, though, if students have already read the explanation of closed and open forms that follows the directions for the "For Writing and Discussion" activity.

Students are likely to need your guidance to complete this activity. First, ask the class if anyone can define the terms "metaphor," "simile," and "analogy." Even though the distinctions among them are insignificant for the purposes of this exercise, students may be distracted during this exercise if they do not know these terms. They may also be confused if they hear the teacher or other students in the class using them synonymously but they were taught differently in high school or in an introductory literature course they may now be taking. It's worth a moment's time to explain that a metaphor is a comparison drawn between two or more seemingly unlike things without using the terms "like" or "as," that a simile makes the comparison with help of these terms, and that an analogy is usually more complex, needing an explanation before the comparison can be understood. You may want to come to class prepared with an example of each for a topic like "writing" or "college" so that they can better understand what the activity is asking them to create. Tell them it is not important whether they choose to do a metaphor, simile, or analogy. It is only important that the similarity be made to something that is not another text; that is what will distinguish their idea as more than a literal comparison, and therefore, in some way metaphorical.

Metaphors, similes, and analogies are often the result of spontaneous insight. With luck, during the class discussion or in each small group, many students will experience this insight. Yet students do not need to wait for the muses to alight. If they are stuck, tell them to make a list of three to five adjectives that describe one of the passages. Once they've generated that list, they should then not think about the passage at all for the moment but look only at the adjectives and try to think of something else that is fittingly described by all or most of the adjectives they've listed. They can then express the connection between the passage and the second artifact they've identified as a metaphor, simile, or analogy, without necessarily referring to the adjectives that helped them make this connection.

Metaphors, similes, and analogies are useful learning strategies because they reveal students' subjective reactions as well as their intellectual understanding. As you listen to your students' responses, pay attention to the underlying emotional reactions. Do their metaphors imply that closed-form texts are boring or lifeless? Do they indicate that open-form texts are less important, less mature, perhaps exclusively "feminine"? Do they assume that open-form texts must involve stories or that any narrative must be open form? Some students' metaphors may communicate negative attitudes about writing more honestly than the student would be willing to do directly. When students interpret their metaphors during the second part of this activity, ask them to consider how the attitudes their metaphors convey may help or hinder them in their future writing. Most teachers who use this textbook will want students to gain experience writing both closed- and open-form essays, so if students' metaphors are far more positive for one form of writing than another, this would be an ideal time to explore the reasons why.

As you respond to students, be aware that this is a difficult activity. Moreover, at this early stage in the course, before their first work is graded, they may be just as invested in impressing you and learning how you respond to students as they are in learning the rhetorical concepts of closed and open forms. Strive to include as many students in the discussion as possible, to correct misunderstandings quickly and with encouragement, and to let students see your excitement when they are inventive. The most common problems students might encounter, which can be minimized if you address them briefly when they are assigned this activity, are as follows: they may offer a response that describes the form but does not create a metaphor, simile, or analogy (e.g., "The open form is friendly"); they may give a response that is a literal comparison, not metaphorical (e.g., "The open form is like a short story"); or they may provide a response that bases its metaphor on the subject matter of these passages, not their form (e.g., "Rockwood writes about obstacles to the use of wind power, something that is as unlikely to happen in the United States as pigs flying.").

The activity on pages 11–12 is a good getting-acquainted activity, as it asks students to tell stories about their previous writing experiences and attitudes. It's an efficient way to generate lists of the genres students have experienced and to connect their college writing experiences with their prior writing, in or out of school.

The activity on page 11 is a relatively simple exercise that gets students to practice forming questions. It is usually easy for groups to generate lists of questions, and this activity can be done sitting at desks or using computers or the blackboard. The exercise brings in visual material and thus can open up questions about the relationship between graphic and print literacy (a topic which is likely to recur later in the semester). If students start lists of questions either on the board or at a computer terminal, other students can tour the room, adding on to others' lists. This is an easy way to generate many ideas. The activity does not ask students to do anything other than list questions; you can build on their questions by inviting them to present their questions to the class, and then discussing which questions are the most controversial, most interesting, or most dull. This will help students start to reflect on their early inquiries, and it is another activity that will encourage students to get to know each other.

The activity on page 25 is helpful for teaching students that it is not the topic but the writer's presentation of the topic that determines the purpose for writing. This exercise is also a useful way to test students' ability to distinguish between the six purposes clearly (and it's usually a fun activity to do: some students will be very creative about the scenarios they imagine!). After you have given students time to write their scenarios, you could ask students to read theirs without identifying the purpose and see if the class can discern which purpose each student is trying to convey. This exercise can be useful to encourage brainstorming about appropriate topics; it can also be useful later in the writing process, when students are refining their approach to an essay.

Guiding Students through the Writing Project

The writing project for this chapter has two options, each of which offers students a different way to give students practice with brief assignments exploring the relationship between purpose, audience, and genre. These assignments can be done in or out of class, and both options ask students to focus their questions in some specific observations or experience.

Project 2 lends itself to in-class work; students are likely to find the work profitable in a small group, and class discussion is a good opportunity to explore whether students have begun to make the chapter vocabulary their own.

If you are assigning Project 1, consider assigning everyone a shared topic at this early stage in the semester. Particularly at the start of the semester, shared topics promote conversation among class participants. Another promising topic that all students are likely to be able to pose questions about is education. As college students, the educational system has already shaped them greatly and will continue to do so. If you use education, make sure students understand that the textbook's remaining guidelines for the assignment hold true.

For the topic of education, for example, it wouldn't be sufficient to ask what "study abroad" programs your institution has, if any, because even if the student doesn't currently know the answer, it can easily be obtained. If you decide not to use the topic of automobiles and fossil fuels for this assignment, you may still want to discuss it in-depth so that students can better assess and revise their own work.

The most common error students are likely to make when completing this assignment is answering the question they ask. Even though the textbook stresses repeatedly that the brief essay should not answer the question—note the directions in the assignments on page 22 and the absence of conclusive answers in the example by student writer Brittany Tinker—students will still have trouble resisting years of indoctrination that the purpose of school assignments is to show what they know, to answer questions correctly. Take time in class to stress to students that in this case, "what they know" is their ability to ask questions thoroughly and thoughtfully. Consider creating an evaluation sheet that lays out your criteria for grading or responding to this assignment, and work with it in class as students are drafting. Thus you can show them that the primary criterion for success in this activity is *asking a question*. Providing an answer to that question in this assignment is not something important. Other activities later in the course will help students present answers to questions, but this activity focuses on the importance of framing questions.

Another common approach students may take to this assignment is to treat the sample student essays in the textbook as a boilerplate, making only minor content substitutions for their own topic. Instructors who consider imitation a useful learning strategy may not object to such mimicry, while other instructors may penalize students for not being sufficiently original. To prevent misunderstandings on this issue, discuss with students how closely they may acceptably model the sample completed assignment.

Clearly state what criteria you will use to judge students' brief problem-posing essays when you initially announce the assignment. You may choose not to grade the assignment, and use it as a lead-in to a longer assignment. Or you may use it simply as an exercise in creativity and invention (if so, it is best completed very quickly). If you will grade the piece separately, be clear about your criteria. For example, when grading, will you consider the originality of the question or only the thoroughness of its discussion? You may wish to require that the question be narrow, not monumental queries like "Why are people so cruel to animals?" You may also want to direct students to word their questions without bias; for example, "Is it ethical to keep animals in a zoo?" rather than "How can people be so selfish as to keep animals in a zoo?"

A brief writing project assignment is used to conclude each of the first four chapters of *The Allyn & Bacon Guide to Writing.* Your syllabus should indicate how heavily you will weigh these shorter assignments, but you may need to explain to your students now whether you will be using letter grades, a check system, or perhaps even comments without an accompanying grade. To further convey to students your own criteria for the assignment, you might discuss how you would grade the sample student assignment at the end of the chapter, or invite students to participate in grading, evaluating, or discussing the sample.

Because this is likely to be the first writing that students submit to you, you may also want to use it for diagnostic purposes. If a student turns in work that has severe and major weaknesses, make a note (to yourself and to the student) that to do well in the course he or she should conference with you about the problem and perhaps work regularly with a tutor.

Chapter 2
Thinking Rhetorically about Your Subject Matter

Understanding the Chapter's Goals

This chapter builds on Chapter 1 by continuing to emphasize the importance of resisting simple answers or conclusions about interesting topics. In this chapter, students are taught how to pursue their questions and intellectual problems with persistent diligence, what the text calls "wallowing in complexity." Rather than reaching quick conclusions, students can use writing and talking to explore their ideas more thoroughly. The chapter introduces students to numerous, specific techniques that can help them reach new understanding about their subject matter as they shape a thesis that relies on surprise or tension to engage readers. The chapter thus introduces key principles that run through every writing project in the text. It introduces students to the task of developing support for a thesis. Equipped with these tools for managing their subject matter, students will be prepared to adapt their ideas to their purpose, audience, and genre, as discussed in the next chapter.

Reinforcing the Chapter's Rhetorical Principles

William Perry's Stages of Intellectual Development

Perry's research on the stages of intellectual development—particularly as it relates to the issue of what professors want—has important implications for writing teachers of first-year college students. According to Perry's findings, most first-year students are dualists, readily accepting what they are taught and doubting the validity of opposing views, if they recognize alternative positions at all. For a dualist, issues are black or white, right or wrong. A composition student who is a dualist, then, may not understand the importance of providing adequate evidence in a paper because to the student, the point may be self-evident. Also, a student who is a dualist thinks more rigidly and thus is likely to take fewer intellectual risks when writing. Such students will be challenged by the opening part of the chapter on complexity and ill-structured problems.

Understanding Perry's scheme can help you know what cognitive obstacles students encounter when writing and can help you develop realistic expectations for their work. Encouraging students to use the exploratory techniques in this chapter can prompt their intellectual development; yet Perry explains that cognitive development occurs slowly. It is unreasonable to expect that students will change drastically in just one term. In fact, Perry found that some individuals may not achieve the highest stages of development until long after college, if ever. Nevertheless, the strategies for exploratory writing and talking presented in this chapter are instrumental in creating doubt for a student at the dualist stage and prompting the student's intellectual development.

Perry's developmental scheme may also help you respond to the work of older students more appropriately. Intellectual development occurs through life experience, not just college courses, so it is likely that older students in your course will be at a more advanced stage of intellectual maturity. If they write significantly better papers, one major reason may be this difference in their intellectual maturity. Your responsibility as a teacher is to prompt their development too. Try to identify where they fall on Perry's scheme and provide appropriate challenges. You might, for example, assign them to one of the more difficult roles in this chapter's simulation activity (see "Using the 'For Writing and Discussing' Activities" below).

Inquiry

The principle of inquiry forms an important bridge between the previous chapter and this one. The chapter's opening sections stress that asking questions is crucial to the academic experience professors seek to foster. Lists of questions on pages 31–32 will help students see that this type of inquiry is cultivated in departments across campus. You can use the questions listed here to help students develop additional questions about some of the areas listed; this can also tie in to a class activity that asks students to share what their major areas of academic interests are.

Freewriting

Freewriting is the technique of exploratory writing that is used most often throughout *The Allyn & Bacon Guide to Writing*. For students who have never engaged in freewriting before, writing without stopping might seem silly or futile. The best way for students to understand the usefulness of freewriting is to give them an opportunity to do some freewriting during class when the technique is first introduced.

Before they begin, explain that you won't be collecting their freewriting so that students won't be overly concerned with matters of correctness, which defeats the purpose of exploratory writing. Announce a common topic about which students can freewrite. You could ask them to write about a campus issue or, in keeping with the topic of this chapter, you could ask them to answer the question, "What hinders you from regularly pursuing problems?" Then remind students that the benefit of freewriting is the ideas that surface in nonstop writing. Warn them that as they freewrite, you will watch them all carefully and remind those who stop moving their pen or pencil to keep writing ("Doris, keep writing." "Luis, I don't see your pen moving."). If they run out of ideas, they can simply write a statement like "I don't know what to write next" or they can recopy the final few words of their previous sentence until a new thought comes. Time them for ten minutes. You may find that bringing an egg timer to class helps keep track of time.

Afterwards, discuss their reactions to freewriting. Begin by asking for students to raise their hands if they had to write at least one sentence for the sole purpose of keeping their writing implement moving. Then ask these students how many thought of new ideas faster than they would have expected to if they had stopped writing when stuck. Ask the entire class if anyone discovered ideas through freewriting that had never occurred to them before. Invite students to share any insights gained about their topic as they freewrote (bearing in mind your original statement that this writing need not be made public if the students don't want it to).

The chapter also describes focused freewriting, which other textbooks may call looping. To use this technique, a writer first freewrites for ten or fifteen minutes. Then the writer reads the freewriting and underlines the brief portion that seems the most promising for further exploration. On page 34, Ramage, Bean and Johnson refer to these places as "hot spots, centers of interest, centers of gravity, or simply nuggets or seeds." The writer then recopies this brief selection and uses it to begin a second freewriting session. This sequence can be repeated indefinitely, with the writer always underlining the most critical insight and then freewriting to explore it in more detail. Subsequent freewriting sessions may be shorter than the initial one, but the writer should set a prescribed time in advance. Otherwise, the writer may be tempted to stop solely because the ideas seem exhausted. If the predetermined time has not lapsed, the writer can instead use text fillers ("I don't know what to write") and possibly generate more ideas. Focused freewriting is highlighted in later chapters as a way to organize reflection in sustained writing projects.

Freewriting can form a nice ritual beginning to a class period. You might invite students to freewrite for a specified period of time at the start of each class period, using similar questions each time (such as "what was difficult for you as you prepared for today's class period?"). Alternatively, you can shape questions based on the current writing project, or even ask students to suggest a focus for freewriting. Doing some writing in class every day is a good way to prepare for the activities that will follow.

Idea Mapping

Another name sometimes given to this exploratory technique is clustering. Using the idea map in Figure 2.1 as an example, point out to your students that the ideas in the center of the map are the broadest, and that the ideas become more specific as they move to the perimeter of the idea map. Talking through this sample idea map with your students can help them understand how to construct their own. The most common mistake students make when writing idea maps is that they tend to expand the branches of the diagram vertically but not horizontally. That is, they track one thought with increasing specificity but are less likely to consider a wide range of possible alternatives. Thus, their idea maps appear more like lists than clusters. Stress to students that they can benefit from idea maps most if they develop them both vertically (adding branches to become increasingly more specific) and horizontally (writing many branches with equal specificity). It can be helpful to ask students to work in pairs on an idea map in order to take advantage of the quick flow of ideas that can emerge in conversation.

The idea map can be useful as the subject for a class discussion of grading and responding to writing, in addition to its utility as a representation of a heuristic. At the start of a writing class, students are often concerned about grading (especially if you are using a portfolio grading system or some other arrangement that defers grading until after a specified period of revision). Working with this idea map can be a way to get students' attitudes about grading on the table, which will improve the class atmosphere and offer additional opportunities for problem posing.

Explain to students that rarely do all ideas in an idea map get included in a finished text. A writer generates an idea map to thoroughly explore a problem, but once the writer decides on a thesis, whole branches of the idea map may be omitted from the draft as irrelevant. An idea map can be quite helpful in developing support, though, because the writer can look at the map to determine if all the branches coming from the center that will be included in the paper have been developed to an adequate level of specificity. The ideas that are most important to the thesis often follow the branch that extends farthest away from the center of the map.

Encourage students to develop a wide repertoire of exploration strategies. Consider assigning students to write an idea map for the same topic they used when learning to freewrite. They may find one technique more helpful than the other now; however, for a different topic, the other strategy may work better. Students can also regularly use multiple techniques (including the others explained in this chapter) to pursue problems for writing. One way to combine freewriting and idea mapping is for writers to create an idea map first in order to identify various aspects of their topic, then freewrite about one branch.

Some composition theorists have speculated about the relationship between exploratory writing techniques (often called "heuristics") and cognitive styles. One speculation is that people who are more skilled at cognitive activities performed by the left hemisphere of the brain find linear forms of written exploration, such as brainstorming and freewriting, especially useful. Writers who are right-brain dominant seem to find more spatial, associational means of exploration—such as idea mapping—of greater assistance. Although such speculations are not conclusive, certainly students learn differently and thus should be offered a range of techniques for written exploration.

Strong Thesis

Many of your students may already be familiar with the term "thesis" from earlier writing courses they have taken, but don't assume that every student will have heard this term before, or that every student shares the same meaning for the term. You might ask students in the class to define this term in their own words and to explain the significance of a thesis in writing. Make sure they know the distinction between a topic and a thesis. You may also want to facilitate a class discussion on differences in what they have been taught, and what they believe, about the nature of a thesis. For example, some may have been taught in high school to write thesis statements that identify three major points they will develop, a sort of mini-outline for a five-paragraph theme. Do they think that a thesis needs to be expressed as only one sentence, like the examples in this chapter? Must a thesis statement be placed in a particular location of a text (the introduction? the last sentence of the introduction)? Is it ever acceptable to not state the thesis explicitly, and if so, when? These latter questions point to major differences between closed- and open-form texts and will be discussed repeatedly throughout the text. Raising such questions now, however, can help students probe their understanding of thesis.

Formulating a thesis is often the first step a writer takes in consciously considering audience. As writers pose and pursue problems, they are often attentive only to their own inquiry. When writers produce texts with this mindset, they generate what writing theorist Linda Flower terms "writer-based prose," that is, prose that is presented in keeping with the writer's sequence of thought. Flower juxtaposes writer-based prose with reader-based prose, prose that more successfully accommodates the needs readers have when processing text. Perhaps the most essential need of readers is the need to know what core idea a writer is trying to communicate. This is the need that a thesis fulfills. Although readers may disagree with the thesis, they should all be able to identify it.

The discussion of thesis in this chapter is stronger (no pun intended!) than in many other rhetoric textbooks because Ramage, Bean, and Johnson recommend that a thesis not only direct a reader, but that it also surprise the reader. The element of surprise can be what makes the text satisfying for a reader. Surprise is what interests and intrigues a reader. Surprise is what helps an audience perceive subject matter differently after reading a text than they did before. This change of perception, in turn, is what makes a text significant for readers. The term surprise can be a difficult one for both teachers and students; taken to an extreme, the need to surprise can seem silly or impossible. It's important to connect the surprise in any given thesis with the rhetorical context: who is the audience, and what does that audience likely know or believe about the subject of the project? Handled properly, the element of surprise will help students shape their writing projects in a satisfying manner. Surprise and tension help writers and readers connect and pay attention.

Ramage, Bean, and Johnson delineate a number of forms this surprise can take. Encourage students to try many possible forms. On page 41, Ramage, Bean, and Johnson provide a template sentence students can use to create tension in a thesis statement: "Before reading my essay, my readers think this way about my topic:/After reading my essay, my readers will think this different way about my topic." Other useful templates might include:

- Whereas most people believe X, this essay asserts Y.
- Although many people know X, they do not know Y.
- If you are uncertain about X, what you need to understand is Y.
- You may feel certain about X, but as I explain Y in this essay, you will understand that X is far more complicated.

- You may believe X, but this essay will convince you that X is improbable/impossible.
- You may disagree with X, but this essay will convince you that X is correct/true.

Such templates can help students experiment with other types of surprise: enlarging readers' views; clarifying readers' views; problematizing readers' views; entirely restructuring readers' views. It's important to be clear with your students whether you expect their thesis statements to use the forms of the templates exactly or not.

Points and Particulars

In this chapter, students learn that it is not just the *quantity* of support that is important to their writing, but also its *relevance* to their thesis. The particulars are what make a thesis convincing. In return, the thesis is what determines what support is needed: which points and particulars to include and which to exclude.

This list of facts on page 45 helps illustrate the distinction between *information* and *meaning*. You can work with this list in class to show students how a *point* is essential in order to help readers understand what otherwise disjointed (but true) facts add up to. Points are a writer's way of interpreting and analyzing what evidence or data means, and students should come to realize that part of being a writer is moving back and forth between points and particulars. On pages 46–47, the text has a helpful discussion of how particulars can be removed in order to create summary. This short section is very helpful in teaching students how to summarize. You can distribute a text and ask students to summarize it in groups, and then compare versions across groups.

Using the "For Writing and Discussion" Activities

The activity on pages 38–39 invites students to practice the variety of exploratory writing strategies the chapter introduces. Although the textbook suggests switching topics while switching strategies, you might try having students loop through the exploratory strategies while using the same topics. This will likely illustrate the ways in which some strategies work differently for different students. The activity involving close observation of an artifact (chosen by you, or the artifacts presented on page 39) is probably best done as homework. That will give students time to ponder the artifact without so much time pressure. Class discussion can explore what the homework accomplished.

The activity on pages 44–45 gives students practice in creating thesis statements, although as the opening of the activity notes, it is often difficult to come up with good thesis statements in class because there is little time to prepare. Writers ordinarily develop their thesis statements after considered reflection. Nonetheless, the activity asks students to build on the reading earlier in the textbook in order to practice generating and then evaluating thesis statements. This activity is a good way to introduce the notion of audience and to have students begin to evaluate their classmates' work. You can ask students to work through the assigned task in groups, and then have each group write their tentative thesis statements on the blackboard. Then have the class circulate and discuss which are the strongest thesis statements, and which ones could benefit from revision.

The activity on page 47 gives students additional practice in close reading. Students will probably note that the particulars given to support that middle point (about unsolved problems in wind-generation facility production) are more general than those offered for the other points. Given that the letter to the editor was written for a general-readership newspaper, it makes sense that the most technical material is presented in the least detail. The particulars seem crafted to help a not-necessarily scientifically knowledgeable audience understand a scientific argument.

Guiding Students through the Writing Project

This brief writing project gives students practice in resisting definitive conclusions. The believing and doubting game can lead students toward a more relativist stance, a recognition that few arguments have clear, easy answers. The writing project is named a "game," in keeping with Peter Elbow's wording, to encourage students to playfully explore far-reaching possibilities, yet it is a game they should undertake honestly. Point out to students that they are not being asked to write the pros and cons of an argument. Instead, the directive to "believe" asks them to imagine holding arguments that they may not, in fact, believe, and the directive to "doubt" asks them to reject views they might in fact value. Thus, unlike a listing of pros and cons, this assignment prompts students to more rigorously question their personal commitment to their beliefs. Hopefully, through such role playing, they can convince themselves of the validity of other positions in an argument.

If you want to make this writing project even more challenging, you can ask students to first complete the project as it is described in the textbook, then choose one of the assertions they have examined and freewrite once more, articulating a position that is a compromise between the more extreme "believing" and "doubting" descriptions. If students have difficulty reaching a compromise, they can freewrite about why. This additional requirement can teach students that even though issues may be more complex than they realized, after careful consideration they can still draw conclusions—William Perry's final stage of "commitment in relativism."

This writing project is designed as a brief activity (the text recommends fifteen minutes on believing and another fifteen on doubting). You may adapt this project for other uses at later points in the term. For example, you can use it as part of a peer response to student writing, or you can use it as part of a reflective sequence for writers to uncover more of their own assumptions. The believing and doubting game can be a good way for students to test the strength of an emerging thesis statement, to engage with a peer's essay, to brainstorm additional ideas, or to explore the complexities of their own thinking.

Chapter 3
Thinking Rhetorically about
How Messages Persuade

Understanding the Chapter's Goals

This chapter focuses on a more theoretical understanding of rhetoric, looking at how messages persuade. This chapter encourages students to analyze the choices they make in all kinds of communicative situations, formal and informal. When students understand why some communications succeed and others fail, they are better positioned to make good choices about their writing.

Reinforcing the Chapter's Rhetorical Principles

Angle of Vision

Exploratory writing and discussion should help students understand that individual approaches to issues are determined by many factors. Our political leanings, our family backgrounds, our cultures, and our experiences all shape the way we see the world. The political cartoon that appears in Figure 3.1 illustrates the way individual positions affect the angle of vision regarding the current debate on stem cell research. You can spend some class time on this cartoon, and invite students to bring other cartoons to class. The visual representation of different viewpoints makes an easy opening for discussions of this complicated principle. Students often want to rush to conclusions or make quick decisions about how to support points with particulars. Spending time exploring how their positions are affected by their social and family backgrounds will help them consider the complexities involved.

The political cartoon also provides a nice lead-in for the discussion of visual rhetoric that begins later in this chapter, and this section connects well with material to come in Chapter 5, on interpretation.

Appeals to Logos, Ethos, and Pathos

Classical rhetorical theory contributes the terms *logos*, *pathos*, and *ethos*. Some points to stress:

- *Logos*, the root of the term "logical," focuses on the content of a communicative act. The reasons and evidence used in support of a point of view are the logical appeals in any argument.

57

- *Ethos,* the root of the term "ethical," focuses on the communicator and trustworthiness. Ethos is communicated on several levels: content, tone, ability to listen, and ability to be accurate are all related.
- *Pathos,* the root of the term "pathetic," focuses on appeals to values and emotion. The connection to "pathetic" can distract students, as "pathetic" has negative connotations. Students should understand that the emotional basis of an argument can be as important as the other elements.

These three terms come together in the rhetorical triangle (pictured in Figure 3.2). As the questions within the figure make clear, the rhetorical triangle can help writers make decisions about a text, and can also help readers and listeners make judgments about the communication acts they encounter. In different situations, one point of the triangle may be more important. Effective communication usually grows out of all three points.

Nonverbal messages

The rhetorical approach outlined in this chapter applies to more than words. This section of the chapter illustrates connections between rhetoric and visual images, clothing, and other consumer goods. Ramage, Bean, and Johnson explore the connections between news, images, and popular opinion. You can ask students to watch for good examples of visual images in the newspaper, keeping a log for a week of what pictures attract their attention. This can be a good way to help students attend to the pervasiveness of visual images in their world.

Students arrive in college with years of experience in analyzing the messages sent by clothing choices. Students who are parents will likely have additional perspectives on this issue, as they will have made choices (and perhaps argued about those choices) on behalf of their children.

Using the "For Writing and Discussion" Activities

The "For Writing and Discussion" exercise on pages 53–54 asks students to compose letters of recommendation in a complicated situation: they are to imagine that they are professors recommending a former student who is striking and unusual. Working both individually and in groups, students can develop lists of points they might cover in a letter. This exercise should make the notion of "angle of vision" much more concrete for students. As they work through choices about how to recommend a student, or debate what different aspects of Riddle's former performance mean, they will explore their own angles of vision. The table on page 54–55, showing different strategies for creating an angle of vision, will help you and your students further your analysis.

The activities on pages 60 and 62 emphasize visual rhetoric and culture. They are well suited to an in-class activity, and should elicit additional discussion of angle of vision.

Students' experiences with technology and health care will have had a profound impact on their initial willingness to trust new advances in medicine or trust health care professionals. Ask students to explore what experiences affect their responses to the images. Similarly, their experiences with the consumer goods and the communities associated with them in Figures 3.5–3.8 will affect their initial interpretations.

Guiding Students through the Writing Project

The brief writing project here gives students additional practice analyzing angle of vision. This can be used as a short homework assignment, and then discussed in small groups as a way of assessing how well students can work with the terms introduced in this chapter. Because it requires careful reading of the short sample texts, it will work better as an overnight assignment than as an in-class assignment. Ramage, Bean, and Johnson provide useful context for the excerpts on page 64 and you can use that information to help prepare your students for the activity. Those who have not attended to debates about nuclear power may need some help getting into the analysis.

Students' analysis should explore the differences in the two pieces. Why does the second passage raise questions about the topic in ways that the first does not? Remind students that starting by considering basic questions such as "Who wrote this?' "Where did it get published?" and "Who was the primary audience for this passage?" will lay the foundation for analyzing the more particular rhetorical elements listed in the project tasks. An op-ed piece addresses the general public with a very different aim than a government report does. If students start with the rhetorical basics of audience, purpose, and message, they will be able to use the principle of angle of vision well. The rhetorical triangle will also be of help, as well as the questions in Figure 4.1, which will help students begin their analysis.

Chapter 4
Thinking Rhetorically about Style and Document Design

Understanding the Chapter's Goals

In this chapter, students learn that effective writing entails managing not only the subject matter (discussed in Chapter 2), but also the style of the document, from word choice to page layout. These elements are shaped by the writer's understanding of purpose, audience, and genre. This chapter can be a touchstone throughout the semester. The general principles that it introduces are explored in specific ways with each writing project, and you may wish to return to this chapter to refresh students' understanding of key assumptions in the text. In addition, you may wish to return to this chapter as students reflect on their learning and polish their final work near the close of the course or grading period.

Reinforcing the Chapter's Rhetorical Principles

Style

Style is a multifaceted component of writing that involves voice, tone, and position. Style is very much rhetorical, and you should encourage students to think about the ways in which style grows out of consideration of genre, audience, and purpose—all concepts introduced in Chapter 3. Figure 4.1 (a new addition to this edition) is an excellent prompt for class discussion. Invite students to look at the star and the table underneath it, and ask them to use the figure to analyze a text you provide (some parts of the campus newspaper, perhaps).

Rhetoric and the Scale of Abstraction

Although editing for word choice is a topic sometimes left for the very end of a writing course, thinking about word choices is another excellent way to prompt students to see how they act rhetorically at every step of the writing process. Connect the material in this chapter with Chapter 3's presentation of points and particulars. The graphics on page 70–71 are excellent models for class activity. You can model activity guides for students by giving them charts to fill out about their own writing. Having students consider, for example, how they would place one of their own pieces of writing on the scale of abstraction will help them evaluate their own style.

Emphasis and Style

The chapter's section on wordiness will extend students' work with the scale of abstraction. Considering how sentences are structured—what phrases or clauses are subordinated, what words are highlighted in positions of importance—will invite students to shape their text in light of their rhetorical goals. Connect all discussions of word choice and revision to students' articulations of their purpose, audience, and genre.

Document Design

This chapter includes attention to document design as an element of style or genre. It's important to be clear about your own expectations for document design, and to invite students to experiment with design as appropriate for your assignments. This chapter devotes attention to fonts, space, and color and offers several examples for students to consider. Especially if your class has access to a computer classroom, you can invite students to change their document layouts and consider the effect this has on readers' reactions. Consider making some of your design expectations part of your formal writing assignments. Let students know what you expect and why; this is another occasion for showing students how teachers think rhetorically about writing.

Using the "For Writing and Discussion" Activities

The activity on page 69 focuses students' attention on writing style (and prefigures the chapter's later discussion of document design). The sequence of questions will move students into a detailed analysis of the effects of style. Many students will quickly identify a few prominent style differences (the difference in vocabulary and the presence of personal details in one piece, for example); the question sequence should prompt more detailed examination of the samples in the text. You can continue this style analysis on the texts they provide.

The activity on page 72 reinforces the previous chapter's material on points and particulars. While some students may feel that they lack the specific knowledge to invent details about either the sports or women's magazine examples, if the students work together they should be able to pool enough knowledge to generate examples. Help focus discussion on both the content of the details (what should be mentioned) and the style (how the different genres might elicit different types of vocabulary or tone). The e-mail example makes different demands than the college newspaper example, and students usually enjoy plumbing the differences among genres.

The activity on pages 75–76 is very effective as an in-class exercise. You can use the blackboard or computer screens to allow groups to share their work and compare efforts. The fact that no two groups will come up with exactly the same revision is a wonderful teaching device. Ask each group to provide a rationale for its revision. This will prompt discussion of the core rhetorical principles in use.

The activity on page 82 also works particularly well as a group activity, since the elements of document design are so plentiful that group discussion is easily stimulated. While the questions focus attention on layout, you can emphasize the ways in which other rhetorical principles are at work here. For example, the differences in font use in women's and men's magazines are connected to assumptions about purpose and audience.

Guiding Students through the Writing Project

This assignment asks students to condense and adapt a passage from *The New England Journal of Medicine* for readers of *Reader's Digest*. In the instructions for the assignment, Ramage, Bean, and Johnson write, "Although the style of the medical article may seem daunting at first, a little work with a good dictionary will help you decipher the whole passage" (84). If your students are not skilled users of dictionaries, they may need more assistance than this advice—in fact, this assignment can be a fun one to do in class, as it will allow students to help one another and allow you to intervene with any students who get overwhelmed by a lack of medical knowledge.

Begin by asking students to bring their own dictionaries to class on the day you will assign this project for homework. If your class meets in a computer classroom, you will find online dictionaries a useful resource. You might want to borrow a few hardback college dictionaries from colleagues for the class period in case most of your students own only paperback editions, or in case some students don't own a dictionary or forget to bring one. Ask students to work in groups to note the differences in their dictionaries. You might ask them to look up any word in each dictionary and see how the definitions differ in their degree of detail. Then ask students to list the next fifteen words defined in each dictionary to see if the dictionaries differ in which words they define. Finally, ask students to look at any special sections in the front or back of the dictionaries to see how they differ in their other features. Many first-year college students don't realize there are major differences between dictionaries and without this activity may not know what Ramage, Bean, and Johnson mean by a "good dictionary." Tell students that most bookstores—including the one on campus—sell several different college dictionaries, and if they own only a paperback one, buying a better dictionary now is an investment that will benefit them throughout college and long after.

Because the mini-article students will write for this assignment is quite short—the sample is only three sentences—students may be tempted to skip over whatever parts of Patrono's article they don't understand. Emphasize to students that they need to understand, at least generally, everything Patrono writes in order to translate this article for other readers accurately. As their first step in understanding this passage, they can rewrite it in less scientific language, without yet condensing or adapting it for a *Reader's Digest* audience. Sometimes a word they are familiar with may be used differently in this passage, such as the word "loading" in "a single loading dose of 200–300 mg." Students may then need to use a dictionary to find alternate definitions of words they know. If no dictionary definition seems suitable, perhaps they can deduce the meaning of the word from its context: "a single loading dose of 200–300 mg followed by a daily dose of 75–100 mg" suggests that "loading" is the initial dose of what will become a regular regimen.

Also tell students that if they can't find a medical term in the dictionary, they may be able to determine its meaning by breaking the word into its syllables and then looking up each. This will be true, for example, for the words "pathophysiologic" and "antithrombotic" in the introduction. Other medical terms, such as "platelet," have no ready synonym. Students must then decide when they define the word whether to also retain the original word along with its explanation. They may even want to check their medicine cabinet to give a more familiar interpretation to the doses cited: how many aspirin tablets would someone need to get 200–300 mg or 75–100 mg?

Once students have paraphrased the passage for their own interpretation, they can then decide how to present these findings for a *Reader's Digest* mini-article. They will need to decide what is most important in the excerpted portions of Patrono's article so they know what to include and what may be left out. Students need not restrict their mini-article to three sentences, the length of the example, but it should still be quite brief. By rereading Ramage, Bean, and Johnson's advice on pages 66–67 of the textbook, students should realize that the best structure for this mini-article is closed form: it should communicate efficiently and clearly to readers who want to access information quickly.

Students also need to make decisions about style in adapting this medical article for a *Reader's Digest* audience. They can use the four broad aspects of style identified on page 57 of the textbook to analyze the style of the sample *Reader's Digest* mini-article. Assuming that John Hargreaves (the scientist whose work is reported in the quoted *Reader's Digest* passage) also reported his study findings in a medical journal, it is unlikely that the study used language like "a piece of hard cheese the size of a sugar cube" or even "a healthy, cavity-free smile" ("teeth," perhaps, but probably not "smile"). The writer of this mini-article has made such stylistic decisions to render her text friendly in tone. In the third sentence, she explains the scientific phenomenon explained in the medical study in lay terms, keeping the mini-article educational. Urge students to similarly consider how they might make their mini-article stylistically entertaining as well as informative.

Even the titles of these sample texts are very different in style. The mini-article is titled "For Teeth, Say Cheese," whereas the medical study is titled "Aspirin as an Antiplatelet Drug." Ask students to write a title for their mini-article that would interest *Reader's Digest* readers (Chapter 18 on revising closed-form prose has a nice exercise on title development). Encourage students to test the success of their mini-articles before turning them in by asking several people not enrolled in this course to read them. If possible, students should ask people who are familiar with or regularly read *Reader's Digest*. Students can then ask these readers if the mini-article is both clear and enjoyable to read.

Chapter 5
Seeing Rhetorically:
The Writer as Observer

Understanding the Chapter's Goals

Chapters 5 and 6 have related goals. Together, these chapters instruct students that using language necessarily entails interpretation. Thus, whenever students write or read, they should be aware of how the text represents "reality." They must also consider what the implications are for a given interpretation compared with other possible interpretations. As students learn to write (Chapter 5) and read (Chapter 6) with greater awareness of how language shapes understanding, they will become more critical thinkers. In particular, Chapter 5 builds on the notion of angle of vision to help students become more conscious of the ways their perspectives affect what they observe.

Reinforcing the Chapter's Rhetorical Principles

Angle of Vision

Discussing rhetorical observation teaches students that even the most factual accounts are necessarily slanted by what they include and exclude and by what they emphasize. The term "angle of vision" (first introduced in Chapter 3) adds to this understanding by explaining why a text may be slanted in one direction rather than another. This chapter offers students a chance to work with the material from Chapter 3 in a more specific context. This chapter should help students see that, at times, writers may consciously assume an angle of vision that is consistent with their political interests. The opening portion of the chapter richly illustrates this connection between perspective and content.

The text offers an extended set of materials on proposed oil drilling in Alaska, featuring text and photographs illustrating how angle of vision drives rhetorical choices. You can work with verbal descriptions of the Arctic National Wildlife Reserve (ANWR) in Exercise 1 and visual descriptions of the ANWR in Exercise 2. Depending on whether the authors of the texts support or oppose drilling and exploration, they highlight different themes or pieces of information. It can be instructive to work with these exhibits sequentially, asking students to first look only at Figures 5.1 and 5.2 (in Exercise 2 on page 91) and then to freewrite their reactions to the pictures. Class discussion might then compare reactions of students who are somewhat familiar with the debate over ANWR and those who aren't. You can then ask students to move to the next images—Figure 5.3 on page 92—and then do another freewrite about their impressions. Similar sequences of freewriting in response to the exhibits can help students see how their own views are affected by each text.

Later in the chapter, the text demonstrates that the angle of vision may be unconscious and/or inescapable, derived from the position of the observer. For example, Ramage, Bean, and Johnson provide two passages by female anthropologists describing women in the !Kung tribe foraging for food (pages 95–96). The anthropologists differ in their interpretations of how the tribe and the women themselves feel about the women's work. Marshal's description of the women's relationship to their work is predominantly negative; however, Draper's description of the same phenomenon is predominantly positive. You may want to ask the class to speculate about the causes for these different interpretations. Perhaps the anthropologists were observing the tribe during times of different food availability, and the foraging was much less productive when Marshal did her studies. Or, perhaps Marshal went away from the encampment with the women while they gathered food and observed how hard they worked, while Draper may have stayed in camp, causing her to notice the excitement of the children more than the women's labor.

The possible angles of vision are limitless. Yet another anthropologist studying the same behavior may focus not on women's attitudes toward their work but on whether the women work collaboratively or individually. Still another anthropologist might study whether all women work equally or whether a tribal hierarchy determines the women's division of labor. Ask students whether they think a male anthropologist might describe the women differently, even whether a male anthropologist might be as likely as a female anthropologist to study !Kung women's work. A non-anthropologist observing the !Kung tribe would have a different angle of vision altogether. This observer may pay more attention to individuals and not notice patterns of group behavior as much.

You can also discuss whether as outsiders, anthropologists may be raising questions that the !Kung do not consider themselves. Perhaps the !Kung women think only about completing the tasks necessary for their survival, without expecting fulfillment or personal satisfaction from their work. Ask students to consider whether the children are likely to perceive the women's work differently than do the adult men in the tribe. Conclude the discussion by stressing again that multiple "truths" may exist because of different angles of vision. Yet, this does not mean that all statements are true. For example, based on the information provided by both Marshal and Draper, it would be false to assert that the food gathering done by the women is of only minor importance to the survival of the tribe.

On pages 93–94, Ramage, Bean, and Johnson identify several of the factors that affect an observer's angle of vision: the extent of the observer's prior knowledge; the observer's cultural understanding; the observer's beliefs and values. In Chapter 6, when Ramage, Bean, and Johnson discuss differences in audiences, the traits they identify can equally affect a writer's angle of vision. You will be able to build strong links between Chapters 5 and 6 on this point. Ask students to brainstorm a list of other possible influences on a writer's angle of vision. These might include age, level of education, time in history, place of residence (e.g., rural/urban), personality (e.g., introverted/extroverted;

optimistic/pessimistic), personal history (e.g., childhood experiences), physical ability, and health.

It is important for students to understand that they cannot entirely control their angle of vision, that it is intricately tied to their identity. The writing project in this chapter will allow them to see that writing always entails an angle of vision; however, you will need to reinforce that writers' angles of vision are far more complex than what writers purposefully contrive.

Also discuss with students the implications of the concept "angle of vision." No single angle of vision can fully depict the subject being examined; therefore, writers must strive to be aware of, and responsible for, their angles of vision. Because the nature of language mandates that observers select, omit, and give emphasis when writing, writers must make ethical choices to represent their subjects fairly.

It may seem like a limitation that no single vision of a subject can be complete. Yet this phenomenon also has many merits. Writers aware of their limited vision gain humility about what they write, knowing it is not the final word, and may even explore their ideas more fully in an attempt to understand other possible angles of vision. Writers can also gain tolerance for others' views, recognizing that other angles of vision may be as valid as their own. Writers who realize that multiple angles of vision are necessary to understand a subject thoroughly will be more eager to listen empathetically and learn from others. They will be more willing collaborators. Finally, because the more angles of vision that are available the more a subject can be understood, each individual's vision has value. Each individual's vision adds to others', if only in some small way, giving each person a compelling motivation to write.

Rhetorical Observation

It can be difficult for students who are educated in the empirical tradition to understand that facts can rarely, if ever, be presented completely objectively. Even when what is stated is empirically accurate, which facts are selected for presentation and which are emphasized will still bias the presentation. Such bias is a normal part of writing, not a flaw. As Ramage, Bean, and Johnson explain to students on page 105, "authors *create* an angle of vision through rhetorical choices they make while composing." Stress that the writing assignments in your course require that students consider the angle of vision they create through their choices.

Ten minutes into the class period on the day that you begin this chapter, you might ask each student to briefly write a factual account of everything that has happened in the past ten minutes, using "I" to describe his or her own experience. Write a description from your perspective also. Then call on several students to read their accounts aloud; read yours too. This brief exercise can quickly show the impossibility of a fully objective record even when the event being described is fairly straightforward.

Students may have noted different conversations among classmates that took place as the class began, and some may have looked at what you were carrying when you entered the room, to see if you had assignments to return. As the class began, you may have noted who was absent, who arrived late, even who was sitting in a seat different from where he or she usually sits, and you have probably already begun trying to assess the students' energy level. Students' accounts of the beginning of class are likely to differ from yours and also from one another's. Discuss with students whether any of these written accounts are truer than others. Some accounts may be more complete, more detailed than others, but are any more factual? Using this exercise can help students understand that there are many simultaneous truths—each accurate from its own perspective—and that just because complete objectivity is impossible does not mean "anything goes." False accounts of what has transpired during the first ten minutes of class could still be written.

Rhetorical Strategies

As the table on page 97 highlights, students can see five rhetorical strategies that affect how a text conveys a particular angle of vision. Advise students to read passages they wish to rhetorically analyze several times, at least once for each of the five features. They can consult this chart during composing or peer-reviewing sessions to apply these strategies fully in their own work.

You may want to point out to your students that the second strategy—selecting or omitting details—is far easier to discern when there are two passages that students can contrast, as in the example given of the two anthropologists' reports and this chapter's writing project. When students do not have an easy basis of comparison, they must be more creative in imagining what details have been omitted. One strategy you might recommend to students is that they apply the following journalistic questions to determine what the writer may have excluded from the text:

- Who is involved? Include all those who are observing or who may be affected.

- What is happening? Include what is happening on the periphery of the writer's angle of vision, what a wide-angle lens would capture.

- When and where is it happening? Include the historical and cultural context.

- By what means is it happening? Include what limitations prevent other events from occurring.

- Why is it happening? Include an analysis of the expenditures and gains of those involved.

For features three and four—which deal with word choice—and feature five—on sentence structure—tell students to pay attention to the mental images that emerge as they read or write. Once they have identified words with strong connotations and figurative language, students can determine the commonalities of these images and better judge the writer's intent.

The chapter's section on composing (pages 101 ff.) will also help students understand the rhetorical features for analysis. It can be helpful to teach those pages together with the presentation of the techniques for analysis to give students the greatest number of examples at the start. Looking at the discussion of generating details (pages 100–101), for example, will help students recognize words with positive and negative connotations in the text they are analyzing.

Using the "For Writing and Discussion" Activities

The "For Writing and Discussion" activity on page 98 of the textbook requires students to perform a rhetorical analysis of two paragraphs. This activity will help them to study closely how one student has used various techniques to convey contrasting impressions of the same scene, which will prepare them well for writing and analyzing their own paragraphs (this chapter's writing project). Once students have had a chance to read both paragraphs, instruct them to analyze both for one rhetorical feature at a time. The analysis below is not inclusive, but does give examples for each rhetorical feature of some differences students might note between the passages.

One feature students should analyze is the writer's overt statements of meaning. In the first paragraph, the writer conveys positive descriptions directly through phrases such as "guarded with shiny rubber boots and colorful umbrellas," "splashes happily," and "radiant orange, yellow, and red leaves blanket the side-walk." In the second paragraph, overt statements of meaning include "steady drizzle of rain" "dismal weather, dull grayness," and "tread grimly on." Students might note that in these paragraphs, the overt statements in the first paragraph refer to general conclusions about the scene, whereas in the second paragraph there are more overt statements that refer to particular elements of the scene. Ask students whether this affects which description is more convincing. Do they think that fewer comprehensive overt statements were possible for the first paragraph because the scene being described is hard to depict? Can they add any particular details to the first paragraph that would embellish the description and its effect?

Another feature students should analyze is what details the writer selects and omits in each passage. In these descriptions of a street corner, issues of weather, commuter behavior, and light are treated very differently in each paragraph. Students should look for details that are included in each paragraph, such as the references to what people are doing on the street and what that might imply about their attitudes. The first paragraph argues that the people observed are happy, while the second paragraph views the people quite differently.

Students should also look for more subtle differences in what is included or omitted. Some of the differences in detail are adjectives that are included in one passage but omitted in the other. Note how the clothing and the toddler are described in each paragraph: "colorful" or "rain soaked," "splashes happily in a puddle," or ""stomping in an oil-soaked puddle."

Figurative language, the fourth feature students must analyze, is less common in these paragraphs. The first paragraph uses several cheerful metaphors, including making a comparison of the toddler's rain gear to that of a tugboat captain. This figurative language evokes a positive atmosphere. The second paragraph does not contain an easily identifiable instance of figurative language, although the descriptions of the pedestrians as "sleep-swollen" connects with the tired, unhappy view of this scene.

The last analysis students must complete of these paragraphs is of their sentence structures. The structures of the first and last sentences of the two paragraphs are virtually identical; the descriptions start with a comment about the weather as seen from the window and end with a description of the mother and child. In the intervening sentences, however, the writer controls the emphasis of the sentences more deliberately. In paragraph 1, the sentences all contain positive conclusions about mood. In contrast, paragraph 2 uses the ends of sentences to emphasize negative images, accenting the ways in which the weather—cold temperatures or oily puddles—makes it difficult to be out on the street. In both paragraphs, the writer uses the accumulation of adjectives to strengthen the intended impact.

"Exhibits on the Arctic National Wildlife Refuge" (pages 90–93)

The three sets of texts here involve students in the analysis of verbal and textual rhetoric. Students can work together or alone to move through the question sequences that have been tailored to the different texts (on page 90, there are questions about the written ANWR descriptions and, on page 92, there are questions about the photographs and pamphlet images).

The questions on page 90 direct students to engage in close reading analysis. Use the table on page 97 to help students analyze what strategies these authors have used, connecting the strategies to the authors' views of the ANWR drilling controversy. The questions here are set up to prompt students to return to the text in order to carefully examine those strategies. These questions ask students to analyze word choice in the two descriptions. The questions segment an exploration of word choice nicely, drawing students' attention to some of the particularly evocative words in use (like "smoke-belching oil rigs" and "American jobs." Students may find it easier to do this exercise if you skip to the "For Reading and Discussion" activity on page 107, which uses a more familiar scene to explore similar rhetorical territory.

The questions on page 92 direct students to analyze the visual texts, connecting visual and verbal arguments. In effect, they must identify the claim or point conveyed by each picture. Students will likely develop more than one idea for each picture, and you can discuss the ways in which students' own positions make them more or less likely to identify those ideas. In addition, you should ask students to support their claims with reference to details in each photograph. For example, a student who says that the visual argument in Figure 5.1 (page 91) is that polar bears are vulnerable and need protection might stress the prominence of the bear cubs in the upper right, and the cubs' dependence on the mother bear at left. A student who says that the photo argues that the ANWR is pristine might point out that the only things visible in the photograph are the bears; there is nothing else to see because nothing else is there. In Figure 5.2, students can plausibly argue that the photograph conveys the caribou's coexistence with the oil industry. "Commerce threatens the caribou" or "Machines don't belong in the wilderness" are arguably the claims made by Figure 5.2.

These questions focus students' attention on angle of vision. Point students to the similarities and differences in the texts, since that is one way to compare what elements are included (or not) in each text. Advocates of drilling point out the ways that the Arctic winter makes the ANWR a forbidding environment for people and animals, and they also point out the ways in which similar environments exist in other Arctic regions. They highlight the human occupants of the ANWR and the human need for jobs. Opponents of drilling focus attention on the presence of animal life and "unspoiled wilderness." They don't mention human needs much and focus on the animals' experiences alone.

"Henry Morton Stanley's Account" (page 108) and "Mojimba's Account" (page 105)

A useful approach for discussing the first question following this pair of accounts is to design a chart on the chalkboard, listing "Stanley's Account" and "Mojimba's Account" vertically and listing the five strategies of a rhetorical analysis (identified in Question 3 following the reading) as horizontal headings across the top of the chart. Then lead a class discussion prompting students to fill in the chart. The contrast between the two accounts is most striking when students can see the chief differences summarized. Although this is the third question in the set, it can be useful to start with this question, since it will help students review the basic rhetorical principles displayed in the texts before moving to other issues.

For example, Stanley's account offers overt statements of meaning in these descriptions: "a sight that sends the blood tingling through every nerve and fibre [sic] of the body"; "Our blood is up now"; "It is a murderous world"; and "We hate the filthy vulturous ghouls." Mojimba's account is different in his overt descriptions of the tribe's reactions: first excitement—"We were open-mouthed with astonishment"; then joy—"We will prepare a feast . . . and escort him into the village with rejoicing!"; and finally fear—"We were paralyzed with fright." Mojimba's account does not include overt statements of hatred, as does Stanley's account.

In charting how the two accounts differ in their selection and omission of details, make sure students notice that both writers emphasize the destructiveness of the other party while minimizing the destructiveness of their own. Stanley includes the information that those in the canoe "let fly their spears" and refers to "the fight in the village streets," inferring that the violence is reciprocal. In contrast, Mojimba omits any reference to a counter-attack, claiming that the tribal member's actions included only retreat and surrender: "We fled into our village. . . . We fled into the forest and flung ourselves on the ground." The most significant difference in the accounts' information is that Stanley does not acknowledge that the explorers killed Africans and destroyed ("plundered and burned") their village in this encounter.

The connotations of words and figurative language used by Stanley and Mojimba also differ. Whereas Stanley describes "a flotilla of gigantic canoes bearing down upon us," Mojimba writes of "the great canoes" used for ceremonial occasions. Stanley describes the tribe's singing as "a swelling barbarous chorus," while Mojimba describes it as "songs of joy." Collectively, Stanley's choice of words is threatening and violent in connotation: "gigantic," "bearing down," "barbarous," "murderous," "daring," "cannibals." His figurative language—"a monster canoe," "vulturous ghouls"—has similarly violent connotations. Mojimba's word choice is more harmonious early in the passage: "brothers," "ceremonial," "honor." Later in the passage his words reflect the tribe's terror—"fled," "flung ourselves," "fearful"—but are not as violent in their connotations as the words used by Stanley. Mojimba's figurative language is also less aggressive: "We were paralyzed with fright."

The final rhetorical strategy used by Stanley and Mojimba—the ordering and shaping of sentences—cannot be analyzed entirely because the accounts that are provided contain many ellipses. Nevertheless, students should notice that Stanley emphasizes "It is a murderous world" by making this statement a main clause at the beginning of a sentence. He also takes emphasis away from "sound the retreat" by placing this phrase in the middle of a long sentence.

The sentence structure of Mojimba's account emphasizes the relentlessness of the aggressors by closely duplicating a key sentence: "We fled into our village—they came after us. We fled into the forest. . . ." The sentence structure of Mojimba's account is also especially effective when reporting the result of the explorers' attack: "When we returned that evening our eyes beheld fearful things: our brothers, dead, dying, bleeding, our village plundered and burned, and the water full of dead bodies." The colon in this sentence is a dramatic introduction to the gruesome detail that follows. The omission of weak verbs in this list—such as "our brothers *were* dead, dying, and bleeding, our village *was* plundered and burned, and the water *was* full of dead bodies"—contributes to its stark power.

The second, fourth, and fifth questions on page 106 ask students to identify a factual version of the two accounts. Some students may want to include all the information from both accounts without obvious bias. Notice, however, that the two accounts are contradictory in revealing who initiated the attack. Stanley reports that the Africans launched spears before the British explorers retaliated with musketry. Mojimba's account, however, describes the explorers as firing first and does not describe the tribe responding with weapons at all.

The sixth question on page 100 of the textbook refers to "the believing and doubting game," which was introduced in Chapter 2. To complete this exercise, students would first say or write, "I *believe* it is possible to create an objective and unbiased account of the Congo phenomenon" and then generate as many reasons as possible to support this statement. When they have exhausted their ideas, students would then say or write, "I *doubt* it is possible to create an objective and unbiased account of the Congo phenomenon" and then generate reasons for this impossibility.

Ultimately, this question prompts students to consider the extent to which complete objectivity is possible in language. In essence, such writing would seek to nullify the effect of the textual features explained on pages 97 of the textbook, the five elements of a rhetorical analysis. It would contain no overt statements of meaning. It would be balanced in its detail, with no extraneous information but also no notable omissions. The word choice would be highly denotative, with as little connotative value as possible. The writing would be devoid of figurative language. Also, the sentences would be structured so that all information received equals emphasis. After students discuss the extent to which they believe such objectivity is possible, you may want to raise the question of what political interests may underlie a seemingly neutral angle of vision. What stake might someone have, for example, in discouraging the formation of judgments? Writers who encourage a seemingly neutral angle of vision may want readers to avoid assigning blame or responsibility, to instead accept information passively. This may be especially true if the writer is the person at fault.

"Two Descriptions of the Same Classroom and a Self-Reflection" (page 106–108)

This student example introduces a sample reflection, so it will be a useful model when asking students to engage in peer-review activities for this chapter's writing project. The reflection focuses on student Tamyln Rogers' use of words and particular details. Students might explore, in answering Question 1, how sentence structure is a particularly interesting aspect of the two paragraphs. The structures of the first and last sentences of the two paragraphs are virtually identical; the descriptions start with the basic size of the room and end with a reference to the view out of the windows. In the intervening sentences, however, Rogers controls the emphasis of the sentences more deliberately. In paragraph 1, the third and fourth sentences end with specific descriptions of students' academic work. In contrast, paragraph 2 uses the ends of sentences to emphasize negative images, accenting the ways in which it is difficult to accomplish work in this environment. In both paragraphs, Rogers uses the accumulation of adjectives to strengthen the intended impact.

Students might also note that in these paragraphs, the overt statements in the first paragraph refer to general conclusions about the scene, whereas in the second paragraph there are more overt statements that refer to particular elements of the scene. Ask students whether this affects which description is more convincing. Do they think that fewer comprehensive overt statements were possible for the first paragraph because the scene being described is hard to depict? Can they add any particular details to the first paragraph that adds to the description and its effect?

Figurative language, another feature students might analyze, is less common in these paragraphs, but useful nonetheless The only clear instance in the first paragraph is the description of the room as being like "the jeans and favorite sweater you put on to go out for pizza with friends." This simile adds to the favorable impression of the scene by connecting with students' social experiences with friends, evoking a positive atmosphere. The second paragraph does not contain an easily identifiable instance of figurative language, although the classroom is described as "baked by the sun," which connotes an oven, an inappropriate working environment.

Guiding Students through the Writing Project

Students can follow the advice on pages 99–104 of the textbook when drafting and revising this chapter's writing project. The first half of the assignment is for students to deliberately alter their angles of vision by providing one pleasant and one unpleasant description of the identical scene. If you would like to make the assignment even more challenging, you can tell students to write two descriptions of the same scene, but rather than making one description pleasant and the other unpleasant, ask them to role-play a change in their identity while writing the two descriptions. This role playing will allow students to "defamiliarize" their subject of study. The introduction to the assignment, which discusses different rationales for the two descriptions, is worth spending some class time on to help students understand why and how they are practicing description.

Students might, for example, give two descriptions of the college football stadium: one from the perspective of a spectator who played football in high school and the other from the perspective of someone who has little or no experience in organized sports. How is a trip down a grocery store aisle perceived differently by an adult and a child? How is a local singles bar perceived differently by a straight person and a gay person? How is a nearby park perceived differently by a groundskeeper and a person recently released from prison?

If students approach the writing project in this way, assuming the identities of different observers, they can still use the advice Ramage, Bean, and Johnson provide on pages 100–101 for composing descriptions: generate sensory descriptions for each observer; use words that "show" rather than "tell"; use precise words with strong connotations to create a dominant impression. As in Ramage, Bean, and Johnson's guidelines, the writer must still describe the same scene at the same time. But rather than writing one pleasant and one unpleasant description, the descriptions will vary according to the identity of the observer. Both descriptions may thus be pleasant or both may be unpleasant, yet they will differ in the details that create these impressions.

If students complete the writing project according to the directions in the textbook, writing one pleasant and one unpleasant description, you may still require them to examine how their perception is affected by their identity. As part of their rhetorical analysis, they may want to freewrite about what observations are missing from both of their descriptions. They can consider how someone else might observe the same scene in still other ways. Such inquiry may help them to reflect upon how their own perception is affected by their prior knowledge, culture, beliefs, and values. You may also want students to address in their final reflection the extent to which what they've learned by writing these descriptions is true for other writing they do, even when they are not deliberately altering their angle of vision. They should realize that even when they are not aware of its presence, they still write with an angle of vision.

This is the first chapter of *The Allyn & Bacon Guide to Writing* that includes guidelines for peer reviewers. You may want to ask students to read the fourth skill set in Chapter 17, on using peer review effectively, before their first experience with peer reviews. You may also want to review the first section of this instructor's manual, on general teaching strategies, for advice on how to best assign students to groups

The complication of peer reviews when students face an identical task is that students will naturally incorporate one another's ideas into their own work—in some ways that may strengthen their thinking and in some ways that may obscure it. For this assignment, students are likely to choose different scenes to describe, and their rhetorical analyses will obviously differ. Yet their final reflections could be interchangeable. During peer reviews, a student who had few ideas for the final reflection section of the writing project may like the ideas in another student's paper and adapt them for his or her own use. You can ask students to write an additional reflection after the peer-review process is complete to explain how the peer-review process affected their own work. You may also want to have students submit drafts of their assignments. That way, if the papers of two students who worked together have very similar reflections, you can examine their drafts to see who deserves credit for those ideas, and you can begin an important conversation with students about acknowledging the influence of peer reviewers on their finished texts. You can also begin a conversation about the appropriate use of others' ideas.

If you ask students to turn in copies of the reviews they received when they turn in their revised writing project, occasionally the writer of the work may not be able to find the reviews, which unfairly penalizes the reviewers. Instead, you may want to require students to bring two copies of each peer review they write: one for the writer and a photocopy (or additional printout, if they write the review on a computer) for you. You can then promptly give students credit for the reviews they write.

Chapter 6
Reading Rhetorically:
The Writer as Strong Reader

Understanding the Chapter's Goals

Chapter 5 taught students how to observe rhetorically, aware of how their angle of vision affects their text. In this chapter, students learn to read rhetorically. They will learn how to vary their reading practices according to their purpose for reading, how to summarize both open- and closed-form texts, and how to read against the grain of a text, which allows them to write a strong response. The writing project for this chapter is for students to write a summary and strong response for a reading; the chapter supports either the use of readings in the chapter or the use of instructor-provided readings.

Reinforcing the Chapter's Rhetorical Principles

Reading Processes

Ramage, Bean, and Johnson identify ways in which skilled readers vary their reading processes. The opening section of this chapter explores rhetorical reading strategies, and offers students the chance to compare strategies of expert and novice readers. You can help students understand the rhetorical nature of reading by helping them to connect their choice of reading strategies with their purpose for reading—just as in the last chapter, you chose class activities to help them see how their writing strategies are connected to their purpose for writing.

You can make use of a short reading later in the textbook to illustrate these principles very effectively. Ask students to turn to the short essay on page 231 of the textbook, entitled "How Much Does It Cost to Go Organic?" Then provide this sequence of directions:

- Scan the essay to find the answer to this question: "How much more would it cost a family of four to buy organic versus non-organic vegetables in an average year?" When you know the answer, stop reading and raise your hand. Time how long it takes for two-thirds of the students to raise their hands. When most of the class has finished this task, give the next instruction.

- Now skim the same essay to determine its main ideas. Although you don't need to write them down, you should be able to summarize the essay's main points in a few sentences. When you are finished, again stop reading and raise your hand. Time how long it takes for two-thirds of the students to raise their hands. Announce the next direction when most of the class is finished.

- This time, read the essay to make sure you completely understand it. Raise your hand when you are finished. Time students again, based on when two-thirds of the class is finished. Announce the last direction when most of the class is ready.

- As your last task, read the essay closely, analyzing its details, trying to notice anything you may have missed during an earlier reading. Again raise your hand when you are finished. Time students once more, clocking when two-thirds of the class is finished.

Now ask students to discuss how they varied their reading for each of the given tasks. How did they find the answer quickly for the first task? Did they scan the page hoping that a critical word like "organic," "vegetable," or "family" would stand out? Or did they read the first sentence of each paragraph? How did they instinctively decide what to skip? What process did they use to skim for the essay's main ideas? Did they just read more quickly, or did they omit reading some sections of the essay? If they decided not to read the essay in its entirety, how did they decide what to overlook? For example, some students may have skipped over quotations.

Also ask questions based on the last two reading tasks. How do students distinguish their processes when skimming, reading for comprehension, and reading for detailed analysis? Based on your timing of their readings, how greatly do these processes differ? Mention to students that if they had been given a different text to read each time, the time differences between these skills would probably have been greater. By the time students were asked to work with the same text for the fourth task, the essay was quite familiar, making its analysis speedier.

After students have sufficiently discussed their variations in reading processes for this activity, ask them if they regularly vary their reading processes. If so, on what basis do they decide how they will read each text? Do they employ reading strategies other than those they have used during this activity? If so, what are they? In what circumstances do they use each? As in this exercise, do they ever read a text multiple times in order to comprehend its meaning? Again, under what circumstances?

Have they ever used a multidraft reading process for a text not assigned in school? For example, most cookbooks recommend that the cook read the recipe completely before beginning, then read the recipe again to follow the steps. Students may have done multidraft readings of assembly instructions for a new product they purchased. Or they may have needed to repeatedly read for comprehension difficult explanations in a computer manual or tax preparation manual. Because "multidraft reading process" refers to reading the same text more than once in rapid succession, this term would not necessarily describe students' repeated reading of a favorite novel in consecutive years. Yet readers will still be likely to reread a novel differently, knowing what will take place, than they read it the first time. Ask students to describe how being well acquainted with a text changes their reading practices.

In addition to varying reading processes to match reading goals and engaging in multidraft reading, skilled readers also vary their reading strategies to match the text's genre. Ask students to brainstorm a list of different genres they have read, and the different strategies they use for reading. Note that some genres make very different demands on readers—some are rarely read from beginning to end, for example, even though many students will say that readers start at the beginning of a work and go to the end. But a discussion of genre and reading strategies usually helps students realize quickly that they already have a wide variety of experiences with genres and different strategies. They likely know, for example, many genres that are usually not read from beginning to end. Their lists might include store catalogs; reference works such as dictionaries, encyclopedias, almanacs, and telephone books; most magazines and newspapers; many literary anthologies and anthologies of critical essays; religious texts such as the *Bible* and the *Torah*; and many legal works, such as the *Constitution*. If you'd like, you might even take a few minutes to explore with them how computer innovations such as hypertext affect people's reading habits.

Now lead students to discuss how their reading practices differ according to the genre they are reading. For example, do they read a novel differently than they do a textbook? Can they identify any differences in how they read a newspaper from how they read a magazine? Certainly the material they would read in *U.S. News and World Report* differs greatly from what they would read in *Entertainment Weekly*; do students engage in different reading processes for different magazines? Students may also read textbooks for different disciplines differently. Ask them how they might read *The Allyn & Bacon Guide to Writing* differently than they would an algebra textbook or a history textbook.

You may even want to ask students to describe the process by which they have been reading *The Allyn & Bacon Guide to Writing* so far in the course. Do they use the headings to help them preview and review each chapter? Do they read the material under each heading carefully or skim it just enough to detect Ramage, Bean, and Johnson's main points? Do they read or skip over "For Writing and Discussion" activities or essays that you don't assign? Do they read the chapter more than once? Assure students that you are not asking these questions to reprimand them for inadequate preparation, but to openly discuss with them how to make the best decisions about reading practices. If a topic is discussed adequately in class, it may be in their best interest to skim a section and devote the time they save to beginning their writing project.

Also discuss with students the chapter's suggestions (on pages 115–116) for reading strategies. The chapter presents experts' reading strategies and offers advice for students about how those strategies can be applied in academic contexts. Ask students how many of these strategies they already use and which suggestions they think could most improve their own reading. You may particularly want to discuss the first strategy, locating rhetorical context, since many students simply plunge into reading assignments in order to get the assignment over with, rather than starting with some reflection about the nature of the text they are to read. Similarly, you may want to discuss the multidraft reading strategy with students because they may not be used to thinking of rereading as an expert strategy; they may associate rereading with failed first readings, rather than with informed exploration.

You may want to require students to apply some or all of the reading strategies on pages 115–116 to a particular passage as a homework assignment so that they gain experience with these skills, working with a later reading from *The Allyn & Bacon Guide to Writing* or with a piece you provide. Or you could assign students to apply the reading strategies to a reading assignment they have received in another course (if you have a student who is not enrolled in any other courses, that student could apply the reading strategies to a section of *The Allyn & Bacon Guide to Writing*, perhaps pages 110 ff. on writing a summary and response). You can assign students to turn in a brief account of how well each strategy worked.

Note that later in the chapter, on page 136, there are strategies for rereading. You can create class activities for these strategies based on the ones described here. You can require journal or in-class writings after directed uses of the rereading strategies, and you can invite students to compare their own rereading strategies with those described in the chapter.

Writing a Summary

Although students may have some initial responses to a text as they read, it is imperative that they fully understand the meaning of the text before writing a response. This chapter first introduces characteristics of an effective summary on page 117–118, 9, using a bulleted list to summarize this section. Later in the chapter, on pages 131 ff., Ramage, Bean, and Johnson offer a more extended discussion, complete with sample analysis of Andres Martin's essay about tattoos that appears earlier in the chapter. The authors recommend that students prepare to write a summary by analyzing what each paragraph of a text says (its meaning) and does (its function within the text). Ramage, Bean, and Johnson provide examples of this on page 1313?? of the textbook, and it is worth spending class time working on these examples, as students may have a difficult time separating the "gist" of a paragraph from its "function." To give students practice with this technique, you may want to give them time individually or in groups to complete this analysis for paragraphs 3, 6, 7, 8, 9, and 10 of Martin's essay (which appears on pages 110–113 of the textbook)—the paragraphs which Ramage, Bean, and Johnson did not analyze. Students will need to read the essay in its entirety to understand the function that each of these paragraphs serves, what it "does." When students have finished, discuss as a class any differences in their analyses.

Once students have a paragraph-by-paragraph synopsis of a work, their next difficulty is deciding what information to include and what to omit in their summary. In part, their decision will be based on the desired length of their summary. Ask students what the advantages and disadvantages are of summaries written at different lengths. In what circumstances might each be best?

Paragraph-by-paragraph analysis is less effective when summarizing open-form prose. In effect, summarizing an open-form text requires students not only to condense the length of the text, but also to reconstruct it as closed form. They may, for example, summarize different themes or character sketches in an open-form piece.

Strong Response Writing

The section of the chapter that addresses strong responses is set up in the reading processes section on reading with and against the grain (pages 116–117). Students are likely to have difficulty fully comprehending the term "reading against the grain." This concept means more than merely agreeing or disagreeing with the text. Students are probably more familiar with the phrase "to read between the lines," a reference to looking for a text's covert meaning. Yet "reading against the grain" is even more goal directed. As Ramage, Bean, and Johnson explain, it entails articulating and critiquing the writer's (or editor's) values, assumptions about the subject matter, and preconceptions of the audience. It may take some class time, and much focused discussion, in order to help students see that reading against the grain is not the same as disagreeing with the text.

Reading against the grain entails examining a text for cultural messages that may not even be the intended subject of the text. Reread with your students the examples Ramage, Bean, and Johnson provide on pages 138 in the first paragraph, under the heading "Articulate Your Own Purpose for Reading." Ask students if they can recall any times when they have participated in such an endeavor. Even if they have not read a text in this way before, they may have watched a movie critically, more interested in how gender roles were being presented than in the movie's plot. Or perhaps they have noticed more about how children are presented in television commercials than they have learned about the products being advertised.

To read a text against the grain is to examine the "angle of vision" of the writer, a concept discussed in Chapters 3 and 5. Often, reading against the grain entails examining the angle of vision not only of the writer, but also of the writer's group affiliations or society. To use the examples Ramage, Bean, and Johnson cite on page 136 in the last row of strategies for rereading, it may not only be the writer of the text who assumes readers will be heterosexual or Christian. Such assumptions are commonplace in contemporary American society. The predominance of such assumptions does not make a writer any less responsible for his or her predispositions; in fact, when such assumptions are widespread, a reader's critique may need to be stronger. Emphasize to students that when they read, even if they identify with the intended audience, they should be alert to ways that other readers might feel excluded. Defying the marginalizations of peoples is in the best interest of everyone, not just those who are excluded.

You can use the question-asking strategies that Ramage, Bean, and Johnson provide in the tables on page 124 and 130 to help students develop responses to the texts with which they are working. You can use some of the questions as the focus of class discussion of essays in the textbook or other material you provide. Remember that as students pursue their readings, they can build upon skills they learned in Chapters 1 and 2 of *The Allyn & Bacon Guide to Writing.* Writing a strong response requires students to ask good questions and explore ideas—strategies discussed in Chapter 1. To assist them in this process, in addition to the strategies recommended in the present chapter, students may want to use any of the techniques of exploration introduced in Chapter 2 (freewriting, idea mapping, dialectic talk) or Chapter 17 (active reading and research, journals or learning logs, e-mail discussions, or focused study groups). The believing and doubting game that serves as the basis of the brief writing project in Chapter 2 can also help students generate a response.

Some additional questions for discussion might include:

- What questions does the text trigger for you?
- What places in the text are particularly thought provoking? Why?
- What is excluded from the text that may bias its conclusions?
- What aspects of the text's data, evidence, and arguments are not persuasive? Why not?
- What can you observe about the author's perspective or "angle of vision" that the author does not directly acknowledge?
- What is questionable about the writer's values, beliefs, and assumptions, both stated and unstated?
- What will you gain by accepting the writer's view? What will you lose?
- What assumptions does the writer make of the readers' values?
- Do you feel excluded from the intended audience of this text? If so, how? If not, who might and why? How do these exclusions limit the text?

Ask students to work through such prompts for the essay "On Teenagers and Tattoos" on pages 110 ff. of the textbook. This activity may be done individually, in small groups (with the groups then reporting their responses to the class), or as a full class discussion. In addition to the analyses in the student response on pages 127–129, what insights have these questions provided that could be useful when writing a response to "On Teenagers and Tattoos?"

Using the "For Writing and Discussion" Activities

For the activity on pages 114–115, students will be quick to identify the political references in the passage as topics for which more background knowledge is needed (and indeed, many students may feel at a loss on the political context!). Before they complete the exercise, however, they should have also identified references that would require cultural explanation for a student from an undeveloped area, most notably the phrase "like a man agreeing to throw in the washer-dryer along with the house." Someone from a preindustrialized culture may not realize that the reference here is to the purchase of a house and that appliances such as washers and dryers are often a point of negotiation. Readers—including many students in your class—would also need more information to understand the passage's final phrase, "retreat into neo-isolationism."

The activity on page 120 asks students to analyze three summaries, the first of which is rated excellent by Ramage, Bean, and Johnson. This summary serves as the comparison for the other two summaries. Students can use the criteria on page 119 to evaluate the other summaries. Ask students to look at the different ways the other summaries divide information into paragraphs (what is the effect of the multiple paragraphs in the second example? How does it guide readers' attention to Rayner's main ideas?). Also ask them to look at the ways in which the word choices in both summaries convey something of the writers' attitude toward Rayner. You might ask students to use highlighters to identify where in each summary the author draws a conclusion about Rayner, or identifies a main or supporting point in Rayner, and identifies particulars from Rayner.

Note that the original article does not appear in the textbook anywhere, although with the complete publication information provided in the exercise, you could locate a copy through a newspaper database at your library. The exercise presumes that the first summary can act as enough of a comparison point. You could, of course, design your own activity using this as a model, selecting an opinion piece from a local or campus paper to use as the point of analysis.

The activity on page 134 asks students to compare their summaries of a common article. This activity will work very well with a computer classroom, where students could walk around the room and see everyone's summary on the screen, or in a classroom with plenty of blackboard space where groups might post a summary. Alternatively, an online forum might also offer a good format for discussion and sharing between class periods. An alternate way to work with these concepts would be to have the whole class brainstorm a list of main ideas from the reading. Have one person be the class scribe and write everything on the board, and you can facilitate a discussion of the points and particulars as the class progresses. Then have groups compose a summary and continue with the activity as presented.

The activity on page 139 is a fairly self-explanatory activity that will help students probe the qualities of successful thesis statements. It is an excellent class activity, best done just before students move to developing their own thesis for a strong response essay.

In the introduction to the activity on page 138, Ramage, Bean, and Johnson write, "This passage often evokes heated responses from our students." If your students also respond heatedly, ask them to explain why. Some students may share Dillard's views and be grateful that someone has expressed them so cleverly, explaining a messy home as a morally correct choice, not a character flaw. Other students may be offended by Dillard's comment. Ask these students whether it is Dillard's housekeeping habits or the way she describes those habits that most disturbs them. Does the use of the word "tidy" make cleanliness seem diminutive, trivial? What is the impact of the clause "I made my own cheese balls," especially at the end of this passage, a place of emphasis? Do students interpret this example as humorous or as mocking? Do students who do attend to housework think this passage accurately reflects their lifestyle? In what ways do they feel they are being misrepresented? They may object to Dillard's implication that those who do housework view it as their highest priority in life and accomplish little else.

You can conclude this activity by asking students what Dillard risks and gains by her characterization of her audience. Perhaps some readers who object to Dillard's personal habits are nevertheless amused by her examples. Other readers may keep reading simply because they enjoy the catharsis that a disagreement can bring when little is at stake, such as differences in housework. Are there students in your class who are so put off by Dillard's remarks that they would not continue reading the text from which this passage is excerpted? Would they keep reading but only with the expectation of increasing their dislike for Dillard? Finally, you might ask students whether they think Dillard expected some tidy housekeepers to read this passage. Is she blatantly criticizing them? Perhaps the clause "I made my own cheese balls" is Dillard's way of telling these readers, "Don't take offense. I'm not referring to you. You're not nearly so extreme."

Discussing the Readings

"On Teenagers and Tattoos" is discussed thoroughly on pages 117–119, in the student example of a summary/strong response essay. The four remaining readings in this chapter are not discussed here because they are included in the chapter only as sources for the writing project. The essays need not be discussed in class. Note, however, that the chapter contains an additional student sample essay (by Stephanie Malinowski, on pages 143–145) in response to Thomas Friedman's essay (on page 142–144). Two readings here are political cartoons, so you have considerable latitude in incorporating responses to visual text and verbal texts.

Guiding Students through the Writing Project

You have several options for assigning students' writing projects:

- You can choose one of the two essays or two cartoons at the end of the chapter for all students to use when writing a summary and response.

- You can allow students to choose any one of the texts at the end of the chapter to use when writing a summary and response.

- You can select any other reading for students to use for this writing project.

- You can use part of a longer reading for students to use (such as one chapter or the preface of a book the class is reading).

One consideration to keep in mind is that if students all work on the same reading, when they do peer reviews, they may find it easy to help one another generate different readings of an essay. Discussion is often fostered when students have readings in common, although you may want to discuss the ethics and strategies associated with incorporating ideas from a peer review into an essay. On the other hand, if students have a variety of readings from which to select, you should be able to group students so that they can review the project of a student working with a different essay. You may want to provide both options for your class so that they experience peer reviews with students who know their text, and students who don't.

Several of the readings that Ramage, Bean, and Johnson provide as options for this writing project are at least partially open in form. Remind students that when they wish to write a summary of an open-form essay, the summary itself should be closed form, making the essay's covert meaning overt, particularly at the beginning and end of the summary. To depict the mood of the open-form piece, students can also briefly cite the most compelling examples and images the writer used.

Clarify all the requirements of the assignment. Ramage, Bean, and Johnson specify that the summary should be approximately 150–250 words. Students can use the example on pages 120 (which is about 200 words) to get a sense of how detailed such a summary should be. Make clear to students whether you expect their summary to be written with attributive tags, as in the example in the textbook. Are direct quotations acceptable as a part of the summary for this assignment? If so, explain to students how much quoting you think is too much.

Ramage, Bean, and Johnson do not specify any length for the response section of the assignment so you may wish to do this yourself. Also decide whether you want to limit in any way the type of response students write for this project. On page 121 and following, Ramage, Bean, and Johnson discuss the common academic forms of strong response essays (rhetorical critiques, idea critiques, reflection, and blended responses). If you have particular preferences about the balance of summary and response, and if you want students to focus their attention on analysis or response, you should make this clear when you explain the assignment. Whatever your preferences, you will likely find that some students veer in the other direction (they include more summary and less response than you deem appropriate, or so much response and so little summary that the text they're responding to gets lost, for example). You can use peer response sessions to focus attention on the balance of summary and response in the text, and to highlight the students' developing thesis statements.

Chapter 7
Writing an Autobiographical Narrative

Understanding the Chapter's Goals

This is the first chapter of *The Allyn & Bacon Guide to Writing* devoted to an open-form writing project. In this chapter, students are taught how to select appropriate topics for autobiographical narratives and create autobiographical tension within their texts. The two writing projects in this chapter provide flexible possibilities for incorporating autobiographical writing into the semester, with a literacy narrative presented as a distinct form of autobiographical writing. Chapter 7 should be read in conjunction with Chapter 19, "Composing and Revising Open-Form Prose." Together, the two chapters teach students to manage the literary techniques of plot, character, setting, and theme. The autobiographical narrative that is assigned in this chapter is also significant because it is the first writing project in *The Allyn & Bacon Guide to Writing* that is a full-length essay (although you may have chosen to teach the project in Chapter 6 as a full-length essay).

Reinforcing the Chapter's Rhetorical Principles

Topic Selection

Ramage, Bean, and Johnson offer extensive prompts throughout the chapter to help students select topics for their autobiographical narratives. The numbered, boxed, or bulleted lists on pages 154, 156, and 160–161 (for open autobiographical narratives) or 164–165 (for literacy narratives) suggest numerous possible topics for students who think they have few experiences worthy of narrative development. Encourage students to thoroughly consider all of these lists' suggestions before committing themselves to a particular topic. The most dramatic topic will not necessarily be the best for this project; the autobiographical significance of an experience is often more poignant when it is not overshadowed by the extravagance of the event itself.

If students still cannot think of a topic for an autobiographical narrative, you may want to suggest that they generate a "time line" of their lives, brainstorming key people, places, and events for every few years. If you want to devote class time to this activity, you can provide the prompts for this gradually. Begin by asking students to list key people in their lives from birth to age five, then key places for this time period, then key events. Before moving on, ask the class to reveal some of the people they listed (parents, grandparents, siblings, babysitters, neighborhood friends, daycare attendants), then some of the places, then some of the events. (These suggestions can easily be applied to a literacy narrative topic selection, too; simply instruct students to construct their time lines or lists with an eye on people and events relating to literacy at home and at school, such as important writing teachers or memorable writing experiences, good and bad.) When students share some of their responses aloud, the memories of other students may be piqued. Next allow students time to list key people, places, and events in their lives from ages five to ten, then ten to thirteen, then thirteen to sixteen, then sixteen to nineteen, and so on in three-year increments until students' present ages. If you have many older students in your class, you can adjust the increments to make sense for the amount of time you want to devote to this activity.

If your class is working with a particular theme, you may want to do a focused time line to prompt ideas. For example, a work time line can help students chart the various kinds of work they have done in their lives (starting with household chores or teenage volunteer work and moving forward to paid employment), just as a literacy timeline can help students chart the evolution of literacy activities in their lives. Such focused direction can help students prompt one another's memories as they compare experiences.

Ramage, Bean, and Johnson's lists of subjects and this "time line" activity will help students think of many possible topics for their essays; however, students also need guidance in determining which of the topics they are considering have the most potential for this writing project. Advise students to choose a topic from which they have some emotional distance. Some students in your class, for example, may have had highly traumatic experiences quite recently, such as the death of a family member in the previous month. Students may want to write about that experience as a tribute to their loved one or to facilitate their grieving process, yet unless they have had time to gain perspective on such an emotionally charged event, it is unlikely that they will be able to present the experience clearly and meaningfully to readers.

An additional hazard when students select traumatic experiences for this writing project is that you may feel uncomfortable assigning grades to such essays. It can be difficult to convince students that you are grading their *essays*, not their *experiences*. Imagine, for example, a student who writes about having been physically abused as a child or one who writes about having been date raped. The experience the student suffered may be heartrending, whereas the student's essay may be poorly written. A student who receives a "D" or "F" on such a paper might feel that the trauma of his or her experience has been belittled.

Early during your work with this chapter, it is best to discuss openly with students the importance of distinguishing their academic investment in this writing project from their personal investment in any topic. Certainly it is ideal for students to write about topics that they care about deeply, but for the purposes of this writing project, when most are receiving their first introduction to autobiographical narratives in an academic setting, students may have trouble judging the appropriateness of possible topics. Therefore, while students are selecting their autobiographical topics, encourage them to imagine the possible academic ramifications of each topic they consider. Is the topic one they will feel comfortable sharing with another student for peer review? How will they feel if the essay they write on that topic receives an average or below-average grade? If a low grade on that topic would devastate them (more so than a similarly low grade on papers with other topics), they should probably select different subject matter. The textbook advises throughout that students choose topics well when they choose issues that are engaging to them; at the same time, students choose topics well when they realize that some topics may simply be too personal to share in class. Use individual contacts with students as well as class discussion to help students be aware of the fine lines they may sometimes draw about topics that are personal, yet not too sensitive.

Students sometimes confuse personal and academic agendas in autobiographical assignments when they write about religious conversion experiences. The common difficulties in such papers are threefold: students sometimes lack the skills to describe such events well enough for a reader who has not had similar experiences to understand; students often develop such papers in ways that begin as autobiographical narratives, but quickly move to religious instruction and/or persuasive attempts to convert readers; some students have difficulty seeing a critical response to their essay as a critical attack on their religious beliefs. For these reasons, some instructors prohibit students from writing about religious conversion experiences. Another option is to permit students to write about religious experiences, but to warn them of these difficulties. Tell them that papers on this topic should focus on their own experience and should develop that experience as concretely as possible. The essay by Kris Saknussemm on pages 168–169 deals with a moment of revelation, although not a religious or spiritual one. Students who are writing about internal developments may find it a helpful model.

Yet another way in which students make poor decisions about autobiographical matter is when they choose a topic that is not sufficiently narrow for the subject of the writing project. For example, a student who is an immigrant may chronologically review his years of hardship in his homeland, the difficulty of his decision to immigrate to the United States, his attempts to gain financial security through various jobs after his immigration, his subsequent decision to attend college, and his anticipation of a more hopeful future. A student athlete who had a highly significant relationship with a coach may attempt to chronicle the evolution of that relationship over a four-year period, starting with the decision to try out for a sport, the difficulties of the try-out process, and then several years of skill development stories. Certainly all of these experiences are connected and form a cohesive narrative, but only a highly skilled writer could convey the breadth of these experiences successfully in a relatively short essay. Most first-year writers would be better advised to choose a more limited time frame and develop just one segment of this autobiographical journey. Encourage students to pare down their focus in order to develop depth with their work. Some students may be reluctant to cut material out once it is written, but organize class activities to help students outline and analyze the scope of their essays.

After students use the prompts scattered throughout Chapter 7 to brainstorm possible topics for this writing project, you may want to have students write a brief paragraph describing the topic they plan to write about and why they have selected it. You can then steer students away from topics with the potential difficulties explained above. You might also display for students the transparency at the end of this chapter in the manual, which provides a more extensive list of criteria to help students decide between possible topics for their autobiographical narratives. Students can answer these questions for themselves or, using these questions for guidance, can give each other feedback in small groups on their probable topics.

Autobiographical Tension

More discussion and examples of narrative tension are provided on pages 552–553 of the textbook. Tension is important in autobiographical narratives because it is the source of growth, change, and insight. Transformation is what interests readers, even if their own experience is removed from that described in the narrative.

Tension is easier for students to identify when they are writing about an experience that has been upsetting than when they choose a topic that is joyful. For example, you may have students who want their narrative to describe the happiest day of their life, which might be their high school graduation, their wedding day, or the day their first child was born. These events are all pivotal turning points in people's lives, but without any tension, the narrative is dull, a generic account that holds significance only for the writer. Your advice about choosing topics shouldn't force students into writing about upsetting events, of course. You can help students discover tensions worth exploring in happy events as well.

Using one of these sample topics, discuss with the class how narrative tension can be found in a happy occasion. The word "tension" often has negative connotations, but it does not need to imply that there are problems, only juxtapositions. Any turning point in someone's life, even if it is a step toward a brighter future, is simultaneously a relinquishing of the past. Whether the writer views moving to a new stage in his or her life as a relief or as bittersweet, the juxtaposition of past and present is a fertile source for narrative tension. As Ramage, Bean, and Johnson explain, sometimes a student cannot identify the source of tension until he or she is in the midst of drafting. Students can question one another about their topics in small groups, however, so that writers can begin to explore what tensions are inherent in their narratives.

Elements of Literary Narrative

Ramage, Bean, and Johnson identify four elements of literary narrative: plot, character, setting, and theme. You might encourage students to explore these elements by considering how they relate to the components of a story, discussed in Skill 15 in Chapter 19 (pages 547 ff.): depiction of events; connectedness; tension or conflict; resolution, recognition, or retrospective interpretation. Whereas the elements of literary narrative identify techniques used to convey a narrative, the story components identify the prerequisites necessary for something to be defined as a narrative. To some degree, however, the terms overlap. The plot, for example, can be defined as both the events and their connectivity. The theme is conveyed through the story's tension and resolution.

Character and setting can contribute to all four elements of the minimal story: they can be the impetus of events, can enhance the connectedness of the story, can be the source of tension, and can provide the resolution.

Plot, character, setting, and theme also deserve discussion in their own right. Novice writers are likely to view plot as a given: what happened is what happened. To correct this misconception, you may want to discuss with students the relationship between plot and story, explained in Chapter 19. As explained there, a sequence of events does not alone constitute a plot, at least not a satisfying one. The depicted events must share a thematic connection, and include a central tension/conflict and resolution. Pacing—how much or how little any one event is developed—is also an element of plot. As you discuss the readings in this chapter, prompt students to speculate about what details the writers left out in conveying a sequence of events. Also lead students to discuss why the writers developed particular incidents in the plot as little or as much as they did. For contrast, have the students read pages 576–578 of the textbook. If students were assigned to strengthen the plot of this autobiographical narrative, what would they leave out? What would they develop more? Would they alter the sequence in which the events are conveyed? If so, how and why?

In discussing characters, ask students the means by which readers learn about characters in texts. Readers judge characters on the basis of how the narrator presents them (physical descriptions and explicit evaluations of them), how the characters themselves behave, what the characters say, and how other characters in the text react to them. To examine these methods of characterization, you might ask students to analyze more closely the excerpt from *Black Boy* on pages 157 of the textbook. As brief as this passage is, the author uses several of these techniques to characterize himself as a child and the librarian he encounters. If you have time, you may want to teach students techniques for writing dialogue. The transparency master at the end of this chapter of the manual outlines some key advice.

Ramage, Bean, and Johnson explain that setting is not only the place where a story occurs, but often it is also the physical embodiment of the narrative's theme. To emphasize this point to students, remind them of the writing project they did for Chapter 5: a composition and analysis of two descriptions of the same scene, one positive and one negative. Students should remember from that project that writers can "see" the same place differently depending on what overall impression they want to convey in their narrative. Even the extent to which the setting is described in a narrative is an important decision in crafting an open-form text.

The final element of literary narrative examined by Ramage, Bean, and Johnson is theme. They explain that a narrative's theme "goes beyond the events of the story to point toward the larger significance of those events" (page 159). As illustrated by the examples provided of a plot summary and thematic summary, although the theme emerges from the plot, characters, and setting of a narrative, it can be stated in more universal terms. In other words, thematic significance is integral, but not restricted to, the specific incidents of a given story. Other stories will share the same theme, even though the characters and events of those stories will develop the theme differently. For another discussion of theme, especially as it relates to the depiction of a narrative's events, see the discussion of the reading "Berkeley Blues" in this instructor's manual in Chapter 19.

Literacy Narrative

A literacy narrative, a new addition to this chapter for this edition, asks students to explore their experiences with literacy—reading and writing in and out of school. This section of the text references prominent published literacy narratives (such as Helen Keller's story) and also pushes students to consider their own experiences. On page 164, Ramage, Bean, and Johnson list the key features of a literacy narrative. In essence, the literacy narrative's subject is more defined than more general autobiographical narratives might be. Literacy narratives can be excellent first assignments, for they help students get to know each other and provide valuable insight into what kinds of experiences and attitudes students bring with them to the college writing context.

Using the "For Writing and Discussion" Activities

The activity on page 174 focuses on setting, combining an analysis of pictures with instructions for vivid description (and the invitation to add characters to that setting). If you had students do the activity in Chapter 5 (page 98) on descriptions of a place, you can make connections here to the power of specific words to shape impressions.

The activity on page 164 involves students in analyzing choices made in the drafting on a literacy narrative. As students answer the very focused questions provided in this exercise, they are likely to notice things like the evocative adjectives used in the first description (the different book covers used in the different reading groups; the contrast between the narrator's meekness and the teacher's verbal strength). The second excerpt relies on a subtle description that shows how the narrator's own views towards reading shifted with the gentle encouragement of a relative. The ending questions here will prompt students to mine their own memories for appropriate topics.

Discussing the Readings

"Phantom Limb Pain" (pages 168–169)

The questions on page 169 of the textbook identify several features of Saknussemm's selection you may wish to discuss with your students. The sparseness of this narrative is particularly important if, like Saknussemm, students plan to write about a topic that is almost entirely an internal experience. Although the narrative is spare, the language Saknussemm uses has great impact, and you may want to emphasize the ways in which the revelatory words in this passage (such as "mythic" or "haunted") connect with the concrete language ("poster of Raquel Welch," "stump of limb," "aquarium full of vodka") to help emphasize Saknussemm's internal struggles.

Ask students to reread the selection looking for ways that Saknussemm's commentary on the narrative is set up earlier in the piece. The first paragraph contains very little detail about Miller King, but the reference to "that mythic kid we all know" allows readers to interpret and imagine Saknussemm's neighbor. What associations does that paragraph raise for your students? In the later paragraphs, Saknussemm's description of his physical labors (he "lumbered" through the area; he did "Marine push-ups") highlights his assumptions about physical prowess, but in paragraph 3 he begins to notice his neighbor's emotional strength ("he didn't cry.") In the closing paragraph, he notes that he "grew a little bigger," which raises questions about his former notions of growth and success.

Saknussemm's passage is also helpful in illustrating how students can use the scale of abstraction (discussed in Chapter 3, pages 60–61, and also Lesson 2 in Chapter 19) to support their commentary with details. Here is a scale of abstraction in paragraph 2:

- "All summer long I worked out."
- "I ordered a set of barbells that came with complimentary brochures…."
- "I lumbered around our neighborhood wearing ankle weights loaded with sand."

When students read each other's drafts, they should watch for occasions where similar scales of abstraction can be developed. Tell students that when they make a generalization, they should make it both more specific and support it with precise examples, as Saknussemm has done.

Saknussemm's commentary in paragraph 6 explains the meaning he associates with this experience. You can invite students to read the story to see whether they draw other lessons from it, making the point that the writer's own analysis is one reading of the story, but readers' experiences may see other lessons (such as about the ways boys are taught to communicate with one another or about gender-based assumptions, for example). His explicit commentary contrasts with the spareness of his narrative, and you should talk with students about the ways in which these two features are connected. Would a richer narrative support the commentary more effectively?

"No Cats in America?" (pages 170–171)

Patrick José's narrative contrasts nicely with the preceding reading because its significance is not explicitly stated. Rather, the author contrasts two memories of a movie soundtrack to illustrate his shifting attitudes towards life in America. The first memory, in paragraph 1, illustrates his idealistic view of the American dream; the second memory, in the closing paragraph, illustrates his considerably changed view of American promise as he struggles with humiliation at school.

This essay is rich is descriptive language. The descriptions of Filipino food in paragraph 2 ("lechon, adobo, pancit, sinigang, lumpia, and rice") may not be familiar to some readers, as one of the discussion questions notes, yet they evoke particular images. The discussion question about José's decision to include specific names of foods and party games is a good one for a class activity, for it highlights the role of audience and culture in relation to narrative. Other descriptive details, such as the lunchroom scenes ("I opened my Tupperware," "I walked my way towards the trashcan, opened the lid, and watched as my lunch filled the trashcan") reveal José's actions in vivid detail. Invite your students to read the narrative, looking for ways in which the narrative reaches out to readers familiar with Filipino culture and to readers who are not.

Ask students to reread the narrative, looking for ways in which the descriptive details help support the theme suggested by the images of "No Cats in America?" Which details suggest José's changing attitudes? The specificity of this narrative guides readers' interpretation of the story. A good group activity is to break the narrative up into component parts (life in the Philippines, life in America before school, the lunchroom, for example) and to ask students to describe what José's attitudes are toward America and toward his own life at each point. Have each group list what particular associations they make with each detail they list to support their analysis. This will help students answer the second and fourth questions following the reading, about setting and details.

"Masks" (pages 172–174)

The questions on page 174 are useful for discussing several of the most important considerations for autobiographical narratives: autobiographical tension, theme or significance, and detailed support. Begin discussing this essay by asking students to identify the main contrarieties, as Question 1 asks. You may want to direct students back to page 154, where Ramage, Bean, and Johnson identify the most frequent contrarieties of autobiographical narratives. "Masks" clearly articulates the second of the three listed there: "Old view of person X versus new view of person X."

Beyond this primary tension, however, this student writer accentuates the tension in the narrative through a number of other critical comparisons and contrasts. An important source of tension in the narrative is the duration of seeming difference between the narrator and Kathy. The narrative depicts three time periods: kindergarten (paragraphs 1–6), seventh grade (paragraphs 7–9), and high school (paragraphs 10–20). Hence, at the heart of the narrative are both contrasts (the differences between the narrator and Kathy) and comparisons (the similarities in the narrator's perception throughout all grade levels, until the last paragraph of the essay). Ask students to consider how the effectiveness of the essay would change if the writer had restricted her narrative to their high school years. It is the duration of the contrast between the writer and Kathy that makes the writer's final realizations so weighty. The descriptions of their differences over years further emphasize the contrast between the past (the writer's prior impressions of Kathy, consistent for at least a decade) and the present (the writer's new realization).

Question 2 asks about the conclusion of the essay. Rather than providing a definitive answer to whether or not the writer should state the realization so explicitly in the final paragraph, discuss with students the effects of retaining, eliminating, or expanding this paragraph. One asset of the conclusion in its current form is that it doesn't allow for misinterpretation. If the narrative ended with paragraph 19, readers might think the author was still feeling jealous or hurt. Another strength of the conclusion as it is written is that it shows that not only has the writer's opinion about Kathy changed, but so has her opinion of herself. In fact, her perceptions of Kathy and herself have reversed: Kathy is now "alone and vulnerable"; the narrator is now "the powerful one" and "independent." A benefit of eliminating the last paragraph would be that the significance would be conveyed more subtly. A benefit of expanding the last paragraph would be that the writer could then *show* the significance, rather than merely *tell* it, as she does now.

"Once Upon a Time" (pages 174–177)

This student example illustrates what a literacy narrative can accomplish. The questions following the essay on page 177 direct students to consider how the text engages readers and how the essay deals with conflict and breakthrough. The juxtaposition of commentary about Jennifer Ching's father smoking and her literacy is a surprising opening. That beginning, and the fact that she was so young when the events that open this essay happened, bring an unexpected feel to the piece. Students may have looked to more advanced school experiences as key to the development of a literacy narrative, but this piece illustrates how even very young experiences can be powerful. Dialogue through this piece illustrates the power of personal relationships to affect the narrator's priorities. Students will likely note that Ching identifies both students and teachers as people who had an effect in helping her move beyond obstacles.

Effective details run through this piece. Students may comment on the inclusion of very early writing samples. The quotation from particular pieces from Ching's past does a lot to build the credibility of her narrative. The resonance of the memories she reports comes from the very particular details she provides in the telling.

Students will likely see several different lessons that Ching has learned from her literacy narrative. Possible themes here include an awareness of multiple definitions of argument; the need to overcome obstacles in school; the kinds of power inherent in words. You might ask student groups to provide evidence for the interpretations they select. This is a good option for class discussion.

Before discussing Question 3, you may want to ask students to explore their responses in writing. Direct them to create two columns—one titled "narrator" and the other titled "Kathy"—and to record the details that serve as contrasts between the two characters for each of the grade levels identified in the essay: kindergarten, seventh grade, and high school. Students should notice that several kinds of detail recur in each section, such as Kathy's hair and clothes and boys' responses to the characters. These patterns add continuity to the narrative. Also ask students which details best characterize the narrator and Kathy.

You may also want to discuss the effectiveness of *excluding* expected details. The name of the person who is the chief subject of this narrative is not revealed until paragraph 10, halfway through the essay. Do your students think the writer delayed this information purposefully? What is the effect of postponing this detail? When Kathy's name is revealed, it is done so in the context of her clothing, not her relationship with others. No one calls her by name throughout the narrative. How does this omission underscore the theme of the essay?

Finally, point out to students this writer's skill in indicating the time period of each segment of her narrative. She begins each part with a physical description of Kathy that suggests her age and only later explicitly indicates the grade level. Even then, though, the announcement of the grade is incorporated into further description. At the end of paragraph 1, the writer states "She was very wise, sophisticated beyond her kindergarten years." In paragraph 8, the grade level is incorporated into the description as follows: "My mom wouldn't let me go out on dates until I was a sophomore in high school. We were only in seventh grade and she was always going out with guys." In paragraph 10, the writer gives this indication of the time period: "She held her head up high, befitting one of her social standing: top of the high school food chain." Encourage students to be similarly thoughtful in conveying essential information subtly.

Guiding Students through the Writing Project

Begin your direction of students' projects by providing them with feedback on their topic selection, in accordance with the criteria explained in the textbook and in this manual. Students can then use the "For Writing and Discussion" activities on pages 172, 173, 174, and 176 of the textbook to generate material for their writing projects, as well as the "Composing Your Essay" advice on pages 186–188.

After working through the activities and readings in the chapter, just before students begin to shape their plans into a draft, you may wish to allot a portion of the class session for students to convene in one of four small groups, each devoted to a narrative technique: plot, characters, setting, and theme. Students should join whichever group focuses on the narrative technique they find most difficult (at least for this assignment). In each group, students should take turns identifying their topics, sharing the ideas they already have for applying the narrative technique to their topics, and seeking further ideas from others in the group. If many students have trouble with one particular technique, discuss it more extensively as a class. Ask for a few volunteers to share their topics so that the class can discuss together how that technique can be applied to the specific narratives students are writing.

If any of your students are writing on extremely sensitive topics, you may need to give special care to facilitating peer reviews for this writing project. Make sure that the students are well suited not only in their writing abilities and the other factors discussed above, but also in their emotional maturity. You should observe these groups especially closely during in-class reviews of these drafts. If the groups are reticent in their discussion of difficult topics, intervene just long enough to get conversation going.

If you sense that writing a narrative about a tragic experience has caused any student undue distress, make sure the student is aware of the counseling services available on your campus. If you have several students whom you suspect would benefit from professional support services, take a few moments of class time to describe your college's counseling services. Stress that the services are confidential and, on most campuses, free. Explain how to make an appointment, as well as the counseling center's staffing, hours, location, and phone number.

Deciding on a Topic for
Your Autobiographical Narrative

1. Have you narrowed a broad or lengthy experience so that you can describe it adequately in this essay?

2. Did the experience happen long enough in the past that you have had time to understand its impact?

3. If the topic is emotional, will you feel comfortable sharing the draft for peer reviews?

4. Will you be able to be objective about your grade if you write on this topic? Remember that the grade you will receive reflects your writing skills on this assignment, not the merit of your experience.

5. If the experience is one that is more internal than external (a change in self-image; a religious experience), will you be able to describe it for readers in ways that are not too abstract?

6. If the experience or person is a topic common to many people's experiences (your high school graduation; your loving grandparents), will you be able to develop it so that readers do not find it generic or clichéd?

7. Is the topic one that will allow for autobiographical tension (opposing values or points of view between characters or divided feelings within the narrator)?

8. Is the topic likely to generate a theme (larger significance) that readers will find relevant to their own lives?

Tips for Writing Dialogue

1. Begin a new paragraph each time the speaker changes.

2. Punctuate dialogue correctly by putting the necessary punctuation **inside** the final quotation mark.

3. Use the speaker's words or the succession of paragraphs to clarify who is speaking. Don't always name the speaker.

4. Avoid the monotony of "he said" and "she said" by using more descriptive verbs and adverbs to convey how the dialogue was expressed.

5. Occasionally interrupt a prolonged exchange of dialogue by having the narrator comment on what is taking place.

6. Try to make your dialogue match each character. The characters shouldn't all sound alike.

7. Test that the dialogue sounds natural by reading it aloud.

Chapter 8
Writing an Exploratory Essay
or Annotated Bibliography

Understanding the Chapter's Goals

This chapter focuses on the process of exploration that occurs when a writer begins with a question or problem, researches the subject, then uses the results of this research to refine the question and continue the research. Two writing projects offer different approaches to exploration. The first requires students to chronologically recount their exploration, and may result in a more open-form piece. The second requires students to write a bibliography with comments, a more closed-form piece. Either project can be successfully taught as a precursor to the writing project in another chapter of *The Allyn & Bacon Guide to Writing*. Two of the reading selections in this chapter are examples of preparatory assignments for writing projects in later chapters: proposing a solution (Chapter 16) and a researched paper (Chapters 20 through 22). Any writing project involving research could also be assigned in conjunction with this chapter: an informative essay or report (Chapter 9), an analytical or synthetic essay (Chapter 13), a classical argument (Chapter 14), or an evaluation (Chapter 15).

Reinforcing the Chapter's Rhetorical Principles

Exploratory Purpose

Although the exploratory purpose is not difficult to grasp, students may experience some confusion simply because exploratory writing is not a common academic writing assignment. Most teachers hope that an exploratory process takes place whenever students undertake a project, yet rarely do teachers reward the process itself, independent of its outcome. If you explain to students how the exploratory purpose relates to what they have already studied in *The Allyn & Bacon Guide to Writing*, students will be more comfortable with this chapter.

The exploratory purpose was first introduced in Chapter 1 of the textbook. In Table 1.1, pages 20–21, exploring is listed as one purpose of writing. To explore is to deliberately wallow in complexity, to postpone closure on an issue. Chapter 2 of the textbook, in Concept 5, stresses the importance of exploratory strategies, offering various techniques students can use to identify complexities. More rigorous research further enhances a writer's exploration. Chapter 21 explains how a writer can gather information using library resources, interviews, personal correspondence, and questionnaires.

Exploratory writing is not always intended to be shared with others. Students—and even some teachers—may see exploratory writing as entirely process oriented, appropriate only for informal exercises on the way to a more polished piece. There are, however, examples of published exploratory writing that can help students see the varied purposes to which exploration can be put. An example of formal and finished exploratory writing that is not included in *The Allyn & Bacon Guide to Writing* but that might help you and your students better understand the exploratory purpose is Virginia Woolf's *A Room of One's Own*. Throughout the text, Woolf recounts her exploration of the topic "women and fiction." As she describes the process of her research, she emphasizes the obstacles to scholarship she encounters because of her gender and the scarcity of women's writing. Wallowing in complexity caused Woolf to change what she wanted to explore: she realized the topic "women and fiction" cannot be divorced from a consideration of women's social conditions. She concludes that women need fixed incomes and time apart from the responsibilities of child rearing to produce art.

Exploratory writing can be a "formal, finished product" that is consciously written for an audience. Often, formal exploratory texts are written to identify assumptions and omissions that span an entire discourse community. As such, they aim to challenge a paradigm. Formal exploratory writing often shares the goals of rhetorical reading, already discussed in Chapter 6. For both, a writer aims to analyze an "angle of vision," attentive to the assumptions and exclusions in scholarly discussions. Chapter 6 illustrates how to perform such an analysis for a single source; the present chapter illustrates how to perform a cumulative analysis for multiple sources.

The exploratory writing students are being asked to complete for this writing project is less ambitious than a "formal, finished product," yet not quite the "unfinished, behind-the-scenes work not intended to be read by others" that Ramage, Bean, and Johnson identify at the other end of the spectrum for exploratory writing. Students will write a paper that recounts their research process—the order in which they used sources and the extent to which each source aided or thwarted their efforts—then revise the draft to keep its pace lively for readers.

Dialectic Thinking

Ramage, Bean and Johnson identify dialectic thinking as an important component of exploratory writing. On pages 180–181 of the textbook, they explain that dialectic thinking is associated with the philosopher Hegel, who posited that a thinker begins with a thesis, the thesis then incites an antithesis, and the opposition between these two leads to a synthesis. Dialectic thinking thus models the exploratory process because it considers multiple solutions, each a reaction to the previous consideration. Dialectic thinking forestalls closure. The synthesis that is derived from dialectic thought becomes a new thesis, which in turn leads to a new antithesis, synthesis, and so on. Dialectic thinking is the prime exemplar of exploratory thought because it is potentially unending.

As Chapter 2 of *The Allyn & Bacon Guide to Writing* explains, exploration is also intricately tied to the stages of intellectual development identified by William Perry. Students who are at the dualist stage may have difficulty genuinely pursuing dialectic thought because they are likely to be firmly committed to their initial thesis. They may pose an antithesis that is artificially simplistic, requiring them to make only inconsequential modifications to their thesis. By urging students to pursue dialectic thinking rigorously and sincerely, you can prompt students' intellectual development. As students undertake the explorations of their topics, you may want to ask them to write a brief justification of their commitment to each thesis, antithesis, and synthesis they consider.

Annotation

Annotations may be purely descriptive summaries, or they may be critical summaries that include an evaluation of the quality of the source and/or its relevance to the students' projected writing activities. The sample bibliography on pages 199–201 should help students understand the nature of an annotated bibliography. Connect back to the presentation of points and particulars in Chapter 2 (Concept 7). It may help to review that concept in Chapter 2 (which illustrates how to write summaries) before proceeding with the annotated bibliography.

It is likely most useful to teach the *evaluative annotation* for this assignment, as this approach (highlighted on page 191 of the textbook) encourages students to examine the rhetorical context of the source and to evaluate the source (both in terms of its inherent qualities and its applicability to the students' writing project).

Using the "For Writing and Discussion" Activities

The activity on page 182 offers a list of sample exploratory questions that could provide class discussion guides for several periods. As you work with students on these activities, connect back to the work you did with Chapter 2, in the first introduction of exploration and writing.

Discussing the Readings

"How Do Online Social Networks Affect Communication?" (pages 194–199)

Because exploratory writing is likely to be an unfamiliar genre to many of your students, you may want to spend ample time analyzing the structure of this reading so they can become more familiar with your expectations for this assignment. The opening paragraphs reveal the writer's motivations and commitment to exploring this topic. Student

James Gardiner's conversations with his friends about their experiences with MySpace and Facebook prompted his curiosity about the ways online social networks affect his peers and communication. In paragraphs 2 and 3, he explains how he moved beyond his personally motivated questions to researching articles and credible online resources. These opening paragraphs illustrate how he moved from a personal question to a broader understanding of his topic.

Paragraph 4 illustrates the way Gardiner's research affected him. This short discussion of what he did not know, and what surprised him, illustrates a good commitment to inquiry. This is the heart of an exploratory essay, which requires the ability to put off commentary and conclusion, and which prizes honest reflection during the writing process.

Paragraphs 5 and 6 show Gardiner continuing to grapple with questions regarding the material he is collecting. With each new source he identifies, he asks multiple questions, often connecting his questions with his own awareness of his proclivity for privacy. Towards the end of paragraph 6, and moving into paragraph 7, Gardiner uses extensive summary to communicate the importance of the sources he is reading.

In paragraph 9, Gardiner groups sources about the ways students use Facebook. This is a synthetic move to classify sources according to subtheme. It can be difficult to teach, so having a good and accessible example is important. Paragraph 10 explains how the information about what students do in online social networks fits into Gardiner's larger inquiry project.

Paragraph 11 moves into a new subtheme—Internet addiction. Sources of statistics are clearly identified, blending a bit of rhetorical context analysis with presentation of facts.

Paragraphs 12 and 13 conclude the essay. While they do contain a tentative conclusion—"that these networks can improve the ability to communicate, but if overused can negatively affect these skills" (198)—the essay's ending reveals a commitment to continued inquiry. It is particularly important that Gardiner has identified questions that must be answered as he continues to write. While not all instructors will assign this sort of narrative exploratory essay, it is important to remember that the attitude of exploration here is something to be encouraged in virtually any writing project.

Draw attention to the different kinds of sources Gardiner approaches. All his research was done online, but he has accessed research reports, newspaper accounts, and journal articles. You can focus students' attention on the different kinds of information provided in each of these sources.

You can ask students to trace Leigh's dialectic thinking process by rereading the paper to see how his opinion on the topic changes. Ask students to chart the places where Gardiner uses first-person accounts of his reaction to the sources and the indications he gives of where and why he chose to pursue additional sources. Reading this sample for insight into the researching habits of a writer is a very useful task for class discussion.

"Indians" (pages 202–210)

This essay by Jane Tompkins is an excerpt from a much longer scholarly essay. It is a good example of the ways in which personal inquiry motivates academic writing. As you introduce this essay to your students, be sure to point out the ways in which the opening paragraphs illustrate the impact of a childhood event on a professional historian. Tompkins' early experiences with Indians (real and imaginary) left her with unsettling questions about the place of Indians in American culture. This essay explores those questions, addressing not so much the answers Tompkins found but the process she used to ask the questions. The key to understanding Tompkins' perspective in this essay lies in paragraph 4, where Tompkins explains "the challenge poststructuralism poses to the study of history." While that is a heady phrase, point students to the rest of that paragraph, where Tompkins uses considerably more lay-reader-friendly language to explain poststructuralism. A poststructuralist assumes that meaning is shaped by observers' (or writers') frame of reference—which is the point Ramage, Bean, and Johnson have stressed throughout the text, calling it *angle of vision*.

This excerpt is fairly long, and takes students through a careful reading of several different historical sources. You may want to make an outline of Tompkins' essay for students, to show them its structure (which may help students follow the discussion of historians they are not likely to know much about):

Paragraphs 1–2: sets up Tompkins' inquiry from her childhood
Paragraph 3–4: explains the significance of the essay
Paragraph 5: explains how Tompkins explored her question and previews the essay's structure
Paragraphs 7–10: summary of Perry Miller
Paragraph 11: reflection on Miller
Paragraphs 12–13: summary of Alden Vaughan
Paragraphs 14–15: reflection on Vaughan
Paragraph 16–17: summary of Francis Jennings
Paragraph 18: reflection on Jennings and the exploratory process
Paragraph 19–21: summary of Calvin Martin
Paragraph 22: reflection on Miller
Paragraph 23: summary of Shepard Krech III
Paragraph 24: reflection on Martin
Paragraph 25–29: reflection on her inquiry and statement of new understanding

This outline matches the graphic presentation of exploratory essay structure in Figure 8.1 earlier in the chapter.

The questions that follow the reading ask students to look carefully at various sections of the essay to look at the angle of vision of particular historians. Question 2, for example, directs students to consider the ways in which Perry Miller's own experiences in Africa shape his analysis of precolonial America. In paragraphs 8 and 9, Tompkins explores Miller's attitudes about Africa, a place he describes as "barbaric," a place he characterizes by its jungles, not its people. In paragraph 10, Tompkins explains, "his failure to see that the land into which European culture had moved was not vacant but was already occupied by a varied and numerous population, is of a piece with his failure, in his portrait of himself at Matadi, to notice *who* was carrying the fuel drums he was supervising the unloading of."

Similarly, Alden Vaughn's historical perspective is shaped by the time of his writing: working before the 1960s, when questions of race and ethnicity became much more prevalent in American academic culture, he could not have seen so many social variations in either Puritan or Indian culture. So his angle of vision, constrained by the period in which he wrote, shapes the tone of his work. Students may have an easier time understanding Tompkins' moves through the different historians' work if you point out that each historian's work is first summarized then analyzed. Tompkins' questions in paragraph 14 are good models for active reading.

Students may struggle with Question 4, as it turns on historical details about Indian religious beliefs and western economic assumptions. Charles Hudson's attack on Calvin Martin appears in paragraph 23, and Tompkins explains the full extent of the differences between Martin and Hudson in paragraph 24. The differences between these two historians are a vivid example of the difference angle of vision makes. If we take Indian religion (or cosmology) as the framework for explaining why Indians participated in the fur trade, then Martin's views make sense. If we take a capitalistic or economic viewpoint as the framework, then Hudson's views make sense. Each author begins from a very different starting place.

Tompkins ends the essay with a meditation on why it is important to live with contradictory explanations for events (a move you might connect to Ramage, Bean, and Johnson's section on wallowing in complexity in Chapter 1). The moral problem Tompkins identifies at the end of the essay is that her exploration of the past does not do anything to address the problems that American Indians are still experiencing. Students who are intrigued by this ending might be encouraged to pursue some research activities connected to this essay with one of the later writing projects. Tompkins' conclusion offers an excellent starting point for a discussion of how exploratory writing can lead to the development of other research projects. Perhaps more importantly, it can lead to a discussion of what difference writing makes. Tompkins realized, at the end of her work, that her study of past didn't change the significant political and social problems that are still faced by American Indians. So how could historical reading and writing be connected to political activism? This is a profitable topic for class discussion.

"What is the Effect of Online Social Networks on Communication Skills: An Annotated Bibliography" (pages 199–201)

The excerpts from this annotated bibliography project will help students see how an annotated bibliography can be laid out on the page. Contrast the introduction of the annotated bibliography with the more narrative approach of the exploratory essay by the same writer.

"Indians: Textualism, Morality, and the Problem of History" (pages 202–210)

The excerpts from this annotated bibliography project will help students see how an annotated bibliography can be laid out on the page. Contrast the introduction of the annotated bibliography with the more narrative approach of the exploratory essay by the same writer.

Guiding Students through the Writing Project

If you are assigning the exploratory essay as a preliminary paper to the writing project in another chapter, you will need to ensure that the topic students chose for this project is suitable for both. Using a research log or other informal writing as a way to check on students' question formation and investment in the activity is a good way to help screen for initial problems and identify early successes to share with the rest of the class. The sample student research log (page 185) is helpful here.

Because students' selection of topics will affect their performance on two major papers, you may even wish to schedule brief conferences with students to discuss their topic selections. Conferences are also valuable at this point in the term for assessing each student's course grade to date and, with the student, collaboratively designing strategies he or she can use to improve future work. Based on prior assignments, does the student have a recurring difficulty that he or she should focus on in subsequent work? Should the student solicit additional feedback on this area during peer reviews? How might tutoring benefit this student? What feedback can you offer the student on his or her attendance and class participation? Does the student have other concerns about the course at this point? However you have structured your syllabus, students are likely to have completed several assignments before this one, and since most teachers will link the exploratory essay to a later writing project, conferences scheduled now would provide an ideal opportunity to summarize students' past performance, approve their current plans (their topics for this project), and guide their future work (what weaknesses they should devote their attention to) based on their past performance.

If students have difficulty thinking of a topic for the exploratory essay, you might suggest that students consider what news items have made impressions on them. Another useful source for topics is reading students may have done, or what topics come up in conversation with friends (which is how James Gardiner decided to write about online networks). Your students might look for topics by considering questions they have as a result of their studies in this course, any of their other courses, or their own reading. Their questions might be directly related to their studies, or their studies may have only provided the spark for inquiry on a tangentially related subject.

Students must keep careful records during their exploration in order to reconstruct the sequence of their research, findings, and opinions. Ramage, Bean, and Johnson recommend that students keep a research log to record such information. Make sure your students realize that the examples are not a complete log, only notes from one article. Although this double-entry notebook format is useful for analyzing their sources, remind students that they must also keep records of their research sequence. This will help you troubleshoot any research problems that may arise.

Recommend to your students that they reread their research notes before they begin writing their drafts to make sure that their reflections reveal dialectic thinking, a movement from thesis to antithesis to synthesis. If the log is inadequate in this sense, students should explore further before they write. Their exploration is most likely to become dialectic if they pose numerous questions.

One part of the peer review guidelines asks reviewers to recommend additional sources or perspectives for the writer's further research. If your students are having difficulty with their research, you may want to devote some class time to small groups for such suggestions even before students write their drafts. Another strategy is that at the beginning of each class session in which you are working with this chapter, you could offer two or three students a chance to briefly share with the class what obstacles they are encountering in their research, so that the class as a whole can brainstorm for other potential resources. If writers don't have time to act on all the suggestions they receive, they can acknowledge their specific plans for continued research in the final paragraph of the paper (review Figure 8.1, on page 188, which outlines how papers might be organized).

If you assign the annotated bibliography option for the exploratory project, you can focus much more class time on summary and short responses or evaluations to individual sources.

Chapter 9
Writing an Informative Essay or Report

Understanding the Chapter's Goals

The chapter focuses on three types of informative writing: that written for readers who need information quickly, that written for readers who are curious and simply want to know more about a subject, with no urgency; and that written for readers who might not even be aware that they need additional information. The first two types of informative writing stress facts, and usually don't include a thesis; the third type is thesis based and focuses on enlarging readers' understandings of the topic or even changing readers' minds about the topic. The key term relating to this type of writing is the *surprising reversal*. Whatever approach you choose for teaching informative writing, the information here may be fruitfully coupled with writing projects from chapters in Parts 3 and 4 of *The Allyn & Bacon Guide to Writing*.

The chapter offers several writing projects: a set of directions, a workplace report, and a magazine-style article. You should decide early in the project how you want to approach the options, choosing one for your students or allowing them the choice depending on their purpose and topic. The directions project can be completed in class as preparation for one of the other two projects.

If you decide to teach this chapter in conjunction with others, there are several especially effective combinations you may want to consider. One possibility is to cover Chapter 19 while students work on this chapter. Although one of the options students will have for the informative essay is to write it in somewhat open and exploratory form (as modeled in this chapter by reading "How Much Does It Cost to Go Organic?" on page 231), most students will probably approach the informative essay as closed-form prose. Therefore, Chapter 18, "Composing and Revising Closed-Form Prose" can complement students' writing on this project (as well as later writing projects) but will not overwhelm them at a time when the writing project itself is highly complex.

Another possible combination of chapters is to teach this chapter along with Chapters 20 through 22 on research. Ramage, Bean, and Johnson explain that one way students may choose to develop their informative essays is through research. With this in mind, if you like you may use this chapter as the basis for a longer researched essay assignment rather than an informative essay. Students can still use the surprising-reversal form discussed in this chapter to structure their researched essays, yet provide support from research to develop their texts more fully. Chapters 9 and 21 are consistent in urging students to begin their writing process with a question. Chapter 20 ("Asking Questions, Finding Sources") and Chapter 21 ("Evaluating Sources"), and Chapter 22 ("Incorporating Sources into Your Own Writing") teach students additional skills that would help them conduct research and incorporate sources into an informative text. You may even wish to include Chapter 8 ("Writing an Exploratory Essay or Annotated Bibliography") as part of this comprehensive research unit. Students could begin with an exploratory essay-writing project that leads to an extended informative (and surprising) essay, i.e., a researched paper (based on Chapters 9, 20, and 21).

One other possibility is to assign parts of Chapter 21, which deal with electronic sources (in Skill 26), along with this chapter. Students could then access the World Wide Web to discover both what is commonly known and what may be surprising about the informative topic they select. Chapter 22 could be assigned as an aid to this informative essay-writing project or as yet another complement portion to the research sequence just described (if you assign it as part of the research sequence, be sure to allot sufficient time to cover the numerous chapters that would comprise the unit).

In summary, there are many options for how you might frame this writing project, from the most basic (this chapter treated autonomously as guidelines for an informative essay or report) to the most comprehensive (this chapter treated as guidelines for an informative researched paper, written within a more prolonged research sequence). Tailor the chapter to fit the needs of your students, your course objectives, and course length. Whatever you choose, this is an important chapter because informative texts are likely to be the kind of texts students will most often be required to write throughout their college curriculum.

Reinforcing the Chapter's Rhetorical Principles

Informative Genres

The chapter offers several ways to consider informative writing—from the point of view of a reader, and from the point of view of a writer. *Need-to-know informative prose* stresses clarity and conciseness, for it is written to provide information that will be used in the moment. Directions about technological products, recipes, directions for crafts or activities, all need to be written so that someone can process the information quickly and act on it. *Informative reports* may simply present information, or present and analyze information, but they stress clear organization and formatting that enable readers to scan and locate information of interest. Often informative reports can be quite long, and the structure and layout of the document must permit readers to browse and read efficiently. With both informative reports and directions, the emphasis is on the reader's need in the moment. The consideration of audience is the most important consideration in students' early rhetorical analysis as they start this assignment.

Informative magazine articles are often thesis-based, ranging from the celebrity profiles in gossip magazines to weighty analyses of political or social trends in more serious publications. These articles require a different sort of rhetorical set-up, for writers must entice readers to pay attention. So a strategy to hook, and then hold, attention, is crucial. Ramage, Bean, and Johnson highlight the importance of creating tension or surprise with the project's thesis, which creates a very different sort of informative purpose.

Informative Purpose

It is important to distinguish informative purposes from persuasive ones (even while considering that the line between them is not always clear). Ramage, Bean, and Johnson note that in informative writing using a surprising-reversal strategy, "the writer's thesis pushes sharply against a counterthesis" (page 216). The emphasis here is not on an argument (as it would be in persuasive writing) but on the subject matter: the writer desires to correct a misapprehension or coax a reader to see something more in the subject than might be clear at first glance.

Other differences between informative (and surprising) discourse and persuasive discourse—specifically classical argument, as taught in *The Allyn & Bacon Guide to Writing*—might be categorized as follows:

Informative and Surprising	Classical Argument
Expands readers' knowledge	Challenges readers' views
Addresses undisputed question	Addresses controversial question
Conveys new information	Prompts debate
Emphasizes facts	Emphasizes values
Requires detailed support for curious reader	Requires vehement support for skeptical reader
Needs evidence derived from personal experience, observation or research	Needs evidence derived from personal experience, observation or research. In addition, needs to appeal to readers' sense of trust and emotional conviction.

To help shape students' projects, you may want to ask students to submit their thesis statements for your approval early in their composing process. The thesis should expand readers' knowledge of *X*, the writer's topic. It follows that the topic shouldn't be highly esoteric: most readers must already have some knowledge of *X* in order to be surprised.

The closed-form essays in this chapter (Rod Crawford's essay about tarantulas, and Cheryl Carp's essay about prisoners serving life sentences) can be paraphrased as follows: "Whereas most people have primarily negative impressions of my topic, what they don't realize is my topic is actually positive/harmless." Students may want to model their thesis after this paraphrase, substituting their own topic, or may want to state its opposite: "Whereas most people have primarily positive impressions of my topic, what they don't realize is my topic is actually negative/dangerous." These are two common patterns for surprise, although thesis statements that convey surprise in other ways are also possible.

Surprising Reversal

Students are likely to be most familiar with informative texts that don't depend on surprise. Encyclopedia articles, technical manuals, budget reports, experimental observations, instruction sheets, and many college textbooks largely present facts without much intention to surprise readers. Ramage, Bean, and Johnson add the element of surprise to the components of traditional informative essays in order to generate greater interest for readers. The surprise is what gives the essay tension and makes it engaging for non-compulsory readers. To illustrate the importance of surprise in hooking readers' interest and keeping them reading, discuss with students the abstract of an *Atlantic Monthly* article on page 216 of the textbook, or the sample thesis statements on page 217. You may want to further emphasize the effectiveness of surprise by assigning students to bring to class an additional abstract of an informative essay in a popular magazine such as the *Atlantic Monthly* or *Harper's*. Students can easily scan past issues in public libraries to learn how frequently and successfully this surprising-reversal pattern is used to enliven informative writing.

In order to compose a text that entails a surprising reversal, students must consider the audience for their essays. Ramage, Bean, and Johnson comment, "You don't have to surprise everyone in the world, just those who hold a common view of your topic" (217). Yet for some topics, students may need help in determining exactly what knowledge is "common" and what is "surprising." Classmates are an ideal resource for this information. Rather than having students discuss their topics in small groups, you might wish to do the following activity, which allows each student to get suggestions for developing his or her paper from every other student in the class.

Begin by asking students to move their chairs into one large circle within easy reach of one another. Then ask students to write their thesis statement at the top of a blank sheet of paper. Once students are ready, ask them to pass their page to the student sitting immediately to their left. That student should read the thesis at the top of the page, then write down no more than three statements in response to the thesis. The statements can be a brief identification of what the respondent already knows about the topic (indicating what "common knowledge" might be) or can be questions that the respondent has (indicating what readers may not know, what would "surprise" them). When the first respondent finishes, the page would then be passed clockwise to the next student, who completes the same process by adding a few sentences or questions. This procedure is continually repeated, with all students adding responses to each sheet, until the pages travel the entire circle and return to their original owner. In classrooms where chairs are bolted to the floor, students may complete this activity by passing their papers up and down the rows in a sequence you suggest.

One potential difficulty with this activity is that sometimes students become so intrigued with others' works that they interrupt the flow of papers by not responding quickly. Especially near the end of the class, students can easily spend five minutes or more reading all the responses and then trying to think of something that hasn't been said. Meanwhile, the next student or two may be waiting with nothing to do. To prevent backlog, encourage students to write their responses after reading just the thesis and the last two or three students' contributions. Even if they end up repeating what someone else has already written, that too can be informative to the writer in showing what knowledge or questions multiple students share.

As students work on this activity, you should monitor the circulation of papers. If one student has several papers to comment on and the next students in the chain are unoccupied, divide the papers needing comments among those students who are waiting. To let a few papers bypass a student who has difficulty keeping up will ultimately increase the number of responses that all papers receive. Whenever students are passing papers efficiently, you can join the circle yourself and add your comments along with other students' comments as the papers circulate. Students enjoy this activity because it allows them to read other students' thesis statements and see how writers enact "surprising reversals" for a vast array of topics. They also appreciate the activity because at the end of just one class session, they leave with many ideas for developing their essays.

Another class activity that can be useful is to invite private writing in the early stages of exploration. Ask students to brainstorm a list of all the topics about which they are reasonably well informed. Some students may profess not to be expert about anything, but remind students that we all have specialized knowledge about a range of topics. Invite students to consider what hobbies they have; places they have traveled; sports they play; interests that are common in their family; family customs; cultural traditions; school traditions, etc. Once students have formed a list, ask them to consider what misconceptions about any of these topics they have encountered (a student who has a stamp collection may have encountered the view that all stamp collectors are unathletic, for example, or a student who rides a motorcycle may have encountered the view that all riders are rebels). Contrasting their "expert" views with these misconceptions may help them see room for creating surprise.

Using the "For Writing and Discussion" Activities

The "For Writing and Discussion" activity on page 213 gives students practice in interpreting and designing directions. Making paper airplanes is a particularly diverting way to begin this chapter's writing project. The activity itself is self-explanatory, and students will easily grasp the problems with poorly explained directions. Note that this exercise introduces a comparison between visual and verbal directions; it is a good time to remind students of any prior conversations about design and layout.

The activity on page 215 creates a role-playing scenario in which the class functions as a focus group. This exercise anticipates material that will be introduced in the following chapter of the textbook, Chapter 10, "Analyzing Field Research Data." You can spend class time helping students brainstorm their questions for the informal questionnaire. More effective questions will include some ranges on time estimates to allow respondents to easily estimate their time on task, and perhaps some suggested game titles for rating. Students will discover that very open-ended questions, while good for discussion, are not good for questionnaires. Respondents like easy-to-answer questions that make their choices clear. Figure 10.2 in the following chapter (page 250) will be a helpful illustration.

The "Thinking Critically About…" questions following each reading offer students practice responding to readings, and that may help them form new questions of their own. Alert students to all of these activities early in the unit so that they may decide upon a topic quickly, begin composing and, if necessary, researching.

If your students have already worked with Chapter 22 of *The Allyn & Bacon Guide to Writing*, "Incorporating Sources into Your Own Writing," or if you wish them to work with that chapter in conjunction with this writing project, you may also want to devise computer-assisted activities for exploring their informative topics. Students can use listservs and the World Wide Web to expand their own knowledge of the topic they intend to discuss. Also, much like circulating their thesis statements in class (as explained above), students could use electronic resources to request others' impressions of their surprising reversals.

Guiding Students through the Writing Project

Ramage, Bean, and Johnson give students ample guidance for writing three types of informative projects. The first option, "Writing a Set of Instructions" (introduced on page 217), could conceivably be done as a group project over a couple of class periods, or as a revised individually written project. This project would allow discussion of layout and document design (connect back to Chapter 4) as well as audience needs.

The second option, the workplace report (pages 219–22), asks students to work within a scenario, each of which requires some research. You may need to supplement the instruction in the textbook with some additional material on how to properly construct a memo, as no memo is modeled in this textbook chapter. Emphasize the importance of a clear and short subject line that clearly reveals the memo's purpose. You could also shift the directions in the text and ask students to write their reports in a style modeled on that of "How Much Does it Cost to Go Organic?" (page 230), which uses a magazine-type style to present information. Part of the richness of educational scenarios is their adaptability, and you should adapt the scenarios presented here—or invent your own—with features to which your students are likely to respond.

The third option, the informative magazine article (page 221), is an essay that uses the surprising-reversal pattern. There are several exercises in the "Composing and Generating Ideas" section that can easily be converted into class activities. You may also wish to draw from other chapters of *The Allyn & Bacon Guide to Writing* to advise students about the writing process for closed-form prose, traditional research methods and documentation of sources, or electronic research, depending on how you have shaped this assignment (see "Understanding the Chapter's Goals" earlier in this chapter of the instructor's manual).

It may also be helpful for students to review Chapter 2 while working on this writing project. Chapter 2's Concept 6, "A Strong Thesis Surprises Readers with Something New or Challenging," includes instruction in writing surprising theses and detailed support. Some principles discussed there, such as using tension to help develop interest for readers, are directly related to the surprising reversal. The pages of this manual that accompany Chapter 2 may also help you guide students as they write this paper.

Discussing the Readings

"Myths about 'Dangerous Spiders'" (pages 210–211)

One of the chief concerns of this chapter is how writers make informative writing interesting for non-compulsory readers. Ramage, Bean, and Johnson suggest that surprise is one way writers do so; descriptive examples is another. Because of this essay's brevity and intrigue, it is a particularly good piece for students to analyze and determine how the writer keeps readers engaged. An effective method for eliciting this analysis is to ask students to assume the role of non-compulsory readers. They should close their textbooks while you read the essay aloud to them. As you read, stop periodically and ask students to rate their level of interest in keeping with the following procedure (students should write down their responses because they will be discussing them in small groups at the end of this activity):

1. Read just the essay's title, then say to students "On a scale of 1 (lowest) to 4 (highest), rate how interested you would be to read this essay if you saw the title in the table of contents of a magazine. Write down the score and one or two sentences, briefly explaining your reason for this score."

2. Read just the first three paragraphs and ask students to again rate the essay: "Using the same scale of 1 (lowest) to 4 (highest), rate how likely you would be to continue reading if you had read these opening paragraphs. Write down the score and a brief explanation of why your interest has increased, stayed the same, or decreased."

3. Read paragraphs 4 and 5. Ask students to use the same rating scale of 1 (lowest) to 4 (highest) to answer this question: "To what extent does this information surprise you?" They should again briefly explain their scores.

4. Before you begin to read again, tell students that you now have approximately one page of the essay left to read. Explain that what you'd like them to do while you read the remainder of the essay is to briefly jot down anything you say that piques their interest, whether that be one or multiple pieces of information, and whether it interests them because of the facts themselves or because of the manner in which the writer presents them.

5. When you finish reading the essay, ask students to rate the essay once more on the scale of 1 (lowest) to 4 (highest) as an overall score of how informative and engaging they found the essay to be. Students should write down this score and, again, a few sentences explaining the basis of their score.

6. Students should now move into small groups to compare and discuss their reactions to the essay. Tell students they may now turn to the essay in *The Allyn & Bacon Guide to Writing* so that they may analyze their reactions more carefully. For example, students may wish to examine more fully the parts of the essay that most interested them (especially those parts that students noted for step 4 above). Did the author disperse the most fascinating points, so that he could regain readers' interest at critical places when that interest might be waning? How did the dialogue—not only of authorities, but also of "ordinary folks" in paragraphs 11 and 13—contribute to the essay's appeal?

7. Finally, ask the small groups to generate some recommendations, on the basis of this essay, that the class can use when writing their informative (and surprising) essays to keep the essays engaging for non-compulsory readers. After small groups have had sufficient time to invent these recommendations, have each group share theirs with the remainder of the class.

"Winery Yeast Preparation Instructions" (pages 226–227)

These short directions lay out the six steps necessary for working with winery yeast, and end with a set of frequently asked questions. Draw students' attention to the plain vocabulary that characterizes this piece. There are very few technical terms used here (*fermentation* being a notable example). You might copy these directions and give half the class the full piece, and the other half only the first portion, with the six steps that need to be followed exactly. Have students compare notes about their reactions to the directions, and then use their reactions to gauge the effectiveness of the frequently asked question section.

"Muslim Americans: Middle Class and Mostly Mainstream?" (pages 228–230)

This excerpt from a Pew Research Center report illustrates clear and concise reporting of survey data. The first question following the report refers students back to the bulleted list of report features on page 220. In class discussion, students will probably easily notice that the report's opening paragraph contains the concise overview of the report, and the second paragraph contains the survey center's research methodology. The report uses two different kinds of graphic displays—a table on page 228 and bar graphs on page 229—to complement the textual discussion of significant findings about Muslim Americans. What students find to be most surprising about the research report will likely depend on their prior knowledge of, or assumptions about, Muslim Americans; point out that the bulleted list is arranged in ways that promote attention to what are arguably the most surprising parts of the study.

"How Much Does it Cost to Go Organic?" (page 231)

"How Much Does it Cost to Go Organic?" shows how students can use graphics in their own work. There are many ways in which student Kerri Ann Matsumoto uses the look of her short essay to emulate a popular magazine piece. In addition to the two-column layout and the graphics, she doesn't use parenthetical citations for all her sources, she uses a short lead paragraph to raise a provocative question, and she situates herself squarely in the paper from the start. These are all choices that signal a more popular, rather than academic, approach.

"Behind Stone Walls" (pages 232–233)

For this informative (and surprising) essay, student Cheryl Carp relies exclusively on her personal experience. Students will find this essay especially pertinent if they feel they are not "experts" about spiders or similarly empirical topics and if you are not requiring that they do research for this assignment. As with the other readings in this chapter, you can discuss with students what they found interesting and surprising about the information this writer presents. Even if some students are not fully convinced that the writer accurately characterizes prisoners serving life sentences, do they still feel this essay has informed them? What other information would they like to know?

Students may suggest that the essay could be strengthened if the writer included in her essay the answers to questions such as these:

- Are all prisoners serving life sentences allowed to participate in the "Concerned Lifers" program, or are there more violent prisoners who are not permitted to participate and to whom the writer has not been exposed?

- How else do prisoners occupy their time?

- What are other interests of the prisoners, besides origami and clowning? What about these unusual and harmless activities do prisoners find most appealing?

- What kinds of topics do the prisoners like to discuss? [Note references in paragraphs 1 and 6 to personal conversation.]

When students draft their own essays, their peer groups can be similarly helpful in identifying aspects of the topic that readers may want to be more fully developed.

"How Clean and Green Are Hydrogen Fuel-Cell Cars?" (pages 233–235)

As Ramage, Bean, and Johnson observe, this essay uses the surprising-reversal formula, raising a question in paragraph 3, moving through common views of the question in the following paragraphs, and placing student Shannon King's thesis in paragraph 5. The essay is informative in providing various angles on hydrogen fuel-cell cars.

Ask students to identify what they find "surprising" about this essay. Students may be surprised, even after all the guidance the chapter provides, that a student puts off a thesis. Using actual examples usually helps complicate the choices students may make with informative assignments, and your students may not believe that it really is OK to postpone a thesis until you have looked at multiple examples from the textbook. Students may also be surprised about some of the content. Ask students to map their own initial answers to the question King poses and then evaluate how well they think the essay presents their views. Another good discussion starter is to ask students what they have learned from this writer's more open-form approach that they may wish to apply to their own writing projects.

"You Have the Right to Remain a Target of Racial Profiling" (pages 236-238)

This essay by columnist Eugene Robinson employs the surprising-reversal strategy to great effect. The essay opens with what may seem to some readers a startling assertion: "Driving while black is still unsafe at any speed." Paragraph 2 would appear to counter that, supplying statistical data that show white, African-American and Hispanic drivers are pulled over by police at roughly equal rates. But paragraph 3 brings in the surprising reversal: readers who assume that paragraph 2 tells the whole story "would be wrong." This surprising-reversal pattern flows throughout this essay, with Robinson patiently alternating reasonable reactions to survey data with the more surprising views that lead to his thesis. Have students look at the ways the paragraph transitions at the start of paragraphs 3, 6, and 10 bolster the surprising reversal. In these paragraphs, Robinson shows how his perspective develops.

This essay is a good one to illustrate the difficulties of making hard and fast distinctions between persuasive and informative writing when a piece uses surprising reversal. This essay might easily be characterized as a persuasive piece, one that seeks to persuade that a social problem exists. Don't let your students be distracted by long discussions about whether this piece is persuasive or not—simply draw their attention to the ways in which Robinson is carefully showing readers that the data they think they know can be interpreted in a different way. That is the heart of the surprising reversal.

Chapter 10
Analyzing Field Research Data from Observation, Interviews, or Questionnaires

Understanding the Chapter's Goals

This chapter deals with field research (questionnaire, surveys, interviews and observations). Field research, while more commonly employed in professional fields and sciences, is also used in the social sciences and humanities. Whether you use this chapter as a source for a full-fledged writing assignment or merely as a supplement to another chapter's project (having students do interviews to augment other kinds of research, for example), students can benefit from understanding how empirical study helps develop knowledge. This chapter supports both research and critical thinking skills. It also supports a short, public presentation of research findings through the scientific poster writing project.

Reinforcing the Chapter's Rhetorical Principles

Field Research Reports

The opening section of the chapter introduces the genre of research reports. The key point to emphasize is that empirical research reports originate in curiosity about the world. On pages 239–240, Ramage, Bean, and Johnson illustrate the curiosities that surround the habits of male and female college students. Once people start wondering whether there are differences in men's and women's exercise habits, they find that there are as many hypotheses (speculative answers to a question) as there are class members. The list of activities on page 240 help students think through some of the issues facing empirical researchers, who must consider questions about how to find out what people's experiences and attitudes are, what ethical considerations must be taken into account, and how well a given set of data represents the larger population. When, for example, can research results be generalized?

Figure 10.1 presents a graphic overview of the eight major sections of a research report: title, abstract, introduction, method, results, discussion, references, and appendices. As Ramage, Bean, and Johnson note on pages 242–243, readers may not read a report from start to finish. The discussion section is almost always read in depth, but other parts of the report may be read very quickly by readers with different needs. This is one reason why research reports tend to rely heavily on subheadings, figures and graphics, and design features that permit flexible navigation through the report.

Scientific Report Structures and the Scientific Method

Ramage, Bean, and Johnson present four stages of the scientific method: posing a question; collecting data; determining results; analyzing results. It's important to emphasize that while empirical researchers form a hypothesis at the start of a research process, the hypothesis is tested before it can be asserted. The research design has to allow for the possibility that the hypothesis may, indeed, be wrong. In the analysis of results researchers sometimes come to a different conclusion, or must pose a new question if the original one has not yet been answered. Forming a hypothesis does not mean closing one's mind to alternate possibilities; it merely means forming an educated guess that can be tested through careful data collection. Additional material on posing questions appears on pages 243–244.

Observation

Ramage, Bean, and Johnson note that the key to successful observation is a clear sense of purpose. When students use observational data, they offer real-life testimony connected to a point they are making. Such data can bring a writing project to life, and make vivid connections between school and workplaces, homes, or public places. But for observation to work well, students must plan their work. The table on page 246 offers solid suggestions. You can connect back to Chapter 5, "Seeing Rhetorically," to remind students about earlier sections of the text which support such work.

Interviews

Interviews can be an excellent way for students to conduct research. It is important for class time to prepare students to interview well, and that includes starting with instruction about how to select an appropriate subject for an interview, and how to politely approach a subject. Show students good invitations to a potential subject, such as:

> I'm Joan Wetherby, a first-year student at State University, and I'm researching the impact of learning communities on student satisfaction. I'm wondering if I could have fifteen minutes of your time to ask you some questions about our university's use of learning communities that have come up as I've been reading about what other campuses do. I'm available most afternoons and I'd be very grateful if you have the time to assist me as I work on this project for English 101.

Notable features of this opening move include:

- A self-description of the student, which orients the potential subject. If the student is already familiar with the potential subject, that part can be omitted, but it is useful to situate the request in the current project ("Aunt Mary, I'm working on a project for my English class, and I'm researching student satisfaction…").

- A brief statement of the project, so the potential subject knows what the student is interested in. This allows the subject to determine whether s/he is really the right person for the interview. Sometimes students will find that their subject declines the interview, but refers them to someone more appropriate.

- A timeframe for the interview, which gives the person an idea about the scope of the time commitment involved.

- Allusion to research previously done, which assures the person that the student is prepared to ask good questions.

- A willingness to schedule the interview at the subject's convenience.

- Gratefulness for the subject's consideration, which indicates that the student will be polite and professional throughout the process.

The guidelines on page 247–248 will help students prepare effective interview questions.

Questionnaires

Questionnaires or surveys are complicated research instruments, but a well-designed short survey can give students a real feel for a common research method in the social sciences. The brief instruction provided in this chapter will allow students to dip into survey research, but not so much so that extensive claims will be able to be generated from the data collected. Still, a small survey can get students engaged in their research process and can generate useful information.

Survey researchers are concerned that the questions they ask not unduly bias respondents, and that the people who fill out the survey are a random sample of the population of interest. It is beyond most students' abilities to generate random samples, so students will likely use what is called a sample of convenience: they will have their surveys filled out by people who are easily available. Encourage students to consider what impact their sample of convenience has on their research results. Who is included in this sample? Who is left out? If students have distributed a survey in their dorm, they may make tentative claims about what dorm residents think about the issue at hand, but they would not be able to support claims about what the population of your town thinks about that issue. Encourage students to think about the limitations of their available sample.

Graphics

You may find that individual students' level of competence with this chapter is quite different from their competence with other chapters of *The Allyn & Bacon Guide to Writing*. Students who are intimidated by writing courses may feel more confident working with visual presentations of material, while students who typically write strong papers may experience "math anxiety" or "artistic anxiety" when they first encounter this chapter. Consider using these variations in students' abilities to your advantage in class discussion.

You may notice that students who don't normally participate in class quite willingly volunteer their responses while working with this chapter. Call on these usually quiet students whenever possible to give them a chance to share their expertise. Assure all students, though, that the chapter contains sufficient information for them to understand the tasks being assigned. Those students who have less experience with visual representations of data may simply need to study the chapter more carefully.

On pages 252–255, Ramage, Bean and Johnson present clear overviews of four types of graphics (tables, line graphs, bar graphs, and pie charts), with the discussion of each presented in terms of what a writer must consider. The discussion here provides good examples of the kind of research questions and methods that students have undertaken, as well as good models for the visual display of research results. Make sure students understand that no one type of graphic—table, line graph, bar graph, or pie chart—is necessarily better than any other. The decision about which to use in any circumstance should be based on three factors:

- The information that needs to be presented (for example, percentages of a whole are best illustrated as a pie chart, whereas the correlation of two variables is best represented as a line graph)
- The rhetorical purpose that the graphic intends to serve (one type of graphic may best highlight points the writer wishes to emphasize and obscure points the writer wishes to minimize)
- The audience for whom the graphic is being designed (some audiences may need more detailed information, which is best presented as tables and sometimes bar graphs, whereas lay audiences may need less detailed presentations with more visual immediacy, which is best accomplished using line graphs and pie charts)

Using the "For Writing and Discussion" Activities

While not officially labeled as such, the activity on page 240 can be a profitable way to introduce this chapter's writing project. Working through the steps listed would vividly illustrate the need to form questions well and to think carefully about the implications of different research methods. The activity on page 245 is another straightforward collection of introductory activities that will help students begin to identity curiosities. Brainstorming in a group will help ideas multiply.

The activity on page 252 is heavily dependent on earlier class activities. Modify the directions based on which field research methods you have emphasized for your assignment. While the activity asks students to talk only with each other, you might want to ask groups to report to the class or have each student make a short summary presentation about his/her plans. It is important to catch any possible problems with research design early, to keep students with flawed plans from disadvantaging their later writing. Students who have poorly designed research plans will miss the chance to collect data that can be usefully mined.

The activity on page 256 invites students to critique an unclear student example. This kind of activity is useful because most students, no matter how uncomfortable they feel producing visual displays themselves, should be able to see some of the problems with the figure. Figure 10.7 lacks good labels for the x- and y-axes, lacks a clear title, and generally fails to communicate what the writer learned. Have students redo the figure using different visual techniques and compare results.

The activity on page 258 stimulates students' free thinking. While it is important to stress that students' ability to speculate is not the same as their ability to support speculative claims, it is also important to encourage students to think broadly. This activity works well as a small group activity or as a warm-up before peer response sessions dealing with drafts of the report.

Guiding Students through the Writing Project

The first writing project for this chapter asks students to prepare a "scientific report" that relies on empirical research to answer a question about contemporary trends or events. It is essential that you be clear about the parameters of the trend or event, and about the extent to which you expect students to research. If you expect library research in addition to the empirical research, leave plenty of time for students to complete their initial investigations.

The section of the chapter on "Analyzing Your Results" (pages 256–258) will help students work with their data. Ramage, Bean, and Johnson explain three ways to work with data: first, by spotting regular patterns; secondly, by exploring the correlations among events; and finally, by direct experiments.

Because the features of the research report are described so thoroughly in the first section of the chapter, the section on writing most of the research report is brief. Direct students back to the earlier parts of the chapter for assistance with formatting and conceptualizing the different sections of their drafts.

The second writing project in this chapter is a scientific poster, which can be assigned as a follow-up to the formal research report, or could be assigned as a stand-alone project. A sample poster appears in Figure 10.8 (page 267). The poster format forces students to compress their ideas. The main point of the poster is to convey the essence of the author's research findings. To produce a successful poster, then, students must have a good sense of what is significant, and why it is significant. Direct students' attention to the bulleted list of poster features on page 266. The most common mistake students make with posters is cramming too much text into a small space. Have students try to do more with less, the better to draw attention to their main findings.

Discussing the Readings

"Women and Smoking in Hollywood Movies" (pages 268–73)

This content analysis, published in the *American Journal of Public Health*, was written for an audience of professionals who have previous expertise discerning the research question at the heart of any project. Students may need some help paraphrasing the essay's main question ("How are women and smoking portrayed in Hollywood movies?" or "What messages do films send about women and smoking?"). The opening section spends its time establishing the significance of the implied question.

The methods section of this essay is particularly detailed, and even if you do not require students to read the whole essay, a collective look at the choices these researchers made is instructive. Their careful presentation of selection techniques will help students see the decisions researchers must make.

Take time to have students look at the figures presented in the report, and to look at what function each figure serves. Note the place in the report where the tables are referenced in words (paragraph 9) and ask students to analyze what is repeated between the table and the text and what meanings are presented in table or text alone.

"A comparison of Gender Stereotypes in *Spongebob Squarepants* and a 1930s Mickey Mouse Cartoon" (pages 274–282) and its accompanying poster (page 283)

This report, written collaboratively by students, is presented in manuscript form and is thus a good format model for students. With either reading in this chapter, students can be directed to identify the different sections of the report and to summarize how each section fulfills the genre features identified in Figure 10.1 The subheads used throughout the paper should make it easy for students to map the text's sections against that list.

Students Lauren Campbell, Charlie Bourain, and Tyler Nishida work from a research question inspired by contemporary criticism of *Spongebob Squarepants*. You can use their abstract and introduction to have students consider the origins of the scientific research report. Although the genre is very closed form and does not reflect much personal writing style, there is a great deal of personal influence or angle of vision in what prompts writers to take up different projects. The source that the students identified on their own—the Kirkpatrick article mentioned in the third question following the reading—is a significant influence of the students' angle of vision.

The review of the literature in this essay is quite brief—it takes only a single paragraph and that paragraph is also the introduction. Some instructors will prefer that students use more of their report to analyze the literature in more detail. Similarly, the discussion section of this report is rather brief, particularly in its discussion (on essay pages 6–7) of the causes of the gender flexibility in *Spongebob Squarepants*. Students may well have additional views to add to these sections, which will help them see how their own reports can be expanded.

This essay is a good example of one relying on student-initiated empirical research set in the context of class readings. If you do not want to have the empirical project take so much time, you can advise students to select smaller questions and do only local empirical research. The resulting project would be more a mini-theme, rather than the full report presented here.

The accompanying poster lays out the students' main research findings. An effective class discussion prompt would ask students to compare the poster to the paper, looking at what the poster leaves out, and what the poster highlights. How might students illustrate some of the specific behaviors they coded on the poster?

Chapter 11
Analyzing Images

Understanding the Chapter's Goals

This is the first of four chapters devoted to analytical writing. While most of the examples that run through the chapter and the writing project itself focus on advertising, the chapter also includes some paintings for analysis, and the language throughout the chapter is flexible enough that you will be able to apply the chapter to a range of visual images. In training students to be more critical readers of advertisements and other images, the chapter accomplishes many important goals. The activities and writing projects in this chapter encourage students to appreciate the creativity of advertisements and visual images, using rhetorical strategies that can be applied elsewhere. The chapter emphasizes cultural criticism. Generally, the work of this chapter invites students to apply their critical thinking and analytical skills to their daily lives, beyond what are traditionally considered "academic" subjects. It raises students' awareness of the vital role audience often plays in shaping texts, and it introduces students to some basic tenets of social constructionism by exploring how advertisements affect an audience's identities and values within a larger social frame.

Reinforcing the Chapter's Rhetorical Principles

Audience Analysis

Advertisements provide an ideal opportunity to teach students that writing is most effective when it appeals to a particular audience. Specifically, the audience of advertisements is consumers. Yet advertisers define the audiences for their texts even more narrowly, as illustrated by the VALS system identified on pages 296–297 of the textbook. The VALS system categorizes consumers by their motivations for purchases (you can make analogies to Chapter 9's classification of readers in relation to their motivation for reading informational writing). You might ask students to examine this system to decide which subdivision they think best describes their own buying behavior, or the buying behavior of friends or family whom they know well. Ask them to explore whether they would categorize themselves differently if they consider different buying behaviors (whether they act differently as consumers of clothing than fashion, for example).

Whereas the VALS system allows advertisers to analyze buyers' values and needs, advertisers also analyze buyers demographically. Ramage, Bean, and Johnson cite several demographic factors advertisers consider: "ethnicity, gender, educational level, socioeconomic class, age, and so forth" (page 295). Advertisements are then created to appeal to people with particular characteristics, and the ads are placed where they are most likely to reach those audiences. Advertisers often hope to create brand loyalty among their customers.

Most students are already aware that products are advertised on television according to which consumers are likely to be watching the program. The commercials during Saturday morning cartoons feature toys; those during mid-day soap operas promote cleaning products and food suggestions for family dinners; those during televised sports are often for cars and beer. Invite the class to discuss other ways in which advertisers adapt their marketing for different audiences. How does the expected audience of a magazine influence the ads in it? How do billboard advertisements differ in neighborhoods with different demographics? You might bring various magazines with different audiences to class and organize a group activity to compare the ads in, say, *Ebony, Good Housekeeping, The Advocate*, and *Sports Illustrated*. Comparing ads across magazines with related audiences (*Ebony* and *Jet*, for example, *Good Housekeeping* and *Family Circle,* or *Parenting, Mothering*, and *Brain,Child Magazine*) can also be a productive group activity.

Of course, advertisements will often be seen by those who are not the intended audience. Ask students to consider how they typically respond when they see advertisements that are obviously created for other audiences. For example, if their limited income while they are students makes them "sustainers" or "emulators" on the VALS system, how do they respond when they see an ad clearly directed toward "achievers"? Do they quickly disregard the ad as irrelevant? Or does the ad make them feel in any way inadequate? How might that feeling foster their purchase of items that are more affordable? Or, if some students in your class consider themselves inner-directed consumers, as defined by the VALS system, how do they typically respond to an ad that is targeted to outer-directed consumers? Do they ignore the ad or do they criticize it in order to reinforce their own values? In other words, even misdirected ads can affect our sense of identity and our values.

After your class has completed this chapter, you may wish to refer back to it to strengthen students' awareness of the importance of audience analysis in all writing. Teach students that writing is most likely to be effective when it is adapted to a specific audience. The writer should appeal to that audience's values and needs, but be alert to how other readers may respond as well.

Image Analysis

On pages 286–293 of the textbook, Ramage, Bean, and Johnson provide extensive suggestions for the analysis of magazine advertisements, followed by their own analysis of an advertisement on pages 298–300. Students will sometimes want to analyze television commercials, and if you permit that option, you will need to support it with in-class activities. You can videotape some commercials that the class can watch together and then discuss, using the criteria in the textbook chapter. Recommend that if students want to analyze TV commercials for their writing project, they should videotape the ads too so that they can watch them repeatedly. If you have good Internet access, Web archives of television commercials (such as the Canadian site http://ihaveanidea.org) can also supply TV ads for analysis (the site requires free registration). Analyzing a TV ad requires the writer to observe the ad just as closely (perhaps even more closely) than one would observe a print ad. Therefore, relying on one's memory is insufficient for this assignment. You may find that it is more convenient for you to focus on print advertising, since students can easily bring their ads to class for review and discussion.

When students analyze an ad, they must study its denotations (explicit content) to determine its connotations (underlying meaning). To draw conclusions about the ad's connotations, suggest that students speculate about the purpose of each element of the ad. Students should be especially attentive to the features of the ad that are most unexpected, those that are most emphasized, and those that are most subtle. Most ads "sell" something besides the product: something people want, like beauty or friendship, or an escape from fears, such as the fear of harm or the fear of others' disapproval. Advertisers hope that consumers will associate their products with these more fundamental needs and thus buy their products to get these needs met.

Urge students to identify what is being "sold," besides the product, in the ads they select for this chapter's writing project. For example, the ad on page 299 of this chapter implies that Coors Light beer sustains friendships and may lead to romantic involvement. Yet what is the causal relationship between Coors Light and the fictionalized friendship of Sam and the ad's narrator? The ad copy explains that they've been friends since first grade, long before their drinking days (one hopes). More importantly, the ad gives the impression that if consumers buy Coors Light, they too will find a comfortable, pseudo-sexual friendship. Similarly, the ad on page 304 implies that Zenith audio products may offer consumers beautiful bodies. Note that the visual images that appear at the beginning of each part of *The Allyn & Bacon Guide to Writing* also offer good examples for class discussion. In addition, remind students that television commercials also bait consumers with promises that have little to do with the products being sold. For example, women are barraged with the message that their husbands and kids will love them only if the kitchen floor glows, the school lunches are packed with the right peanut butter, and their clothes are the whitest white.

As students analyze ads together for practice and begin to analyze them independently for their writing project, encourage them to assess the ad's persuasiveness. Do they find it effective? Do they think others would find it effective? Can it be effective even if, after analysis, at least parts of it are objectionable? What most contributes to its effectiveness? Is it effective because the values and needs it relies on are immense?

Every year, television commercials are competitively judged and the very best are given a Clio Award. A trait common to many winning commercials is humor. If the ads students analyze rely on humor, students should also analyze the contribution this approach makes in the ad's overall persuasiveness. What is the source of the ad's humor? Some TV ads are humorous because they poke fun at themselves, at the grand exaggerations that advertising makes; viewers smile and know to discount the hyperbole, but may subconsciously retain the exaggeration.

Some Internet resources may be helpful in the general presentation of this chapter. Adbusters is one group that presents spoof ads and media commentary in order to encourage public discussion of images in the information age. As the Adbusters Web site (http://www.adbusters.org) explains (in its information section), the group is "a global network of artists, activists, writers, pranksters, students, educators and entrepreneurs who want to advance the new social activist movement of the information age." Adbusters' spoof ads can be compared to commercial advertising for food or fashion, and the analysis techniques presented in the chapter will help students see the assumptions at the heart of each image. A more commercial view of advertising is available at Adcritic.com, which is owned by advertising companies. Here you and your students can find information about advertising agencies and their latest campaigns. This can be useful for creating common images for students to analyze and discuss in class.

Cultural Issues

Ramage, Bean, and Johnson provide numerous examples of how advertising reflects and reinforces gender inequalities. Often, the use of women in advertisements focuses on their bodies (see the ads on pages 305 and 306 of the textbook). This use degrades women by treating them as ornaments, rather than as thinking human beings. Ads that emphasize women's bodies are likely to affect male and female viewers differently. Many male viewers may find the woman's sensuality arousing. Advertisers hope that if male viewers desire her, they will consider the product desirable merely through association. On the other hand, many female viewers may compare the woman in the ad to themselves. There is extensive cultural pressure for women to feel that a chief measure of their worth is their attractiveness. Therefore, if women consumers feel less attractive than the woman in the ad, they may associate the product with becoming desirable, more like the woman featured. In this way, many ads are created primarily for male audiences but consider women secondary audiences. The reverse—ads that target women and appeal secondarily to men—are far less common, which is itself indicative of society's sexism. Increasingly, however, men's bodies are sexualized in advertising, and students may well have lively discussions about the ways in which men and women are visually depicted.

Another expression of sexism in advertising can be seen by contrasting how women and men are portrayed in magazines that are read almost exclusively by one gender. The primary audience for *Cosmopolitan* magazine is female, yet in this and many other fashion magazines with almost exclusively female audiences, often ads still portray women as sexual objects. This practice shows the extent to which many women have been socialized to judge themselves by their appearance: even when male viewers aren't present, women are likely to view themselves through men's eyes. The same phenomenon is not true of magazines targeted to men. Whereas women are often statically posed, waiting for a judgment of approval from others, men are portrayed as decisive, active, and inherently important.

Extreme examples of sexism in print ads can be found on the back cover of every issue of *Ms.* magazine. The ads are clipped from other publications by readers and submitted to *Ms.* for this regular department. Some of the reprinted ads are shockingly misogynist, while the sexism of others is more subtle. Because all are reprinted without editorial discussion (the name of this periodical department is "No Comment"), you may want to take a few back issues of *Ms.* to class so that students can become more attuned to cultural issues by analyzing these ads.

Of course, gender is not the only cultural issue at stake in advertisements. The full spectrum of prejudices exists. It is rare to see people who are visibly gay, disabled, or working class in ads. Although racial minorities are increasingly represented, they are usually accompanied (and outnumbered) by whites in the ads where they appear (unless the ads appear in minority-targeted publications). And one minority is considered sufficient: ask students whether they've ever seen an ad that depicts people of more than one race without including whites. The elderly are used almost exclusively in comic roles (recall the Wendy's fast food spokesperson who would bellow, "Where's the beef?") or to sell life and health insurance plans. The implication is that the elderly should be viewed as the brunt of jokes or as nearly dead. Portrayals of overweight people are also rare in ads, except for humor or to sell weight-loss programs. Both treatments are derogatory in implying that obese people are not worthy of respect at their current weight. Throughout your work with this chapter, encourage students to look for such biases in the ads of magazines they frequently read and television programs they regularly watch. (The "For Writing and Discussion Activity" on page 305–308 offers good guidance for such work.)

You can complicate students' analysis of these cultural factors by bringing in magazines targeted at minority readerships. Using mainstream gay or lesbian publications (such as *The Advocate*) is a good way to explore images of beauty and sexuality in advertising. Images from men's fashion magazines (such as *Esquire* or *GQ*) complicate the presentation of masculinity, since in these magazines men's bodies are frequently objectified (although not perhaps in the same way that women's bodies are in mainstream magazines). You can bring a range of magazines to class for students to analyze together.

Students can apply lessons they have learned from Chapter 6 of *The Allyn & Bacon Guide to Writing* when analyzing the cultural assumptions of advertisements. To analyze, students must "read against the grain," as Chapter 6 explains. Many of the questions for reading against the grain presented in this manual's treatment of Chapter 6 are relevant for this assignment as well. Students should look at what is excluded from the ad (including who is excluded from the ad), what is questionable about the advertiser's stated and unstated beliefs and assumptions, what assumptions the advertiser makes of the consumer's views, and what a consumer will gain and lose by accepting the advertiser's view.

Collectively, advertising creates not only an image of products, but also an image of culture. Advertising affects how people define their identities, their relationships with others, and their positions in the world. You may wish to discuss with your students the cultural implications of advertisers using images to shape societal norms and values, all as a means of enhancing corporate profits.

Using the "For Writing and Discussion" Activities

The "For Writing and Discussion" activities throughout this chapter ask students to create and analyze advertisements or paintings, tasks they are likely to enjoy. In addition to the activities in the textbook, you may wish to ask students to keep a daily log for a week of the advertisements they are exposed to through magazines, television programs, billboards, and sales brochures. In the log, they could write a brief description of each ad, and then one or two observations that interpret the ad. The observations could be analyses of the ad's audience (perhaps as identified by the VALS system), any subtle connotations created by the ad's image, and/or any cultural issues in the ad. You may then wish to reserve the first five minutes of each class session for a few students to describe an ad they've noted in their logs and to offer a quick assessment of its effectiveness. Keeping a log in which they analyze ads will help students become more critical observers of the images they see on a daily basis. This assignment will also give students many ads to select from when they do their writing project for this chapter.

Although not explicitly labeled "for writing and discussion," the exploratory tasks at the start of the chapter (pages 288–289) are a good way to get students working with analysis. The first task asks students to do some preliminary analysis of a set of pictures relating to United States-Mexico immigration debates. The second task asks students to consider how the pictures might be used in support of different arguments. From the start, this chapter links image analysis to rhetorical analysis, and these tasks are a good introduction to what kinds of skills students bring with them to the unit.

The activity on page 291 asks students to analyze images of bears. You can easily replicate this assignment with a cluster of images of your choosing if you prefer to switch the content focus. Asking students to compare different images from college viewbooks often leads to interesting comparisons of college campuses in the region.

The activity on page 293 asks students to apply the strategies introduced for advertising analysis to two classic paintings, one by a Dutch artist and the other by an American. This exercise highlights the flexibility of visual analysis. The tools of this chapter can be applied to various kinds of images, on line, on the page, and on canvas.

The activity on page 297 puts students in the role of futon (cotton mattress) manufacturers who need to boost sales. This exercise asks students to switch roles and think about creating images and supporting texts, rather than analyzing them. Students don't need to actually compose images, of course, but you can ask groups to sketch out sample advertisements to make the exercise more generative. This is a good way to reach out to students with drawing skills, although you should emphasize that artistic merit is not required in order to work with the rhetorical underpinnings of an ad campaign.

The activity that begins on page 300 takes students through a step-by-step analysis of automobile ads. It is a very useful way to help students practice steps they can use on their individual projects. Many students can easily find one or two observations to make about any given ad, but this activity's list of structured questions will help students develop additional ways to see and interpret their images.

The activity that begins on page 305 was discussed earlier in this chapter of the manual, in the "Cultural Issues" section.

Guiding Students through the Writing Project

One of the most important skills students will need to complete this writing project is the ability to analyze every minute detail of an ad. To give them practice with such analysis, you may want to give students a photocopy of one advertisement and ask them to analyze its features using Ramage, Bean, and Johnson's guidelines on pages 291–292. After students complete this individually for homework, give them some time during the next class period to meet in small groups and compile their observations. Then have the small groups report their analyses to the class. In all likelihood, each stage of this activity— moving from individual student, to groups, to the full class—will increase the thoroughness of the analysis. Students can then compare the final analysis of the ad done by the full class to their own individual analyses and can realize how much they initially overlooked. This should motivate them to be persistent in their analyses when they do their writing project, rather than end their observations prematurely.

A flow diagram of an analysis of two visuals appears in Figure 11.17 on page 309. This outline describes one good way to organize this writing project. You may want to develop alternative organizational models for students if you are concerned that a single model will be too restrictive (for example, you might diagram one model that alternates analysis of two images, criteria by criteria, and another model that presents analysis of one image first, then the other). Note that the diagram's advice on the conclusion is that it should contain "final comments about the significance of your analysis or [touch] in some way on larger issues raised by the analysis" (page 309). Advise students that to achieve these goals, they need to focus on something other than the ads in their conclusion. Their analysis of the ads might lead them to an observation about the role of audience in advertising, the cultural significance of the product being advertised, the social construction of people's identities in the ad, or a similarly important point.

Discussing the Readings

From "Visual Persuasion: The Role of Images in Advertising" (pages 311–313)

This reading introduces students to more theoretical research about advertising. Messaris' emphasis on iconicity is something worth spending class time on; the term is likely to be new to students. Some students are resistant to the notion that advertising affects them at all, and Messaris' essay can help them explore the ways in which advertising images affect perceptions of lived reality.

Messaris' excerpt focuses on the ethical issues associated with advertising, and it stakes a middle ground between critics and celebrators of advertising. In paragraphs 2 and 3, Messaris outlines the contrast between earlier advertising, which focused on simple images of carefree consumers, and modern advertising, which often focuses on negative images (such as "heroin chic"). He is particularly interested in images of adolescents and African Americans, and the four ads on pages 314 and 315 are a vehicle for exploring his analysis (students can also identify their own ads involving these groups, of course). Draw students' attention to the ways in which Messaris reads "with the grain" and "against the grain" as he considers the criticisms of abrasive or belligerent teenage behavior or the alleged phoniness of racial depictions in some ads. The discussion questions that follow the reading will direct students to consider the contexts for the advertisements in the chapter, as well as other advertisements they may recall from experience.

"How Cigarette Advertisers Address the Stigma Against Smoking: A Tale of Two Ads" (pages 316–318)

This student essay is a strong model of the assignment students will complete for the writing project in this chapter: an analysis of two ads that sell the same kind of product but appeal to different audiences. This student, Stephen Bean, follows the outline recommended on page 309 of the textbook for organizing this writing project. Rather than describing and analyzing the first ad fully before discussing the second, the writer relates the ads to one another by describing each and then analyzing each. It is important for students to see how they can analyze two ads in relation to each other, rather than crafting two mini-essays.

Major strengths of Stephen Bean's essay are his careful study of the ads (for example, noticing that in the first there is no smoke coming from the cigarettes but that the cigarettes in the other emit smoke), and his thoughtful analysis of the symbolic messages conveyed by the images. He interprets the images in each ad well, demonstrating how the ad's components work collectively to give the ad a dominant message. You might want students to compare paragraphs 2 with paragraphs 5 and 6 in this essay, and paragraph 3 with paragraph 7. Your students should notice that nearly everything Stephen Bean writes in his early descriptions of the ads is critiqued in his latter paragraphs. Stress to students that they should be equally thorough in their analysis.

Perhaps the greatest strength of this essay is that Stephen Bean analyzes these ads within a larger societal context—the current stigma associated with cigarettes and smoking. For this reason, Bean's essay is more revealing than an essay that simply explains how two ads for a product differ. By discussing the differences not only in these advertisers' audiences, but also in their purposes, Bean successfully analyzes the rhetorical decisions of the ads' creators.

Even if your students choose to analyze ads with less socially charged products, the ads themselves may be socially charged. In this essay, Bean did little analysis of the cultural issues presented in the ads. Although the ads are not included in the chapter, even from Bean's essay it seems a critique of class or race would be fruitful in the Benson and Hedges ad, while gender roles could be extensively analyzed in the Richland ad. Bean might have used the chapter's cultural analysis resources to work more carefully with the characters' expressions, gestures, and positions.

Chapter 12
Analyzing a Short Story

Understanding the Chapter's Goals

Although many English teachers enjoy the opportunity to teach literary analysis in a writing course, often students find such assignments intimidating. They may think that only English majors can excel in literary analysis; worse, they may think that literary analysis has no relevance to other writing they may do. This chapter addresses students' concerns by presenting literary analysis as simply another type of reading. Like any analysis, it entails a process of inquiry and interpretation.

Throughout the chapter, Ramage, Bean, and Johnson emphasize that there is no single correct interpretation of a story. Quite the opposite, they provide opportunities for students to explore in small groups how their interpretations of the same story differ, and they urge students to use these differences as focal points of their essays. The writing project for this chapter includes two documents: an essay analyzing a short story, and a reading log that contains responses to fifteen tasks assigned throughout the chapter. The reading-log tasks demystify the analysis of literary techniques (plot, characters, setting, point of view, and theme) and ensure that students gain experience in interpreting all literary techniques, not just the technique they choose to emphasize in their essay. The requirement for students to submit their reading logs along with their completed essay enables you to reward them for their entire interpretive process.

Reinforcing the Chapter's Rhetorical Principles

Literary Reading

In the opening pages of this chapter, Ramage, Bean, and Johnson distinguish between reading literally and reading literarily. You can reinforce this distinction by helping students realize they often read differently, even when they don't consciously change their stances as readers. To do so, bring to class a wide range of texts meant for either kind of reading. The stack might include a telephone directory, an encyclopedia volume, a paperback romance novel, a hardbound "classic" novel, a hardcover edition of a nonfiction book currently on the *New York Times'* bestseller list, a department store catalog, a street map, and so on. Remind students that earlier discussions of reading strategies (which accompanied your work with Chapter 6, "Reading Rhetorically") explored the ways in which different texts require different reading strategies.

As you hold up each volume, ask the class to tell you all they can about it based solely on the cover: whether they would read it literally or literarily; what types of information they could expect to find in it; whether they are expected to read it starting at the beginning and moving to the end, or if the author anticipates that they might skip around in their reading; the extent to which the text is "truthful"; and so on. From this activity, students will see that they already vary their reading strategies depending upon the text they read, often before they even scan the opening lines of the text.

Literary Techniques

The most common error of students inexperienced in literary analysis is that they summarize the plot of a narrative, engaging in little interpretation. To discourage mere summary, you might want to advise students to analyze the plot of a narrative by writing the major events of the story in one column, labeled "What Happens," and then describing what they believe to be the significance of each event in a parallel column, labeled "Why It's Important." Completing the second column teaches students to interpret the plot by identifying how the events are connected and how each contributes to the narrative. The double-entry format helps students realize that they must analyze—not merely summarize—the plot of the short story that you assign for their writing project. This double-columned note-taking strategy is in line with note-taking strategies presented in Chapter 8.

The concept of narrative discussed in Chapter 19 can also help students analyze a short story. There, Ramage, Bean, and Johnson identify the four elements that are necessary for a text to be a narrative: the depiction of events; connectivity between those events; tension or conflict; and resolution of the conflict. In addition to the reading-log tasks assigned throughout this chapter, students may want to try condensing the story they are analyzing to its barest essentials, using the techniques as a guide. They can then explore how this synopsis of the story enlightens their understanding of the narrative techniques. How do each of the narrative techniques—plot, character, setting, point of view, and theme—reflect the narrative's tension or conflict? Which techniques play the greatest role in the conflict's resolution?

Because open-form prose uses many of the techniques of literary narrative, Chapter 7 ("Writing an Autobiographical Narrative") builds on the information about plot, character, setting, and theme conveyed in this chapter. Therefore, you may wish to refer students to pages 156–158 of Chapter 7 to read more about literary techniques, particularly if they choose to focus on a question of plot, character, setting, or theme for their analysis. Chapter 7 does not discuss point of view, an additional narrative technique discussed in the present chapter.

Using the "For Writing and Discussion" Activities

All of the "For Writing and Discussion" activities in this chapter require students to discuss their reading-log entries, either as a class or in small groups. In other chapters, you may decide to use only some "For Writing and Discussion" activities, based on the time you have allotted for that chapter. With this chapter, it is essential that you devote class time to every activity. If you do the activities that allow students to discuss plot and character, but not those that focus on other narrative techniques, you will be putting students who wish to write their essays about setting, point of view, or theme at a disadvantage.

There are five activities in this chapter, all of which must be completed by the time students have done the first nine of their required fifteen reading-log entries. Thus, when you plan the class sessions you can devote to this chapter, consider how to pace the "For Writing and Discussion" activities. Even though students are directed to write each log entry as they come to it in the textbook, without reading ahead, you can still assign students to complete several for homework, all to be discussed during the following class.

For example, on the first day of class devoted to this chapter, you might assign students to read pages 320–326 which open the chapter and provide the framework for students' work. Once students have read the story you select for this writing project, they can complete the first three reading-log tasks on page 327 (collectively, requiring twenty-five to thirty minutes of writing). On the second day of class, you can give students time to discuss their first three reading-log entries, as directed in the "For Writing and Discussion" activity on page 327.

The four remaining "For Writing and Discussion" activities assign students to discuss their responses to reading-log tasks 4 through 9—tasks that collectively require eighty minutes of freewriting. Because students will have little textbook reading to do as they complete these reading-log tasks (only pages 328–329), you may want to have students complete reading-log tasks 4 through 9 for one class session's homework. Although you may wish to distribute students' discussion of these reading-log entries over several class periods, by assigning students to complete the tasks early, students can continue to read the chapter and to complete the six remaining log entries, which need not be discussed in class. This pace will also leave students ample time to begin writing their essay.

To keep students' interest throughout the "For Writing and Discussion" activities, you may wish to vary how you arrange the discussions. The first, on pages 327, might be done as a full class discussion (be careful when using this format that students do not relate to you as an authority who knows the story's "correct" interpretation; you should play the role of a facilitator as they discuss their ideas with one another). In a later class session, students might discuss the plot and characterization reading-log entries in small groups. Still later, students can be directed to switch groups to discuss the setting, point of view, and theme of the story. In this way, students can be exposed to the wide range of ways in which their peers responded to the story and can gain increasing confidence in their own ability to interpret literary texts.

You should consider how to collect and evaluate students' writing-log entries; you may wish to collect them with the essay and grade the whole packet, or you may wish to collect and grade the logs separately. If you are using portfolios and grades are deferred, you may evaluate the logs in some way (using checks/plus/minus, perhaps) as they are completed. It is important that students conscientiously complete the tasks prior to the in-class discussions. If students do not come to class prepared, their discussions of the story will be less thoughtful, less diverse. Students who feel insecure about their ability to understand literature may be tempted to wait until after they have heard other students' interpretations of the story to write their reading-log entries. If that happens, those students will not learn that they too are fully capable of analyzing literature.

Therefore, to ensure that students complete their reading-log entries before they hear other students' interpretations, announce that you will check during class to see that each student completed the reading-log task(s) you assigned. You need not read the log entries now, only scan them to make sure all are complete. You may assign participation points or use some other incentive for homework completed on time. You can attend to such matters quickly at the beginning of the period if the "For Writing and Discussion" activity will be set up as a full-class discussion, or if students are sharing their log entries in small groups, you can walk around the room to check assignments as students meet. If you plan to enforce a penalty for students who have not completed the reading-log entries on time, announce what that penalty will be in advance. Do not collect the individual log entries prior to the due date for the writing project because many students will want to refer to their log as they write their essay.

Discussing the Readings

"The Medicine Man" (pages 321–322)

As the questions that follow this reading indicate, this Navajo legend is included in the chapter to illustrate the difference between literal and literary reading. The first indication that the legend should be read literarily is the opening clause: "There is a telling that, in the beginning . . ." (which students may recognize as similar to the classic opening of many children's books: "Once upon a time . . ."). Because the events in this legend are so imaginative (including the anthropomorphism of animals), it is difficult to conceive of a literal reading of the text.

Nevertheless, students can recognize the differences between literal and literary texts better if you ask them how the legend would change if it were meant to be read literally, not literarily. A literal version of this text might be summarized as follows: "There is a Navajo legend that explains why coyotes howl and why they do not hunt or kill field mice. According to this legend, coyotes howl because they have a perpetual toothache, which they received as a punishment for releasing stars they were entrusted to deliver in a bound pouch. The reason coyotes don't hunt mice is that coyotes are grateful to mice for providing them with medicinal herbs that help to ease their toothaches." Clearly, the events described in the summary are still fictional, but the text of the summary is literal because it directly explains the Navajo legend. In literary texts, a writer uses plot, character, setting, point of view, and theme to give a story immediacy, to help readers experience the story's meaning. In literal texts, the meaning is usually more explicit. Even in non-literary texts where the thesis is implied, not directly stated, the reader is only expected to deduce the meaning, not experience it.

"Everyday Use (For Your Grandmama)" (pages 332–338) and "The Lone Ranger and Tonto Fistfight in Heaven" (pages 339–43)

The two longer stories in this chapter are discussed here together because how you use them with your class will depend upon which story, if either, you assign students to analyze for their writing project. The story that students interpret for their papers should be discussed in class only as directed in the "For Writing and Discussion" activities. The other story may be used by the class to collaboratively practice a thorough interpretation of a story, without risking that doing so will leave students struggling to find something new to write in their own essays. Before you begin to teach this chapter, then, read both stories to decide which you want to assign to students for their writing projects. Keep in mind that a student analysis of "Everyday Use (For Your Grandmama)" is included in this chapter, so your decision may be based on whether or not you want students to have a sample analysis of the story they are required to interpret. If neither of the stories in this chapter seems suitable for your students, you can provide another story for their writing project; in that case, you could use either or both of the stories in this chapter to model a thorough literary analysis.

Tell students they must read any story they intend to analyze several times. The first time, they should read it as directed in the first reading-log task on page 333 of the textbook, stopping periodically to freewrite their predictions of what will happen next. You may want to designate the three places they should stop to freewrite for this reading-log task. Points you might recommend, which will give students enough context to allow them to make plot predictions, yet which simultaneously invite a wide range of possibilities, are after paragraphs 12, 44, and 67 in "Everyday Use (For Your Grandmama)," and after paragraphs 4, 13, 31, and 44 in "The Lone Ranger and Tonto Fistfight in Heaven."

The second time they read the story, students should place a question mark in the margin by anything they don't understand. Explain that before they can understand a story literarily, they must be able to understand it literally. Students should go back over confusing areas, using a dictionary to define unfamiliar words and jotting down questions they can ask in small groups or in class discussion so that the author's literal meaning is clear.

There may be some unfamiliar cultural references or vocabulary words that hinder students in interpreting the literary aspects of the story. For example, immigrant students may have difficulty analyzing Walker's story because they may not know what a butter churn is (an artifact crucial to the theme of the story; see paragraphs 46–55) or may be completely unaware that some people collect and display antique, handmade items like quilts (ironically, these similarities to Maggie and Mama in valuing domestic items only for their "everyday use" is precisely what may prevent such students from being able to analyze the story's thematic conflicts). If your students have immense difficulty understanding the literal meaning of either story, you may want to have them work in groups writing a paragraph-by-paragraph synopsis of the story in their own words.

After students have read the chapter's explanations of plot, characters, setting, point of view, and theme, lead the class in exploring each of these for the story you will analyze together. What does each technique contribute to the story? You might want the class to identify the elements of the story's narrative (see Skill 15, on narrative, in Chapter 19 (pages 547–554) and then discuss the importance of each event. For each of the major characters, ask students what they most liked, what they most disliked, and what most surprised them. Which characters, if any, do they think changed in the course of the story? How so? Also discuss how the setting contributes to the story. How would the story need to be changed if the writer used a different setting? Similarly, how would the story change if it were told from other points of view?

As Ramage, Bean, and Johnson acknowledge in Chapter 7 on autobiographical writing, "The word *theme* is difficult to define" (page 159). Therefore, consider devoting more of the class discussion time to this literary technique than to others. Begin by asking students to volunteer how they would define this term. Then encourage other students to refine the definitions that are offered. Ramage, Bean, and Johnson compare a narrative theme to the thesis of closed-form prose, but a theme is not necessarily the story's moral. Rather, it is the general issue that the narrative explores through the use of specific events and characters. You may want to give students time in small groups to discuss what they think might be the predominant theme of the story before discussing it as a full class.

Assure students that theme is almost always more ambiguous than the other literary techniques. No attempt at identification of a narrative's theme is "wrong" as long as the students have evidence from the story to support their claim. In fact, an analysis of theme often provides a reader great opportunities to understand the relationships between their experiences and what they read.

Resist the urge to point out nuances students overlook in this or other stories you discuss. The goal of this chapter is to foster students' independence in analyzing short stories. Although they may press you for the "right" answer when they generate conflicting interpretations, prod students to grapple with those differences themselves, stressing that having supporting evidence from the story is the only measure of validity.

"Who Do You Want to Be?: Finding Heritage in Walker's 'Everyday Use'" (pages 343–345)

By the time students have finished all fifteen reading-log entries required for this writing project, they will have many ideas for interpreting the assigned short story. One of their biggest challenges will thus be deciding on a thesis for their essay. Their essay will not be coherent if they include every insight they have regarding the story. They must choose one or two interpretive arguments they can best develop. In discussing this essay, then, talk with students about how student Betsy Weiler focuses her essay. She does not discuss all the narrative techniques of the story, but concentrates on its theme. She also discusses the character of Dee/Wangero and specific events that take place in the story, but only because they affect how the readers of the story perceive its theme. Advise your students to similarly limit the narrative elements they analyze. If you allow them to analyze "Everyday Use (For Your Grandmama)" for their writing project, you may wish to require them to write their analysis on a narrative technique other than theme (and possibly, if they choose the technique of characterization, a character other than Dee/Wangero because she is discussed extensively in this sample essay).

This essay is also useful for helping students understand how to emphasize literary analysis over narrative summary. To demonstrate how analysis and summary are integrated, you may want to have students make a photocopy of this student essay, then use two different colors of highlighter markers to distinguish which comments are interpretive and which are summative. Are there any instances of summary given that do not seem to be tied to interpretative comments? If so, what seems to be their purpose? What is the relative proportion of interpretation and summary?

Guiding Students through the Writing Project

Much of the guidance students will receive for this writing project will be in the form of their reading-log tasks and the practice they receive analyzing "Moonlight." Advise them to read the short story they are analyzing several times; each additional reading can yield new observations. Suggest annotating the story as they read to help them remember these connections. Decide how you want students to make use of any research in connection with this assignment; many teachers prefer to have students work only with their own close readings rather than research in order to ensure that students challenge their own analytical abilities. Remind students as well not to spend excessive time summarizing the plot of the story. They should assume that the essay's reader knows the story well. Student Betsy Weiler's essay in this chapter ("Who Do You Want to Be?: Finding Heritage in Walker's 'Everyday Use'") models emphasis on interpretation, not synopsis.

You may also wish to discuss with students how to paraphrase and quote from the story to support their claims. If they need additional assistance with these skills, they can refer to Chapter 22 of the textbook. The section on Skill 28 (pages 615–620) explains when to paraphrase, when to quote, and how to use attributive tags to smooth the transition between one's own voice and others' work. Skill 29 (pages 620–624) explains how to format long and short quotations, how to modify quotations using brackets and ellipses, and how to punctuate a quote within a quote (which students might need to do if citing a passage that includes dialogue). Chapter 23 explains the MLA system for citing sources (both in-text and in the works cited page). You may decide not to require in-text citations because the only source likely to be cited is self-evident—the short story you assign —yet doing so (especially for quotations) can give students good practice for their future writing projects.

Finally, you will need to decide how you intend to grade this writing project. Do you want to assign the reading-log and essay separate grades, or one grade that reflects a collective evaluation of both parts of the assignment? In either case, do you want to weigh the two parts of this assignment equally, or is one more important? What criteria will you use for grading the reading-log entries? What are the consequences if any entries are missing? Make such decisions in advance and announce them to your class.

Chapter 13
Analyzing and Synthesizing Ideas

Understanding the Chapter's Goals

This chapter teaches students important critical thinking skills: they learn to analyze groups of ideas or texts, looking for patterns and connections among them. Synthetic thinking enables students to reflect on how their reading affects their own thinking on the topics they are writing about, and it enables students to develop informed positions through inquiry. This chapter develops ideas about dialectic thinking, first discussed in Chapter 8. The writing project in this chapter has two parts, an extended research log and a formal essay. You will need to decide how much emphasis to give to the research-log activities in class and for homework. Because of the focus on inquiry and synthesis, this project can be taught as a precursor to another formal essay (such as the projects in the chapters that follow). However, the project can also stand alone.

Synthesis is a difficult skill to teach. It involves strong rhetorical reading, active summarizing, solid paraphrasing and quoting, and analytical organization. The Learning Logs support students as they move through extended reading and reflection; they are an essential tool in the development of a formal synthetic essay. This chapter previews the kinds of assignments that students will often be asked to do in other disciplines, and it can be helpful to ask students to profile the kinds of research writing assignments they have been asked to do in other classes, or to ask their instructors in other classes what kinds of researched assignments are common in those other disciplines.

Reinforcing the Chapter's Rhetorical Principles

Focusing Questions

The focusing question, or synthesis question, is the heart of any synthetic writing project, since the writer's own focusing question is what prompts inquiry. On page 351, Ramage, Bean, and Johnson identify illustrative focusing questions for work in various academic disciplines, and on pages 356–57, they identify possible focusing questions for the reading options supported in the chapter. If you are using one of the textbook reading sets, you will need to help students understand why each question is significant. If you are using readings from outside the chapter, you may want to present students with a focusing question, or you may invite students to develop their own. In any event, spending class time with students' focusing questions will help frame the writing project effectively. Taking class time for a collaborative exercise in which students brainstorm and evaluate focusing questions can be an excellent step toward strong analysis (Chapter 17 helps support such work, too).

At the start of your work with this chapter, it can be useful to find analogues to academic focusing questions. Start by asking students what experiences they have with important decisions. When students have faced choices like "What high school or college should I attend?," "What daycare arrangement best suits my child?," or "What volunteer work should I choose to satisfy my school's requirement for community service?", they have likely engaged in analytic and synthetic thinking. In order to make choices about what we should do or think, we naturally turn to analysis and synthesis, although we may not think of it in those terms. Ask students to tell stories about how they have made some major decisions, and then ask them to tease out the elements of that decision. Students will usually be able to articulate the ways in which they compared available options, and the ways in which they identified points of comparison (for example, the costs of different daycare options, the experience of the daycare providers, the credibility of the people who served as references, and the facilities available). As the discussion progresses, help students to see that the focusing questions for their writing assignment will help them make informed choices about a position or action. The Learning Log Tasks will help them make increasingly sophisticated connections among the texts they read. Students will need to understand the focusing question before they move into summarizing, analyzing, and synthesizing.

Analysis of Ideas

Synthesis begins with analysis, which is to say that students' success with this writing project depends on their beginning with a solid understanding of their sources. The first task facing students is to summarize the readings they will be using. Although summary is assigned in Learning Log Task 1 (page 357), do not assume that students will easily and adequately summarize the texts in one sitting. As they work through this assignment, they may need to reread their sources and adjust their summaries. You can support this activity by connecting back to Chapter 6, "Reading Rhetorically," particularly the sections on summarizing (pages 117–119) and reading with and against the grain (pages 116–117).

To prepare for the synthetic elements of this assignment, students' summaries should focus on naming the major themes and ideas that are covered in their sources. It can be useful to give students structured directions for their initial summaries, using Chapter 2, Concept 7, on points, particulars, and summaries (pages 45–48). For example, you can ask students to identify

- The author's thesis (this focuses students' attention on the broadest summary of the source)

- The points that the author uses to support the thesis (this focuses students' attention on the different themes, ideas, or categories raised in the source)

- The particulars, or evidence that the author uses to illustrate the points (this focuses students' attention on the kind(s) of data an author has used—personal experience, statistics, anecdotes, etc.)

- Counterarguments or alternative points of view raised in the source (this focuses students' attention on a range of perspectives about the idea under discussion)

Emphasize that the purpose of summary in this chapter is to understand the text fully from the author's perspective in order to gain an appreciation of all points of view on a complicated topic. Students may want to jump to writing responses (especially if you worked with the writing project in Chapter 6, which required a strong response). You will need to help students see that spending time on summary early in the project helps them form better responses later. In their formal writing project, the summary serves to recapitulate the source for a reader who is unfamiliar with the source, but at the start of the project, the summary serves to help the writer understand the range of issues involved with the topic at hand.

Synthesis of Ideas

Ramage, Bean, and Johnson define synthesis as a technique that lets students "carve out [their] own thinking space on a research question while sifting through the writings of others....[it is] wrestling with ideas from different texts or sources, trying to forge a new whole out of potentially confusing parts" (page 346). The key element of this wrestling is the identification of patterns or connections across different texts or sources. On page 360, the bulleted list of questions will help students begin to identify similarities and differences in the texts they have read. Students may be confused if the texts they are reading do not directly challenge each other. At first glance, for example, the first two readings in the chapter ("Mobile Phone Tracking Scrutinized" and "Reach Out and Track Someone," pages 347–349) don't appear to be argumentative (each piece might be characterized as a piece of informative writing using a surprising reversal, stressing the fact that many Americans may not be aware of the tracking capabilities of cell phone service providers). Neither piece specifically sets itself up as participating in an argument. Yet both pieces are excellent resources for writers interested in the chapter's first focusing question, "How have cell phones affected the lives of American citizens?" (page 356). Looked at through the lens of the focusing question, both pieces provide a number of facts about the current state of cell phone technology and the stands taken by some prosecutors and judges about the need for cell phone tracking. Students should use their focusing questions to help them develop their summaries, and then use their focusing questions to help them develop points of comparison across readings.

A useful tool for teaching synthesis is a grid (see the overhead at the end of this chapter in the manual). Students can graphically represent the relationships between their sources using a simple table with different themes across the top row and with each source treated in a separate row on the table.

Using the "For Writing and Discussion" Activities

The "For Writing and Discussion" activities in this chapter work in tandem with the Learning Log Tasks. Each activity requires students to share the writing done for the task in order to develop additional ideas. In many chapters, it is possible to pick and choose among the activities, depending on your interests, time constraints, and the nature of the writing project. In this chapter, however, it is important to do all the "For Writing and Discussion" activities as part of the Learning Log Task sequence. To skip any of the Learning Log Tasks is to jeopardize students' ability to carry out the project; each task emphasizes a different element of the assignment.

Because the "For Writing and Discussion" activities are so tightly connected to the Learning Log Tasks, they are discussed in the "Guiding Students through the Writing Project" section of this chapter, below.

Guiding Students through the Writing Project

The five Learning Log Tasks (pages 357–364) are an excellent guide to the development of the formal synthesis essay. They offer fairly self-explanatory opportunities for students to engage in exploratory writing prior to drafting the formal essay. The tasks get increasingly complicated, moving from summary to analysis to synthesis, and they open many opportunities for class discussion and reflection.

The first Learning Log Task (page 357) invites students to summarize the main texts they will use, and the second Learning Log Task (page 359) invites students to consider the rhetorical strategies used in each text. Depending on the nature of your class, the amount of time you will devote to this chapter, and the complexity of the texts under discussion, you may want to divide or rearrange some elements of these tasks. You might, for example, have students summarize one text at a time, pausing to discuss each summary as it evolves. Or you might assign parts of the second task first, or in conjunction with the first, asking students to consider the nature of the source along with the summary. It can be helpful for students to consider what kind of publication an article first appeared in as they begin to summarize it.

The third Learning Log Task (page 360) asks students to identify the main issues and themes in their selected text and to begin to compare the texts. Here the grid described above can be helpful. At the end of this chapter in the manual, a transparency with a sample preliminary grid appears. This sample grid illustrates some of the ways in which student Kate MacAuley compared the articles by Ritzer and Turkle. A good class activity is to ask students to create a grid of their sources either before or after this Learning Log. The visual display of the similarities and differences recorded in the log can help students see additional points to add. And if your entire class (or portions thereof) is working with the same sources, students will see how different grids emphasize different themes. This will help students develop additional ideas for analysis.

The chapter's sections on shaping and drafting, writing a thesis, and organizing (pages 365–368) offer some straightforward warnings about the complexities of this assignment. As Ramage, Bean, and Johnson note, "focusing and organizing your ideas for a synthesis essay are challenging writing tasks" (page 365). It is normal for the drafting stages of this assignment to take quite some time; you should plan to devote a good bit of class time to working with students' preliminary readings of the sources. The chapter advises that students should work back and forth between their analysis and synthesis sections and their thesis section. The "For Writing and Discussion" activities following each Learning Log Task can each take up as much as a full class period, depending on your schedule (some can be combined if you need to move more quickly, of course). The Learning Logs can be a valuable tool as you help students move from one section of the essay to another.

One important point: the thesis of a synthesis essay is usually complicated. Sometimes the thesis statement is actually the joining of two lower-level thesis statements, one on the nature of the sources and one on the writer's personal views. The example thesis statements on page 366–367 will help students develop a thesis with tension. The thesis should avoid stating the obvious ("Both these articles agree on some things and disagree on others") and they should include references to the sources and to the writer's own views.

Discussing the Readings

"Mobile Phone Tracking Scrutinized" (pages 347–348) and "Reach Out and Track Someone" (pages 348–349)

These readings are discussed together because the chapter provides them in order to lay the groundwork for synthetic thinking. As you work with these readings, you should encourage students to see the thematic connections between them. It can be useful to assign students to read the essays and do the individual questions on page 350 for homework. Class time can then focus on building more complicated understandings of the relationships between the two pieces. A sequence of guided questions can help illuminate the ways in which each reading becomes richer when considered in light of the other:

- Start by inviting students to list the different issues raised in the first of the pair, "Mobile Phone Tracking Scrutinized" (themes like technological capabilities of cell phone companies, judicial rulings, law enforcement needs for tracking, views on government's ability to gather information on citizens, for example)

- Ask students to read the second article in order to see what light that article can shed on any of those themes (students may note that a watchdog group, the Electronic Frontiers Foundation, is mentioned, and there are more pointed criticisms of the federal government extending its surveillance powers)

- Now ask students what themes in the second article have been left untouched in the discussion so far (personal reasons for wanting to use such tracking technology)

- Have students return to the first article to see how it sheds light on the themes in the second article (the social pressures promoting uses of tracking seem more complex and urgent now)

Following this discussion, you can use the group or whole-class tasks on page 350 to pull things together. Students should see that approaching reading through a focusing question invariably results in even more questions.

"Technology's Peril and Potential" (pages 353–355)

This student reading provides an excellent example of a synthesis essay, and the annotations in the text will help students see the various moves Kate MacAulay makes as she considers the focusing question "What effect is technology having on humanity and the quality of life in the twenty-first century?" Draw students' attention to the ways in which MacAulay starts with a broad question but comes to a more particular focus as she works with the readings by Turkle and Ritzer. Her essay focuses on evaluating the differences between Turkle's and Ritzer's views and on raising questions about values and morality in our attitudes about technology.

You should also help students see the role of summary and analysis in the opening section of the essay. MacAulay has selected themes from the readings to highlight in her presentation in order to answer her focusing question (see paragraphs 2 and 3). The opening section of the essay (through paragraph 6) focuses almost exclusively on the views of Ritzer and Turkle, although MacAulay's own questions have determined the nature of her summary. As paragraph 6 ends, it introduces MacAulay's views, and paragraph 7 begins to emphasize the development of MacAulay's views on technology. For the rest of the essay, MacAulay's informed views dominate, and this is a result of the synthesis she achieved in the first half of the essay.

"Comprehensive Immigration Reform: PROs and ANTIs" (page 370), "Immigration Frenzy Points out Need for Policy Debate" (pages 371–372), "The Global Immigration Problem" (pages 373–374), and "Excerpt from 'Immigration Policy Must Help Economy While Preserving Ideals'" (page 374) and "Excerpt from 'The Progressive Case Against the Immigration Bill'" (pages 375–376)

If you assign these readings—all posts from political blogs, with the URLs for the blogs provided in each headnote—you will likely be using them as sources for students' writing projects, so an explicit set of discussion questions are not provided. You should decide whether you want to require that students use all three of the readings, or a particular pair, or any two. Together, the readings address the focusing question "What lifestyle changes should we make to combat global warming and the depletion of nonrenewable resources?"

Encourage students to use the reading strategies discussed in Chapter 6 as they move through the assigned readings. Those reading strategies, in combination with the Learning Log Tasks, will support students in thorough and careful summary and analysis. Although you will probably not want to discuss the essays in class in advance of the students' Learning Log Tasks, you should read through the essays in advance and have some idea of the thematic connections among them. Your students will see possibilities you did not consider, but you will be better able to help students through the early sections of this project if you are prepared. Some connections you will note are issues of personal vs. corporate responsibility; the motivations for corporate action; the effect of business on individuals; the importance of government, business, or personal priorities; the strategies that cause people to change their habits; the process of gaining weight; the relationship of exercise to consumerism.

A Preliminary Grid based on Kate MacAulay's Learning Logs and Sample Essay

	Health problems	Human connections	Ability to respond to technology	Moral questions
Ritzer	McDonald's food is not healthy and that leads to problems	Technology interferes with human relationships	Society is in a downward spiral b/c of technology	
Turkle		MUDs and other online situations can interfere with healthy identities But self-knowledge can result	People can adjust to technology changes and learn to live with them happily	Cybersex scandals online

Chapter 14
Writing a Classical Argument

Understanding the Chapter's Goals

This chapter begins a series of chapters on persuasive writing. Here students are assigned to write an essay that argues a stance on a controversial issue. In subsequent chapters, when students are given more specific tasks—making an evaluation and proposing a solution—the skills that they learn in this chapter will help them to be more persuasive. Beyond the assignments in this course, knowing how to critique arguments can help students resist manipulation and participate more knowledgeably in public discussions of controversial issues. Knowing how to write persuasively can empower students to create change.

The chapter presents a general introduction to argument. Ramage, Bean, and Johnson emphasize that "argument is an act of inquiry characterized by factfinding, information gathering, and consideration of alternative points of view" (page 378). Your context will determine how much of the chapter you assign. The first portion of the chapter covers claims, reasons, and evidence, and invites students to reflect on assumptions and counterarguments. Later in the chapter, more specialized information—different types of argument and definitions of various fallacies—appears.

Reinforcing the Chapter's Rhetorical Principles

Truth Seeking

Students usually associate argument with wins and losses, and with proving a point. These elements of argument are usually linked to persuasion. An important theme in this chapter is that argument is not wholly about persuasion; it is also about truth seeking. Particularly if you assign research in conjunction with the classical argument, you will want to emphasize that argument is a process that enables readers and writers to construct informed positions. It is important for students to approach argument with something of an open mind. This is not to say that students always change their minds while writing and researching arguments. Rather, students should be open to understanding a range of views on the topics they explore, and they need to look beyond sources with which they already agree. Truth seeking is an important way of wallowing in complexity. To write a successful argument, students must be able to understand varied views on a topic.

Claims and Reasons

To supplement the discussion of claims in the textbook, explain to students the variety of argumentative goals they may choose from for their writing project. If the audience they

150

intend to address holds the opposite opinion than they do, writers may either attempt to fully change the audience's opinion or may strive simply to make the audience more open minded about the issue, so that they will be more likely to change their mind in the future (you can build on the work done in Chapter 9 with the surprising reversal here). Making readers more open minded may be all that is realistically possible if the issue being discussed is broad and/or highly controversial. Writers may also address an audience that has no preformed opinion about the issue. In this situation, the writer needs to provide more background information on the subject before attempting to persuade the audience to adopt the writer's view. A final category of audience is one that already agrees with the writer's position intellectually but isn't acting on that opinion (for example, someone who agrees that natural resources should be preserved but who doesn't regularly recycle). For this final audience type, rather than providing arguments that support the position, the writer needs to develop arguments showing why it is urgent that readers act on the issue. Once students identify what opinion, if any, their audience is likely to already hold regarding the subject, they can then state their claim so that it reflects the appropriate argumentative goal.

This chapter introduces a new vocabulary of classical argument. You should help students see that the rhetorical principles underlying this chapter are the same ones you have worked with all along. The specialized vocabulary helps identify some particular features of argument, which will focus your attention on the development of a good claim. Remind students that the terms *claims*, *reasons*, and *evidence* bear striking relations to the terms *thesis*, *points*, and *particulars* introduced in Chapter 2 and used elsewhere in the textbook.

Qualifiers also help students write more specific, tailored claims. Qualifiers are discussed later in the chapter, on page 393, as a way of making a claim less susceptible to counterarguments. If students are assigned to read this section before they choose a topic and formulate a claim, they will realize that qualifiers can help them to write persuasively about complex issues. Students will be less likely, then, to reject potential topics that would be too difficult to argue absolutely.

Unstated Assumptions

Assumptions about values and beliefs are inherent in all arguments, even when neither the arguer nor the audience is aware of them. The covert nature of these assumptions does not make them any less important in argument. On the contrary, when readers reject an argument, it is often because they disagree with the argument's assumptions. Without the readers' agreement to assumed values and beliefs, a writer cannot convince the audience of a claim, no matter how logical the reason or how thorough the evidence. When writing arguments, then, writers should choose reasons that assume values and beliefs that the audience will share.

Many arguments have unstated assumptions that imply not only what is good or bad (as in the examples on page 384), but also what is better or best, i.e., what values should take precedence over other possible values. There may be readers who accept the assumed values, but not the *hierarchy* of these values. These readers may find merit in the argument but still not be fully convinced. For example, on page 384 of the textbook, Ramage, Bean, and Johnson give the following example of a claim and reason: "Women should be allowed to join combat units because the image of women as combat soldiers would help society overcome gender stereotyping." Ramage, Bean, and Johnson identify the unstated assumption of this statement to be "It is good to overcome gender stereotyping." There may be readers who agree that gender stereotyping should be overcome but who also think that the foremost priority of combat is the safety of troops. If these readers think that troop safety is at all threatened by women serving in combat, they may perceive the underlying assumption for this example to be "Overcoming gender stereotyping is more important than the safety of military troops." Consequently, these readers are likely to reject the argument being made.

As students identify and account for the assumptions relating to their emerging arguments, challenge them to use counterarguments in this way to examine the hierarchy of values implied by those assumptions. Readers can't be persuaded to accept an argument unless they already agree with the assumption's value judgments or the writer convinces them to accept those values. Therefore, if readers disagree with the argument's inherent assumptions, the writer must take one of two possible actions. One solution is to demonstrate why the values and beliefs that the argument implies are the most viable and desirable. Or the writer can support the claim with a different reason, one whose unstated assumptions the readers already wholeheartedly embrace.

Evidence

The body of an argument text consists primarily of evidence. Encourage students to use a wide variety of types of evidence in their argumentative writing, as discussed on pages 385–388. In addition, review with students the exploratory material covered in Chapter 2, Concept 5. Many of the techniques discussed there—freewriting, idea mapping, dialectic discussion, the believing and doubting game—are likely to generate additional evidence for students' arguments. You may want to assign students to use several of these techniques while planning their argument papers and to turn in written evidence of their explorations. In addition, students can explore the evidence for their arguments most thoroughly if they allow themselves to wallow in complexity, as explained in Chapter 2. If students will be doing research for their argumentative writing projects, refer them to Chapter 20 for help with finding sources. The discussion of reading against the grain in Chapter 6 can also help students judge more critically the value of the sources they may wish to cite.

Objections and Counterarguments

Counterarguments help to compensate for the audience's inability to respond to an argument, as they could in conversation, and are a way of bringing the audience's voice into the argument. By summarizing and then rebutting or conceding to opposing views, writers produce arguments that are more thorough and therefore more persuasive. Students can identify possible objections by playing the believing and doubting game (see the brief writing project in Chapter 2 for a fuller explanation) and by discussing their arguments in small groups and having group members play devil's advocate.

Addressing counterarguments also makes the persuasive impact of the argument more lasting. If a text raises a counterargument that readers have not considered and then rebuts it, the readers' opinions won't change if they are made aware of the counterargument in some later experience.

Ramage, Bean, and Johnson recommend that writers concede to counterarguments they cannot refute. Students may view concessions as losing the argument. Explain that, like qualifiers on a claim, concessions acknowledge the complexities of an issue and that truth is rarely absolute. Concessions are also indicative of Rogerian argument in that the readers' values and interests are explicitly acknowledged.

Ethos and Pathos

Ethos and pathos are important to argument because as humans—not machines, not computers—our judgments are affected not only by our minds, but also by our sense of trust and our passions. Advertising serves as a good example of the influence that ethos and pathos can wield in argument. Although arguments based on logic alone can elicit an audience's intellectual agreement, advertisers know that it is often appeals based on credibility and emotion that stir an audience to act. For class discussion, you might ask students to recall examples of appeals to ethos and pathos in advertising.

Another useful activity for exploring these methods of argument is to ask students to bring to class one or two pieces of junk mail they have received recently: appeals for charitable donations, applications for credit cards, sales letters for magazine subscriptions, and so on. Then ask students to analyze these texts, searching for examples of appeals to ethos and pathos. (This is also a useful method for giving students practice in looking for fallacies.) Allow time for the class to discuss examples they find convincing and ones they find superficial or calculating. How do they discriminate manipulative appeals from those that are genuinely persuasive?

You may also want to give students experience in planning appeals to ethos and pathos. To do this, ask groups to choose one of the claims and reasons in the "For Writing and Discussion" activity on page 383 of the textbook. The groups should brainstorm some specific ideas for conveying ethos that they might use if they were to write out the argument for this audience. They can refer to pages 393–394 for suggested strategies. Also ask them to write a short passage that uses vivid language and examples—an appeal to this audience's pathos—as exemplified on pages 394–95. When they finish, ask the groups to share their work with the class. Discuss how these writings would contribute to the effectiveness of their arguments.

Fallacies

After instruction in fallacies, some students begin to identify every unconvincing reason given in support of an argument as a fallacy. To prevent this, emphasize when you first discuss fallacies that they are specific types of flawed reasoning. An argument may be unconvincing for many reasons: it may have insufficient support (*grounds*), may be based on a warrant the audience doesn't accept, or may even include inaccurate facts. All of these situations would weaken or destroy an argument, but they are not logical fallacies.

Occasionally, you may have one or two students who suggest that fallacies should be used in persuasive writing, claiming that they can be a very effective method of convincing unsuspecting readers. Even if no students raise this point, some may be thinking it, so you may wish to initiate a discussion about this stance. Ask students what they think of the purposeful use of fallacies, by others and even by themselves. Would they ever consider using them knowingly? This question can initiate an enlightening discussion about ethical considerations regarding persuasion.

Preferably, students will be able to resolve these ethical concerns through class discussion without much intervention from you. If necessary, however, remind them that persuasion should not be viewed as a contest that results in a "winner" and a "loser." At its noblest, persuasion is instead a mutual search for the best possible position on an issue. Rather than resorting to the deception and manipulation of intentional fallacies, if students find themselves unable to support their position, they should consider changing it. Ideally, persuasion is first and foremost self-persuasion.

After discussing the nature of fallacies generally, take time to talk in class about each of the kinds identified on pages 395–397 of the textbook so that students do not merely skim over them. For this discussion, you might expand on the explanations given, ask students to explain in their own words the logical flaws in the examples, and, where possible, urge students to revise the example so that it is no longer a fallacy. Here are more specific suggestions for the discussion of each fallacy:

- *Post hoc, ergo propter hoc*: Point out that this is a specific type of non sequitur fallacy. Non sequiturs claim a logical relationship when none exists; this fallacy does the same, but the specific relationship that is claimed is causal. Encourage students to identify non sequiturs that imply a cause and effect relationship more specifically as "post hoc, ergo propter hoc" fallacies.

In the example cited, the argument seems convincing because crime declined after a change in police tactics. But perhaps other factors were in play: perhaps fewer crimes were reported, perhaps crime had been on a decline before the tactics changed and the tactics didn't interfere with a trend already in progress. If your students have trouble understanding this fallacy, you may wish to share with them a more blatant example: "Because roosters crow every morning just before sunrise, roosters must make the sun rise."

- *Hasty generalization*: Mention that this is the same logical error commonly known as stereotyping.

- *False analogy*: Students shouldn't be afraid to use analogies all together. Students should, however, use analogical arguments cautiously. In this example, the analogy links two relatively simple things to two more sophisticated things: tulips are relatively plain flowers compared to the complexity of roses; similarly, the qualities of a child are compared to the sophistication and maturity required to be a musician. Yet the analogy is fallacious because, while a tulip can never transform into a rose, many children do become musicians.

- *Either/or reasoning*: Tell students that this fallacy does not always include the actual words *either* and *or*. The fallacy occurs whenever someone presents only two choices, even though there are other possibilities. The arguer does this to stack the deck, hoping that if one possibility is rejected, the other (the arguer's own) will automatically be accepted. In rare situations, there may be only two choices, so presenting them would not be a fallacy. To test for this fallacy, whenever students are confronted with only two choices, they should ask, *"What other possibilities might exist?"*

- *Ad hominem*: Explain to students that judgments of character may certainly be made. They just do not belong in arguments when it is the person's viewpoints or stance that are under question, not his or her character. In this example, Senator Jones' oil holdings do not directly affect her opinions on nuclear power.

- *Appeals to false authority* and *bandwagon appeals*: These are grouped together because both types of fallacies involve deciding the validity of arguments based on who supports them, rather than on the arguments' own merit. Explain that it is acceptable to cite a famous person as an authority as long as that person has expertise on the subject about which they are speaking. In the first example, Joe Quarterback is a false authority on motor oil, but he could be an appropriate and convincing authority on football-related subjects. The second example illustrates a bandwagon appeal.

- *Non sequitur*: Ask students to explain why there is no necessary connection between the ideas in this example. They should realize that to avoid a fallacy, the student must dispute the grade on the basis of his or her performance in this course, not other courses.

- *Circular reasoning*: Tell students that this example would not be a fallacy if this were the first sentence in a paragraph that specifically identified the various ways marijuana harms one's body (although such a sentence might not be considered felicitous!). On its own, however, the second half of the sentence does no more than restate the first half, without providing any evidence.

- *Red herring*: Students may be interested to learn that this fallacy is named after the hunting practice of dragging a herring across the trail of an animal so that dogs tracking the animal lose its scent. In the same way, a red herring argument distracts an audience, directing it away from the issue at hand.

- *Slippery slope*: You may want students to know that this fallacy is also sometimes informally referred to by other names. One is the "snowball effect," because what starts as a small ball of snow at the top of a hill will get increasingly larger as it rolls down, picking up more snow until it is out of control, just as the ideas in this type of fallacy lose all proportion once the momentum is built up. Another name for this fallacy is the *domino effect*, based on the recognition that domino pieces standing on end near each other will all topple in succession when one is pushed, just as this fallacy begins a series of collapses from a single idea.

  Slippery slopes exist whenever the initial action or belief need not necessarily incite the others. In the example given, medical research does not guarantee that reproductive cloning—a technique not even invented yet—will occur.

Using the "For Writing and Discussion" Activities

The activity on page 381 can be used as part of students' writing process to help them identify an issue they may wish to write about for this chapter's writing project. The remaining activities give them experience generating and analyzing key components of an argument: the reasons (page 383), the unstated assumptions (page 384), and the evidence and counterarguments (pages 391–392). Notice that example claims about legalizing cocaine and heroin, energy policy, and gay marriage appear in several points in the chapter, so you may want to use these claims as examples throughout your discussion in class.

Guiding Students through the Writing Project

Soon after your students begin to work with this chapter, ask them to submit a short paragraph describing the arguable issue and audience they want to use for this writing project. You can then briefly respond to their plans so that students don't invest considerable time in projects that are not well suited for this assignment. When you check their plans, make sure their topics are, indeed, arguable, as discussed on page 381of the textbook. If students select a topic that entails making an evaluation or proposing a solution, you may want to suggest that they reserve this idea for a subsequent assignment (Chapters 16 and 17 address these writing projects).

Also respond to the scope of students' proposed topics. Students will have most success if they can narrow their topics by applying them to a local situation. If students want to approach overly used, overly ambitious argumentative issues—e.g., gun control, capital punishment, abortion, euthanasia—work with them to generate a specific angle on the issue (the visuals on women and gun control that open Part II of the textbook are a good example). Invite students to explain their connection with the topic. Their ethos will be strengthened when they can demonstrate their interest in the topic, perhaps with personal experience, perhaps with background knowledge.

When students submit their topic, they should also indicate the audience they will address so that as the class works through the chapter, students will be better prepared to write warrants, reasons, ethos, and pathos sensitive to their intended readers. You may even want to give students the option of writing their paper in the form of a letter.

As students begin to draft their arguments, you may also wish to add to Ramage, Bean, and Johnson's recommendations for organizing texts. Although appeals to ethos and pathos are important throughout an argument, each is particularly important in one part. A writer's ethos must be firmly established in the beginning of the text, in the introduction, or soon after. Readers must know that the writer is well informed on the issue and has the readers' best interests at heart. Appeals to pathos are most needed at the end of the text to help the text resonate with the readers after they have finished and, if appropriate, to stir the readers to action.

Essential Vocabulary for Understanding Argumentation

argument: a combination of truth seeking (a diligent, open-minded, and responsible search for the best course of action or solution to a problem taking into account all the available information and alternative points of view) and persuasion (the art of making a claim on an issue and justifying it convincingly so that the audience's initial resistance to your position is overcome and readers or listeners are moved toward your position) (page 377)

claim: the position you want to take on an issue, stated as a brief, one-sentence answer to your issue question (pages 380–382)

counter-argument	readers' likely objection to a text's arguments; such an objection should be anticipated by the writer and responded to in the text either through refutation (an analysis of the counterarguments' shortcomings) or concession (an acknowledgment of the counterargument's validity) (pages 389–390)
ethos:	textual appeals to gain the reader's confidence in the writer's credibility and trustworthiness; evidence that the writer is knowledgeable, trustworthy, and fair (page 384)
evidence:	particular support for an argument's claim and reasons; may consist of examples, summaries of research, statistics, testimony, and subarguments (pages 385 ff.)
fallacies:	murky reasoning that can cloud an argument and lead to unsound conclusions (pages 395–397)
pathos:	textual appeals that arouse audience interest and deepen understanding of an argument's human dimensions; often manifested as vivid language and examples, and reasons that appeal to the audience's values and beliefs (page 394)
qualifier:	the term used by philosopher Stephen Toulmin to refer to words that limit the scope or force of a claim to make it less sweeping and therefore less vulnerable to counterarguments; examples include "perhaps," "in many cases," "often," "likely," and "may" (page 387–88)
reason:	a subclaim that supports your main claim; usually linked to the claim with such connecting words as "because," "therefore," "so," "consequently," and "thus"; also known as a premise (pages 382–383)
unstated assumption:	a general principle, rule, belief, or value that connects the reason to the claim; must be made explicit and supported with evidence if the audience is unlikely to accept it (pages 383–384)

Discussing the Readings

"Paintball: Promoter of Violence or Healthy Fun?" (pages 404–407)

Student Ross Taylor chose his subject because he was tired of justifying his interest in paintball to other people. Students can emulate Taylor by considering what activities in their lives are the subject of frequent misconceptions. A good brainstorming activity is to have students list some activities and interests, then have the rest of the class record initial impressions or understandings. Whether done as a small or large group activity, it will let students see what their classmates assume about some area of interest.

Taylor's claim appears in paragraph 2, where he briefly summarizes the misunderstandings of paintball and then concludes with his main point: "Paintball is a fun, athletic, mentally challenging recreational activity that builds teamwork and releases tension." Direct students to look at the way he supports his claim: first by describing the game (paragraph 3), then offering three positive features of the sport: athletic challenge, mental challenge, and teamwork (paragraphs 4–6, respectively). Beginning in paragraph 7, Taylor addresses counterarguments, admitting in paragraph 8 that there are powerful arguments against his position.

Taylor uses both research about paintball (in paragraph 6) and personal experience (paragraphs 5, 7, 8, and 9) to make the sport seem appealing. Draw students' attention to the strategies Taylor uses to relate to his audience. He admits, for example, that "paintball is violent, to a degree" (paragraph 9); he describes his friendships with people who critique paintball (paragraph 8), and admits to knowing of injuries that have happened (paragraph 7). He offers counter views to each objection; use class discussion to explore how satisfying students find each objection and reply. This is a good way to draw students into a discussion of warrants, as the students who accept Taylor's views and those who don't are likely to hold different values about violence and sports.

"Why Uranium is the New Green" (pages 407–410) and "Welcome to Sellafield" (page 411), and "No to Nukes" (pages 412–415)

Students can gain a wealth of insight into argumentation by comparing and contrasting these three readings on nuclear power. A full class session could be wisely spent analyzing these readings; if possible, devote more than one day to the discussion. Assign students to read the essays closely prior to the class discussion; it is too difficult to read and parse arguments like this during class. You may want to assign all students to read all three pieces, then have half the class reread and annotate William Sweet's essay, and the other half reread and annotate the *Los Angeles Times* editorial. Tell students that they should come to class prepared to be knowledgeable about both essays but an "expert" on the essay they are assigned to annotate. This division of labor can facilitate informed debate in the classroom while keeping the workload for each student manageable.

You might want to start the discussion by examining the cartoon. As the cartoon can be easily "read" in class it can be used a day ahead to preview the arguments to come, or it can be used at the beginning of a class period to examine some objections to nuclear power plants. Ask students to create sentences summarizing the point of the cartoon, and ask them to explain what parts of the cartoon lead them to that point. What do the multiple arms represent? What does the fact that the sign needs painting represent? What questions do students have about the cartoon?

The cartoon also raises questions about audience. Students who have not attended to the debates about alternative energy formats may find it difficult to interpret the cartoon. Asking students what knowledge the cartoon assumes is a good way into a discussion of warrants. You may want to revisit the cartoon after the other essays in order to permit a more informed discussion.

Sweet relies heavily on logical appeals to make his case. Through paragraph 3, he outlines a series of facts about the state of energy production in the United States to establish that there is a problem with the use of coal. In paragraphs 4–8, he deals with counterarguments (which are implied more than stated: that coal utilities can make clean energy, that nuclear plants are dangerous, that radioactive waste is a problem). In paragraph 10, he concedes that one counterargument (that atomic bombs might proliferate) has some merit, but he quickly dispenses with it. Paragraph 12 does put some limits on his position, and then paragraphs 13–15 add a subargument, that wind power can be added to nuclear power in order to maximize economic benefits.

The *Los Angeles Times* editorial, "No New Nukes," takes a different approach to its argument. It opens with a set of pathetic appeals, using vivid imagery (the magnitude 6.8 earthquake) and striking adjectives ("weak case," "endless controversy") to pull on readers' emotions from the start. Throughout the editorial, stronger language is used. Ask students to look at the different publication sites for theses pieces—*Discover*, the science magazine and a major urban newspaper—and consider how the place of publication may have affected the language choices.

The structure of the editorial is easily discerned thanks to the subheadings. The "Glowing Pains" section, beginning at paragraph 5, outlines four significant risks associated with nuclear power, one per paragraph. The "Goin' Fission" section, beginning at paragraph 12, outlines three reasons nuclear power plants are too expensive (paragraphs 13–15) and then looks at alternatives (in paragraph 17).

Point out to students that both essays treat wind power very positively. This is a good example of the ways in which writers who have very different final conclusions may nonetheless find common ground in one part of the argument. Use this point to underscore

Ramage, Bean, and Johnson's conviction that argument is not about proving right or wrong, but about inquiry and reasoned conclusions.

"Spare the Rod, Spoil the Parenting" (pages 415–417)

Pitts' claim that mild spanking is an appropriate child-rearing practice is not stated explicitly anywhere in his op-ed piece, although in paragraphs 9 and 18 he comes very close to making an explicit claim. Pitts's essay is a good example of one that addresses counterarguments well. In paragraph 12, he addresses two failings of the anti-spanking "orthodoxy," and in paragraph 13, he addresses a possible counterargument to his own position.

Pitts' essay is also a good example of an argument written in response to a reading. It is not clear whether or not his reading of reports of a recent Time/CNN poll or his reading of Diana Baumrind's report prompted his work, but his references to both reports suggest that his argument was motivated by a current issue in the news. His careful use of Baumrind's report illustrates a good focus on a single source for a short argument. Particularly if you are using a microtheme approach to a classical argument, Pitts's essay will be a good resource.

"The Case for (Gay) Marriage" (pages 417–422)

A.J. Chavez' argument for same-sex marriage uses a more explicit structure, with his main claim stated in paragraph 2 after an introductory paragraph using a Human Rights Campaign TV spot to set up the topic. Chavez, who identifies himself as gay in the introduction, offers four reasons to support his claim in paragraph 2, handles counterarguments in paragraph 3, and then moves through a more detailed discussion of each reason in paragraphs 4–7. Students will likely find the structure of this piece easy to interpret.

Although Chavez explicitly lists counterarguments in paragraph 3, he does not refute them one by one. Rather, he uses his four reasons to generally rebut the counterarguments, a strategy which not all readers will find convincing. You can have students map the counterarguments against his reasons to see what, if any, gaps they find at the essay's end.

Chapter 15
Making an Evaluation

Understanding the Chapter's Goals

Chapter 14 introduces persuasive writing by discussing how to structure and support arguments. In this chapter, students get to apply those more general persuasive skills to an evaluative task. Students are taught to approach evaluations as two-pronged persuasion: arguments identifying and supporting the criteria by which the writer's subject will be judged, and arguments assessing whether or not the subject meets each criterion. The use of criteria is what distinguishes evaluative writing from classical arguments, taught in Chapter 14.

Knowing how to use criteria to determine merit is an important critical thinking skill. It helps students understand the importance of standards, that judgments are not unfounded preferences. To better understand the role that learning evaluative writing can play in developing students' critical thinking skills, you may want to reread Ramage, Bean, and Johnson's summary in Chapter 2 of the stages of intellectual development identified by William Perry (pages 29–30 of the textbook).

Perry found that many traditionally aged students begin college in the initial stage of dualism, in which they see all judgments as simply right or wrong, with one single, unproblematic answer. Once they regularly confront the complexity of problems, they become multiplists, believing that "anything goes," that everyone has his or her opinion and that there is no basis for favoring one judgment over another. Only in the two final stages of relativism and commitment in relativism are students able, to cite Ramage, Bean, and Johnson, "to take a position in the face of complexity and to justify that decision through reasons and evidence while weighing and acknowledging contrary reasons and counterevidence" (30).

Clearly, the use of criteria to make evaluations encourages students' movement toward relativism and commitment in relativism. Establishing criteria helps students learn that there are bases for judgment (we are not doomed to relativism), but that the criteria must be carefully determined (they are not as clear cut as dualists expect). Students also discover that while the subject they are evaluating may meet many of the criteria, it may not meet them all. This scenario puts students in positions of relativism and committed relativism: students can support a judgment based on their subject's adherence to the primary criteria, while still recognizing that the subject doesn't meet all criteria. Evaluative writing assignments can thus be quite instrumental in promoting students' intellectual development.

Reinforcing the Chapter's Rhetorical Principles

Criteria Selection

The proper selection of criteria is essential to a successfully argued evaluation. Begin your discussion of criteria by explaining to students that they essentially have two topics for their papers: the specific thing they are evaluating, and the large class to which that thing belongs. Advise students to make their identifications of class as specific as possible so that what they are evaluating will not be judged by unfair standards. The scale of abstraction (introduced in Chapter 4 of the textbook, in Concept 11) can help students learn to move from a more general identification of class to more specific identifications: "a good restaurant" can become "a good ethnic restaurant," which can become "a good Chinese restaurant," which can become "a good Chinese carry-out restaurant." This specificity will help students avoid what Ramage, Bean, and Johnson discuss on page 429 as "the problem of apples and oranges."

Students must know the particular item, artifact, place, or other topic they wish to evaluate in order to identify the class to which that item belongs. However, once the class is identified, they should concentrate mainly on the class—not the particular member of the class they will write about—while they brainstorm criteria. If students focus too much on describing their particular item or topic while generating the criteria, the criteria may be skewed. The criteria may move to include pleasant but unnecessary features. For example, the student may like the fact that his or her fitness facility has numerous television monitors, each set to a different station and tuned to different AM radio stations, so that gym members can hear any show they like on headsets while other members exercise undisturbed. This may be a feature that gym members enjoy, yet it may not be what most people would insist a fitness facility offers in order to be considered good. On the other hand, such a feature might prove to be one that tips the scales in favor of a particular facility if the gyms under comparison are equivalent in all other respects (and a student might argue that a more general criteria—the ability of a fitness center to serve a wide range of people—might subsume these particular details). Encourage students to prioritize their criteria as appropriate.

Thinking too much about the particular topic can bias the selection of criteria in another way, by causing the student to overlook a criterion that the student's topic doesn't meet. To again use the example of a fitness facility, perhaps the one the student belongs to has a staff knowledgeable about exercise routines and the gym's equipment, yet has no one who is trained to assist with diet and overall health. By thinking only of one's own gym while developing criteria, the student may unintentionally omit this important criterion. Therefore, it is important that students concentrate on the class, not their particular topic, to identify criteria that hold true for any and all members of the class.

Another vital task in selecting criteria is to consider the values held by the essay's audience. If the criteria selected do not reflect the audience's values, the audience is unlikely to accept the evaluation, no matter how strongly the "match argument" is made. For example, major box office releases rarely win the Cannes Film Festival because most film critics value criteria that are different from that of the typical American moviegoer. No matter how much an evaluation praises the film's cinematography, if the actors are not widely recognized, many people will not care to see the movie. The audience's values should also influence the relative weight assigned to different criteria.

Finally, the criteria should be manageable in number. After students have brainstormed all the possible criteria for their topic's class and weighted them to reflect the audience's values, students should decide how the criteria can be grouped so that the essay does not resemble a lengthy list. In the extended example in the chapter (an evaluation of Seattle's Experience Music Project), three different sets of criteria are provided (to evaluate the museum as a tourist attraction, museum of rock history, or rock and roll shrine; see page 433; students may want to consult the Experience Music Project Web site, http://www.emplive.org for additional information about the museum). Each set of criteria is focused. Students should similarly construct focused sets of criteria in order to promote deeper analysis.

Matching Criteria to the Topic

If readers agree with the criteria a writer is using to evaluate something, the writer's chief remaining task to get readers to accept an evaluation is to match the writer's specific topic to those criteria. Students must provide numerous examples to demonstrate the extent to which the topic being evaluated meets or does not meet each criterion. To give students practice with this type of support, you could have students develop criteria for a different topic that all students are likely to know and could illustrate with examples. What are the criteria for a good college campus? A good college classroom? A good textbook? Students can then match these criteria to particular characteristics of your college campus, your own classroom, or even *The Allyn & Bacon Guide to Writing*. Have the class generate specific examples they could cite to support their judgments regarding each criterion.

Using the "For Writing and Discussion" Activities

The activity on page 428 gives students experience in identifying, weighting, and grouping criteria (in this case, for careers) and using them to make evaluations (here, of particular careers). Some minor refinements can make this activity even more instructive. In the first step, after students have brainstormed possible criteria, Ramage, Bean, and Johnson direct them to "rank your criteria from highest to lowest priority." You may wish to have students not simply rank their criteria but instead assign percentage weights to their importance. This will help students to consider even more thoughtfully the relative importance of different criteria. They may decide, for example, that their top three criteria are nearly equal in importance, while their fourth is substantially less important. As students begin to match particular careers to the criteria, they can then be more decisive about their evaluations. What percentage of the weighted criteria must a career meet before it is judged to be a good career choice. Is it possible, for example, for a career to receive a positive final evaluation if it meets all the criteria except the most important one? What if it fulfills *only* the most important criterion?

Step four in this activity states, "When disagreements arise, try to identify whether they are disagreements about criteria or disagreements about the facts of a given career." Obviously, disagreements about the facts of a given career may arise because any given career may vary in how it matches criteria, depending upon the particular organization one works for, the supervisor and colleagues one has, etc. During your class discussion, you may wish to take one career choice and apply the criteria to two different locales your students will recognize. Would the criteria be met differently, for example, for a bus driver who transports children to the local elementary school than for a bus driver who works transporting long-distance travelers for Greyhound? Would a police officer for your city match the criteria differently than a police officer who works for your college? According to students' criteria, which is the better career: a physician who works at a community health center or a physician who works in a hospital emergency room?

The activity on page 429 teaches students that the same topic can receive different evaluations depending upon the class and accompanying criteria used to evaluate it. This activity can help students get beyond dualistic, black and white thinking, and understand that most things have both merits and weaknesses. After the students have completed the first two parts of this exercise, you may want to challenge them further by asking them to think of one thing they greatly value and one thing they strongly dislike. Can they think of some category or class for each of these items that might lead them to give the item an opposite evaluation?

The final activity in this chapter, on pages 459–460, asks students to evaluate the extended student example about the Experience Music Project. How does their evaluation compare to student Jackie Wyngard's?

Guiding Students through the Writing Project

Students who look only at the list of topics on page 437 may need to be reminded of the chapter's earlier directive that they evaluate something controversial or problematic. Students should not review a TV show, movie, book, etc., unless they can demonstrate why an evaluation is necessary, that the merit of what they are evaluating is in question. At the same time, students should not feel that the subject of their essay must be the center of a raging controversy. Reviewing a popular book or TV show is an excellent way to come to a better understanding of cultural values. As students select their topics, work with them to identify what draws them to this topic.

You may also wish to supplement the discussion of organization offered on pages 438–439, using the figure on page 439 in class. Encourage students to thoughtfully consider the order in which they should discuss their criteria. If they are writing to resistant readers, they may want to begin with their most important criterion to strengthen their argument. If the audience is relatively uninformed about the topic being evaluated, placing the strongest argument last may be a better way to lead readers toward conviction. Another option is to adhere to a pre-existing, natural arrangement among the criteria. For example, an evaluation of a restaurant might discuss the ambiance, the service, and then the food, mirroring the order of a patron's dining experience. In the essay's conclusion, writers may want to provoke their readers to act on the evaluation by either utilizing or avoiding what has been evaluated. The conclusion is also a good place to stress the significance or implications of the evaluation.

Discussing the Readings

EMP: Music History or Music Trivia?"(pages 440–441)

Student Jackie Wyngard's essay is a good model for students working on their own writing projects. Wyngard uses several strategies particularly important for evaluation arguments: she presents her own connections to the topic in paragraph 1, and at the start of paragraphs 2, 3, and 4 she presents a criterion for evaluation. In paragraph 5, she handles counterarguments (which are applications of additional criteria).

Wyngard's criteria are clear: EMP should cover the history of rock and roll from its beginnings to the present; it should include influential individuals and groups; it should have accessible and relevant explanations. In each paragraph, she uses ample details from her visit to the museum to show the ways EMP fails to meet her three criteria.

Students are likely to get involved in a discussion of the appropriateness of Wyngard's criteria. As Wyngard responds to other views towards the end of her essay, she lists some other features that others may find enjoyable. Students may well offer additional criteria for evaluation (a museum should have interactive exhibits; a museum should contain artifacts from tours, not just personal items of musicians). While students who have not visited the EMP may need some prompting to discuss this essay (they may object that they cannot evaluate Wyngard's argument because they don't know the museum), you can encourage them to analyze the structure of Wyngard's argument and then to apply her criteria to a specialized museum in your location.

"Sesame Street: Brought to You by the Letters M-A-L-E" (pages 442–443)

This essay demonstrates the importance that a single criterion can have when making an evaluation. There is a quick reference in paragraph 11 to the many criteria this children's show meets: "educational value, lack of violence, and emphasis on cooperation." This same paragraph even acknowledges that in terms of the one criterion of non-sexism, the show is partly successful: "the adult characters on the show are admirably balanced in terms of avoiding sexual stereotypes." Aside from this brief, positive paragraph, however, the entire reading is dedicated to demonstrating the shortcomings of the show in its shortage of major female characters and interesting minor female characters.

The third question following the reading asks, "If you agree with the argument that *Sesame Street* is sexist, should that criterion be sufficient for undermining the popular assessment of *Sesame Street* as a model educational program for children?" The authors themselves do not think so. In paragraph 11, the authors proclaim, "Yes, we believe that *Sesame Street* is one of the best shows on television for small children." Their purpose in placing such negative emphasis on the show, however, is revealed in paragraph 12: "But even the best of the bunch has room for improvement."

Ask students how their impressions of the show might change if the authors had begun the essay with their statements about the show's attributes. The delay of these praises until late in the essay accentuates how seriously they view the show's sexism, despite its many other positive attributes. This essay models a technique students may want to try in their own writing project: a thorough examination of one crucial flaw in something that is otherwise quite good. The approach works best if, as in this essay, the flaw is not widely acknowledged.

"Parents: The Anti-Drug: A Useful Site" (pages 444–446)

This student example applies evaluation criteria for Web sites (you can refer students to Chapter 21, Skill 26, for a discussion of the criteria applied). The criteria are laid out near the end of the first paragraph. Paragraphs 2 and 3 explain the ways in which the Web site fails to meet some criteria fully (good disclosure and coverage seem weak). Paragraphs 4 and 5 lay out ways in which the site does meet some other criteria (good range of information, and currency). The conclusion, paragraph 6, is a balanced restatement of a conclusion that was forecast in the opening: the site has some flaws but is generally quite useful.

Chapter 16
Proposing a Solution

Understanding the Chapter's Goals

This chapter can be considered the culmination of many skills developed in the textbook's earlier writing projects. Chapter 14 trains students to write a classical argument. Their knowledge of a general argumentative frame, and the relationship of evidence to reasons and the various ways writers can appeal to readers can help students be more persuasive when proposing a solution to a decision maker. Chapter 15 instructs students how to use criteria to make evaluations, a strategy important to proposals when a writer must justify the merit of one solution over other possibilities. If your students have worked with either of these preceding chapters, encourage them to apply what they learned to this writing project. This chapter adds to what students have already learned by encouraging them to use their persuasive abilities to argue for a specific change. It also provides extended support for translating written argument into an extemporaneous speech with accompanying presentation software.

Reinforcing the Chapter's Rhetorical Principles

Discussion of the Problem

All the questions listed on pages 448–449 of the textbook will help students explore the problem they are writing about more thoroughly. You might suggest that students freewrite their responses to these questions to help them brainstorm possible solutions; however, it is not necessary, or even appropriate, that all of the answers be incorporated into the essay.

Some students may already have sufficient credibility about the problem they have chosen to write about, while others may need to do research. It is important that they understand all of the problem's complexities. For example, if entry-level classes on campus close early every registration period and they want to propose that more such classes be offered, they must find out why the problem hasn't already been fixed. Perhaps there are not enough classrooms available to schedule additional sections because all rooms are used at all periods of the day. Knowing this will necessarily change the writer's solution: proposing that more classes be offered would be naive. In this case, as in many situations, what is identified as the problem changes after some research. There should be more classes, but the greater problem that must be addressed first is the lack of classroom space. Only after the writer has identified the root problem should solutions be explored.

In a proposal, the amount of discussion that a writer should devote to describing the problem depends on the proposal's intended audience. If the audience is already convinced that a problem exists and that it needs to be solved, this section of the paper may be only a few sentences or a paragraph. If, however, the audience is unaware of the problem, the writer must spend more time arguing that the problem exists and has serious consequences, enough to demand the reader's attention.

Discussion of the Solution

On page 449 of the textbook (under item 2: "*Proposal for a solution*"), Ramage, Bean, and Johnson explain that sometimes writers submit "planning proposals" that call for further study of a problem and do not themselves propose a solution. Although it is useful for students to know that proposals can be complex documents requiring extensive study to prepare, discourage them from writing a planning proposal for this writing project. If they do, they will not gain experience with justifying a solution and comparing it to alternative solutions. If students cannot think of a feasible solution to the problem they are interested in, urge them to choose another problem for this assignment, unless they have the time to research the issue more. Following the process of exploratory research described in Chapters 2 and 8 might help them identify a solution they can support.

If your class has completed Chapter 15, "Making an Evaluation," facilitate a class discussion in which students suggest criteria for what makes a good solution. Their list might include the following: it should be detailed; it should be cost effective; it should be effective in terms of time/labor needed to implement it; it should be capable of solving the problem; it should cause no other great harm. How important is it that the solution requires little labor? Must it be a solution that can be enacted immediately, or in some cases is a long-range solution preferable? What other criteria can they suggest? Asking questions such as these gets students thinking about solutions from the position of decision makers who need to consider others' views, rather than as individuals who need to consider only themselves.

When writers rebut alternative solutions, they must be especially thorough but should not "stack the deck" by including clearly outlandish suggestions. Connecting back to material from Chapter 2, on wallowing in complexity, will help students see that taking time to ponder reasonable alternative solutions will strengthen their project. You may want to give students time in groups even before they draft the papers to discuss their proposed solutions. Group members can serve as devil's advocates, examining the writer's solution for weaknesses, and proposing alternative solutions. This activity will help students refine their solutions so that they can write more persuasive, complete drafts.

Advocacy Arguments

Ramage, Bean, and Johnson link advocacy ads (see the striking example in Figure 16.1 on page 455) to proposal arguments. Students may see advocacy arguments as forms of classical arguments; point out that advocacy ads usually highlight some particular action or stance as a solution to a problem. Some ads, like the advocacy ad in Figure 16.2, emphasize key facts in an effort to sway public opinion (the ad does not overtly request action on readers' parts, although it is a part of a campaign to decriminalize drugs). Other advocacy ads overtly present a solution (suggesting that viewers donate money, for example). Point out that most advocacy ads do make fairly specific and focused demands on readers (they want readers to *do* something, such as sign a petition, vote, or donate money). The material in Chapter 4 , Concept 11, on document design and rhetorical context will be helpful if your students' writing projects involve advocacy ad analysis or design.

Proposal Speeches

Ramage, Bean, and Johnson provide an alternative way to deliver an argument: an extemporaneous speech. A proposal speech requires all the same preparation that a written proposal argument would, although the writing process and product is different. With an extemporaneous speech, students would write presentation slides (using PowerPoint) and perhaps a handout for the class or audience. As the textbook notes, the aural nature of a speech may make more closed-form markers important. Speakers must find a way to grab audience attention and then hold it. The strategies outlined on pages 462–463 highlight practical steps for students.

PowerPoint slides are their own genre, and page 465 lays out tips for effective visual aids for speeches. A common mistake is to put too much information on the slide. Each slide should help the audience see what is most important; each slide should be clearly organized and large enough for everyone to see. Note that Ramage, Bean, and Johnson recommend that slide titles be full sentences rather than short phrases, so students will need to change some of the PowerPoint defaults to have room in the title section for full sentences.

If you assign a speech, decide in advance how will you grade it, and make sure students understand what part of the grade comes from delivery and what from content.

Using the "For Writing and Discussion" Activities

The activity on page 480 gives students experience in justifying solutions they propose. If you assign this activity, decide whether you want students to write justifications that both support and denounce each proposal (the claims for the exercise are written positively and negatively), or if students can choose which version of the claim to support. Students will benefit from learning that each type of justification can serve arguments that support and denounce a claim, so you may want to at least ensure that opposing viewpoints are heard in class discussion. Not all students will be familiar with the concept of service learning courses, referred to in the first claim, so you may need to explain that these are courses in which students learn through required involvement with community agencies.

The table on page 452 provides template sentences that can help students invent justifications based on principle, consequence, and analogy/precedent for each claim in this exercise. For "Argument from Principle," Ramage, Bean, and Johnson list some positive words that can help students argue for the intrinsic value of a claim. You may want to brainstorm with students what principle-based words could be used to denounce a claim: bad, unjust, wrong, unethical, dishonest, uncharitable, inequitable, unfair, unimportant, etc. When students work with "Argument from Consequence," remind them to draw on what they learned in Chapter 14 about identifying consequences. "Argument from Precedent or Analogy" encourages students to cite similar situations elsewhere and to use the consequences experienced by others as models or anti-models for what should be done regarding their own claim. If students choose to develop an analogy for this form of justification, remind them that analogies can sometimes be fallacies if crucial differences are ignored in the two situations being compared. Turn to page 396 for a quick review of the "false analogy" fallacy.

Discussing the Readings

"Visual Aids for a Proposal to Reduce High-Risk Drinking through Student Awareness Workshops" (pages 469–472)

These PowerPoint slides are by student Jane Kester, written to accompany a ten-minute speech on a proposal to reduce college student drinking. You can use the tables on pages 462–63 (on effective speech outlines) and page 465 (on effective visual aids) to help students evaluate Kester's work. Slides 1 and 2 grab the audience's interest by highlighting the extent and importance of the problem at hand, and slide 3 summarizes Kester's proposal. Slide 4 describes the proposal, and then slides 5–8 show the benefits of this approach.

You can ask students to use the slides to derive an outline of Kester's proposal argument, and you can also ask students to use the criteria in Table 16.1 (page 464) to evaluate the graphics and layout of Kester's slides. Her slides use the complete assertion-evidence format recommended by Ramage, Bean, and Johnson. Ask students to make notes about the PowerPoint slides they see in use in their other classes over the course of a week, and then have the class discuss the variation they observe.

"A Proposal to Provide Cruelty-Free Products on Campus" (pages 472–476)

This proposal models a campus-based approach to the writing project in this chapter. It begins with a transmittal letter conveying the proposal to the person responsible for the situation. Student Rebekah Taylor's problem is stated in paragraphs 1–3: the lack of cruelty-free products on campus forces students who want to buy such products to go off campus and to spend money off campus. She frames the problem as one not simply about ethics of animal testing, but about student well-being. This appeal is likely to connect with the values and beliefs of university administrators, who are responsible for the quality of student life on campus. This line of reasoning is carried forward in the justification section of the proposal, which continues to focus on the proposal's connection to the university's mission and to student safety.

Taylor's strategies reflect some good exploration of the nature of the problem and the audience for the proposal. In paragraph 4, she notes that she had previously requested the bookstore take action to provide cruelty-free products, but the bookstore had declined because it would be too expensive. Taylor reports this, making clear that her proposal will address the previous objection.

Taylor's proposal illustrates a number of argument strategies: arguments from principle (carrying cruelty-free products supports our university's progressive values, paragraph 14); arguments from consequence (carrying cruelty-free products will be economically successful, paragraphs 13, 15; students will be safer, paragraph 15).

Taylor's proposal addresses the issue of availability of cruelty-free products, although students may find that her proposal for volunteer students to stock the shelves is not feasible. A volunteer program might not have consistent staff available, and the proposal to create the program could, in fact, constitute a whole different proposal. Students may also find that Taylor's proposal fails to address the economic issue previously raised by the bookstore: the products are too expensive. Some students may find her economic arguments persuasive, however, and a debate in class about the merits of this proposal will help students understand the criteria for successful proposals better.

"The Athlete on the Sidelines" (pages 476–478)

Jennifer Allen (daughter of Washington Redskins' football coach George Allen) wrote her essay as an op-ed piece for *The New York Times*. Allen opens the essay with two paragraphs of description, focusing attention on the activities of competitive cheerleading, and raises a surprising question at the end of paragraph 2: "What took so long?" Many readers will not be aware of the history of competitive cheerleading, and so the opening paragraphs introduce some tension.

Allen deals with objections to competitive cheerleading in paragraph 4, and not until paragraphs 6–7 does she fully state the problem: competitive cheerleading is not coherently organized and not recognized by the NCAA as a sport. Her organization gradually leads readers to appreciate the scope of the problem faced by competitive cheerleaders. Paragraph 8 provides national statistics for problems foreshadowed in Allen's personal experience (paragraph 4). She moves from personal experience to more objective evidence, gradually building the case for her claim. Her increasing emphasis on logical appeals as the essay progresses helps support her claim.

"'The Hardest of the Hardcore': Let's Outlaw Hired Guns in Contemporary American Warfare" (pages 494–483)

Fujitani's essay is almost wholly focused on demonstrating that a problem exists. Establishing a solution to this problem is really beyond the scope of a first-year student's abilities. Discuss with your students the value of essays that dwell so much on the existence of a problem.

Fujitani places his claim at the end of paragraph 2: "the use of mercenary soldiers must be halted or brought under intense congressional scrutiny." He lays out six reasons in support of this claim (paragraphs 3–9), each clearly identified in the opening sentence of a paragraph. He heavily privileges logical appeals, carefully documenting his reasons, providing ample evidence for each reason. Fujitani's essay offers many nice examples of attributive phrases used to introduce sources (e.g. "According to *New York Times* reporter David Barstow…") and this couples effective ethical appeals with logical ones. Fujitani clearly presents his research as part of his credibility. Careful documentation and presentation of evidence makes his argument effective.

Note that certain terms, such as "outsourcing" (paragraph 4) or "mercenaries" (used throughout) carry negative connotations. Ask your students to read through the essay and identify other loaded words that help establish connections with readers. Ask them, too, to evaluate Fujitani's language choices: to what extent do his word choices affect his argument? Are they fair choices? How do they shape readers' reactions and appeal to emotions?

Guiding Students through the Writing Project

This chapter's placement in the textbook, as well as its reliance on former chapters (see "Understanding the Chapter's Goals" above), might lead many teachers to assign this as the final writing project of the course. If so, you might want to consider approaching this assignment in less traditional ways. Consider giving students the option to research the problem and write the proposal collaboratively. As students research and draft their proposals, encourage them to use electronic research methods (see Chapter 20) to find solutions used by others that they might cite as precedents.

Chapter 17
Writing as a Problem-Solving Process

Understanding the Chapter's Goals

This chapter provides an overview of the composing process, focusing on four skills of experienced writers that students can emulate and practice. It provides an "eagle's eye view" that complements, but is distinct from, the goals of other chapters in *The Allyn & Bacon Guide to Writing*. The chapters in Part 1 of the textbook, for example, teach students how to pursue and solve a number of specific writing problems: content problems such as thesis and support, as well as rhetorical problems such as purpose, audience, and genre. Also, Chapter 18 discusses the writing process of closed-form prose specifically, and Chapter 19 discusses the writing process of open-form prose. Yet this chapter explains holistic writing processes that apply to all forms of writing. These three chapters form a unit that can be used flexibly throughout the course.

Here, Ramage, Bean, and Johnson emphasize the need for multiple drafts and discuss the strategies that experienced writers use to produce effective texts. If possible, teach this chapter early in your course while students are simultaneously working on a writing project from another chapter. You may want to assign Chapter 17 in conjunction with or immediately following the reading of Part 1. By reflecting on the writing process early in the term, students will be able to benefit from the strategies explained here for all writing projects they do in the remainder of the course. Also, by working on a writing project as they study this chapter, they will be better able to observe and adapt their own writing process to the recommendations given in this chapter.

Another reason to teach this chapter early in the term is that the final section of the chapter offers general advice for peer review workshops. Peer review guidelines that are tailored to each writing project appear at the end of their respective chapters; however, in this chapter, the general function and design of peer review workshops is discussed. If possible, have students read and discuss this material prior to their first peer review workshop.

Reinforcing the Chapter's Rhetorical Principles

The Writing Process

It is possible that one or more students in your class have not been taught in prior writing courses to approach writing as a process. They may have learned about the importance of thesis statements, how to develop paragraphs, and various modes of organization (comparison/contrast, classification, and so on), but may never have had a teacher talk to them about the importance of planning (beyond outlining) or the recursiveness of composing. Even students who were not trained in this manner, commonly referred to as the "current traditional" approach to writing, may nevertheless believe that the written product is all that truly matters because that is often all the teacher reads and grades. Connect the presentation of the writing process to the notion of inquiry (presented in Chapters 1 and 2), and invite students to talk about the ways their previous writing experiences are like—or not—the processes presented in this chapter.

Ramage, Bean, and Johnson explain that writing is a complex activity that exceeds the capacities of short-term memory. The section on Skill 1 (which starts on page 490) addresses why experienced writers use multiple drafts. In so doing, they can focus on one concern at a time. Often, when writing about a topic, the writer comes to understand it more fully, which may mean that parts of the text that have already been written must be changed to accommodate this new understanding. Although novice writers may think of multiple drafts as just more work, experienced writers recognize that expecting multiple drafts makes writing easier: knowing that no one but themselves will read the initial attempts, writers can be more playful in their thinking and tentative in their wording.

Make sure that students understand that revisions are not merely the *number* of changes, but more importantly, the *kinds* of changes. A writer may take a text through many drafts, each time for a different purpose (see the table on pages 494–495 in the textbook for a list of various types of revisions). Even the simplest revisions can require a multi-stage process: writers who commonly make more than one type of grammatical or mechanical error find it helpful to proofread a text they've written several times, looking for one particular type of error each time.

As Ramage, Bean, and Johnson report in this chapter, there is no single, ideal writing process. The process differs from person to person, and even for the same person, from text to text. Just as one person may use different reading strategies for different texts (see Chapter 6), so too will one person use different revising strategies. What typifies good writers, though, is that their writing process is recursive and complex. To authenticate this characterization, allot class time for discussion of individual writers' processes. Students may share accounts of their own writing process, especially how their process may have changed as they have matured as writers. Share accounts of your own writing process. If you write scholarly articles, pieces for community publications, or other types of texts, how does your process differ depending on the genre? How did you go about writing the syllabus for this course? If you are in the midst of writing anything when you discuss this chapter, consider taking it to class and discussing your process for that text with your students.

You might also invite colleagues to your class to discuss their writing processes, to reinforce the fact that, often, different strategies work best for different writers. If possible, invite colleagues from other disciplines to show students that writing processes are important to most fields, not just the province of English classes. You might also invite friends who are not academics but who write regularly, either for their own enjoyment or for work-related projects. You could even ask students if they have friends, family members, or coworkers who spend a lot of time writing and would be interested in talking to the class about their writing processes. Because students rarely have an opportunity to observe experienced writers compose, they may not realize the effort that even the best writers put into composing. Students may falsely believe that they're not "meant" to be writers if writing is difficult for them. Having successful writers describe their own writing difficulties may help students realize that their struggles aren't unusual.

Rather than construing the writing process as linear and sequential—choosing a topic, narrowing it, writing a thesis, outlining, drafting, revising, and editing—Ramage, Bean, and Johnson propose a more flexible way of construing the writing process in Skill 3, on expert writing habits. This skill, which starts on page 496, offers students ten specific pieces of advice—starting with the admonition to use exploratory writing practices (introduced in Chapter 2) and ending with the recommendation to learn to satisfice (or know when to stop). These discrete pieces of advice will help students see what small steps they can take to develop new habits of mind and practice. These tips generally begin with the early stage of a writing project and move through the end, but you can encourage students to use the tips flexibly. If you have described your writing processes to students, or if invited guests have described theirs, ask students to compare those processes to the model described in the textbook. Have experienced writers mentioned any composing strategies that are not mentioned in this model? For example, is there a particular time when writers are most likely to put away a text they are writing in order to gain a better perspective on it through a later, fresh reading?

Students should also compare their own writing process to actions suggested here. Which of the habits do they regularly use? Which do they regularly omit? A useful homework assignment would be to ask students to write a paragraph in response to the following questions:

- Which practices listed on pages 496–497 of the textbook do you think are your strengths as a writer? Why?

- Which practices do you think you most need to improve in your own writing? Why?

Students should also compare their own revising processes to the strategies outlined in this chapters's Skill 2, on global revision (which starts on page 493). Which of the strategies do they regularly use? Which do they regularly omit? A useful homework assignment would be to ask students to write a paragraph in response to each of the following questions:

- Which types of revision (from the table on pages 494–495) do you think are your strengths as a writer? Why?

- Which revision strategies do you think you most need to improve in your own writing? Why?

- What strategy do you think you might try on your next writing project?

Once students have analyzed their writing process and set goals for improving it, you can periodically ask students to evaluate their success in meeting these goals. When they submit their next writing project, ask them to reassess their composing process; if their writing process has not changed, ask them to reformulate goals for themselves. You might ask for another assessment midterm, and again just before the final writing project for the course. Improving their writing process is one of the ways students can most benefit from this course. The material in Chapter 25, "Assembling a Portfolio and Writing a Reflective Essay," will help students carry out this reflection on their own work.

Another strategy for encouraging students to be reflective about the writing process model Ramage, Bean, and Johnson propose, as well as students' own writing processes, is to ask them to think of an analogy for each. This is similar to the "For Writing and Discussion" activity in Chapter 1, which asks students to create a metaphor, simile, or analogy to explain the difference between closed-form and open-form prose. See additional discussion of that activity, most of which would apply to this activity as well, on pages 8–9 of *The Allyn & Bacon Guide to Writing* and its accompanying glossary in this manual.

Students' own analogies will reveal much about their understanding of the writing process. If a student suggests the analogy of an assembly line, for example, he or she is still (mis)understanding the composing process as linear. You might ask students to create analogies in small groups and then share them with the class. As groups contribute their ideas, point out what assumptions about writing underlie their analogies and explore any misperceptions and tensions that arise.

Peer Review Workshops

Ramage, Bean, and Johnson offer many specific strategies for responding to a classmate's draft on page 499. The key goal in peer review workshops is to help students move beyond bland remarks such as "I liked it" or "good job" in their conversations. Ramage, Bean, and Johnson say that the success of peer review practices comes from the ability to see a draft "from a *reader's* rather than a writer's perspective" (page 498). Structured conversation with peers helps enlarge that readers' perspective.

In some places, the chapter suggests that students read their classmates' papers before commenting, but in others, it highlights the benefits of having students read their own work aloud (see pages 503–504 for the rationale for this practice). Experiment with different approaches so you and your students can see what habits work best for your class. This can help students recognize and claim their voice, as they have the physical experience of speaking their words aloud. It can also help them see where they naturally self-correct as they read. Assure students that they need not feel self-conscious as they read. Because a writer in every group will be reading at the same time, the classroom will be noisy and no one but his or her own group members will be able to hear each reader's paper. You can reinforce this practice by occasionally role playing the writer when you discuss an essay in class. In preparation for peer reviews, read aloud a student essay from the textbook and then ask the entire class to serve as your group members, offering you feedback on the essay you have read and using the strategies outlined on page 499 of the textbook, or the response- and advice-centered guidelines on pages 504–505. Resist the urge to provide the "right" answers as the teacher. Instead, use your energy to help students develop increasingly analytical conversations about one another's writing.

The chief difference between response-centered and advice-centered workshops is that in the response-centered workshops, group members describe their reactions to the writer's essay without explicitly directing the writer to make particular changes. This workshop method may be preferred by student respondents who lack confidence in their ability to assess writing. The advice-centered workshop method is more directive in its feedback to the writer. Each major writing project in Part 2 of *The Allyn & Bacon Guide to Writing* includes "Guidelines for Peer Reviewers" tailored to each assignment to help students perform advice-centered reviews. As Ramage, Bean, and Johnson explain, the reviews are best completed by two students writing the review together.

Ramage, Bean, and Johnson also explain that reviews can be written outside of class. When deciding whether to arrange workshops so that students are required to work together outside of class, consider how feasible this requirement will be for students at your campus. If the majority of the students in your class live off campus and have jobs and/or family responsibilities, requiring them to schedule time to meet with other students outside of class may be unrealistic.

Whatever peer review format students use, remind writers to listen with an open mind to suggestions rather than to defend their drafts. If writers find themselves needing to explain or defend their drafts, clearly their draft isn't meeting readers' needs; they should then listen to their reviewers, rather than talking themselves, to discern what would make the draft more clear. Writers should ask follow-up questions to encourage their peer reviewers to be specific in their comments. Writers should also ask their reviewers follow-up questions so they can better decide how to act on what may be contradictory advice from various peer reviewers. Chapter 25, especially pages 698–702, offers further advice on how to promote successful group interaction and resolve problems in group dynamics.

Remember that it takes time for students to become effective peer reviewers. You can help them develop skills by structuring workshops over the course of the semester. Don't simply point your students to a set of peer review questions and turn over the whole class period to discussion. Ask students to turn in some evidence of peer review and perhaps a reflection on the peer review activities from a writer's perspective. Early in the semester, design peer review activities that focus on limited elements of a draft (such as the activity described above, which focuses on a single paragraph). As the semester goes on, gradually extend the complexity of the peer review activities and the time allotted.

Using the "For Writing and Discussion" Activities

The activity on page 495 obviously is most effective if students are working on a writing project from the chapters in Parts 1 or 2 of *The Allyn and Bacon Guide to Writing* as they work through this chapter. If they are not, however, you may still use this activity by asking them to bring to class a paper they are writing for another course or even asking them to use one of the paragraphs they have written for the homework assignment described above, in which they analyze their own composing process and set goals for improving it. Or you can use the activity on page 501, which addresses questions to a draft that appears elsewhere in the textbook.

The straightforward activity on page 498 asks students to reflect on, and discuss, their prior writing experiences. It is an excellent activity early in the semester, and should easily allow everyone to contribute.

Chapter 18
Composing and Revising Closed-Form Prose

Understanding the Chapter's Goals

This chapter deals primarily with the organization of closed-form prose. Students learn what readers expect of closed-form prose so that they can successfully meet those expectations. They also learn many organizational patterns or "moves" that can expand their repertoire of structures and add greater variety to students' texts. The chapter is organized into ten distinct skills. Rather than assigning the entire chapter in sequence, you may wish to assign only the skills that your students need most (perhaps you will want to assign some lessons to the entire class and other lessons only to the students who especially need help with those particular issues); you may wish to assign the skills at various times during your courses; and you may wish to alter the sequence of the skills, based on your students' greatest needs.

Reinforcing the Chapter's Rhetorical Principles

Skill 5: Reader Expectations

This lesson provides an overview of skills that are discussed more thoroughly in later lessons. The skills of "unity and coherence," "old before new," and "forecasting and fulfillment" somewhat overlap. Figure 18.1 presents unity and coherence graphically, and may help some students grasp these terms more quickly. Students can use this skill to diagnose what reader expectations they typically have the most difficulty satisfying. Students can then concentrate on the lessons that best correspond to those reader needs.

Skill 6: Thesis/Support Structures

When a paper just doesn't work, it will often be because it is written with one of these three riskless structures. A chronological structure is troublesome when it lacks a thesis; an encyclopedic structure has no thesis; and a formulaic structure is dissatisfying when it lacks surprise. Remind students of these problematic structures before they write major closed-form writing projects and encourage them to watch for them in one another's essays during peer reviews. If you notice any of these structures when you are grading students' work, in your comments refer the writer to this lesson. As long as students have a clear thesis that surprises, they will avoid these structures.

Skill 7: Structure

This lesson discusses three visual devices that can help students structure their writing: outlines, tree diagrams, and flowcharts. Students who dislike writing formal outlines may find tree diagrams and flowcharts less intimidating. In addition to helping writers plan the structure of a text they will draft, these techniques can also be used to detect organizational flaws after a text is already written.

You may want to distinguish outlines, tree diagrams, and flowcharts from another method of visual planning students were taught to do in Chapter 2: idea maps (an example of an idea map appears in Figure 2.1). In idea maps, students put their topic in the center of the page and explore by drawing branches outward. As their ideas get more specific, they create minor branches off related major branches. Writers use idea maps to generate ideas without self-censorship early in the writing process; however, rarely do writers put all of the ideas from an idea map into their paper.

Like idea maps, outlines, tree diagrams, and flowcharts are visual methods for generating ideas. Yet unlike an idea map, everything that is represented in these three forms of visual planning is included in the text. Also, these visual plans are arranged more deliberately: the ideas are positioned to represent the order in which the points will be made in the text; whereas in an idea map, the arrangement of ideas is more random. Like idea maps, however, the three visual methods discussed here can be generative. As Ramage, Bean, and Johnson explain on page 520, a writer can diagram the points and particulars of a text on branches and sub-branches of a tree diagram and then add question marks to "hold open" spots where the plan needs more development. Place-holding question marks can be similarly used in outlines and flowcharts.

Encourage students to try all three visual devices for planning a text's organization. Through such experimentation they may discover that they like one form most; however, help them realize that the other visual planning devices may prove more useful with other texts they may write (for example, an outline may be most suitable for a text that requires an elaborate hierarchy of ideas). Whenever a student's paper has structural weaknesses, consider advising (or assigning) that student to write an outline, tree diagram, or flowchart of the written text. Such a condensed visual may help the student detect incongruities that are obscured within the full text. Also encourage peer reviewers to use these visual forms to explain organizational weaknesses in drafts.

Skills 8 and 9: Titles and Introductions

Students often write weak titles and introductions. Many students simply don't title essays at all, and introductions can often be difficult if written at the start of the writing process, rather than at the end. This lesson is particularly helpful in getting students to form ideas about titles and introductions, and it offers concrete strategies for action. Ramage, Bean, and Johnson delineate possibilities that are likely to expand students' repertoires:

four conventions for titles of closed-form prose and four common features of academic introductions. Ramage, Bean, and Johnson are also helpful in advising students to write (or rewrite) these parts of a text last, when the meaning of the text is utterly clear. A text need not be written in the order in which readers will receive it.

You may want to have them examine the titles and introductions of several closed-form texts to see how these aspects of the texts affect them as readers. The closed-form readings in other chapters of *The Allyn & Bacon Guide to Writing* are handy examples.

Begin by asking students to turn to the table of contents in the textbook and, looking at the chapters devoted to closed-form prose, identify one or two essays for each of the four types of titles Ramage, Bean, and Johnson list: those in the form of questions, thesis statements, purpose statements, and two parts separated by a colon. After students have had a few minutes to search for and categorize titles on their own, you might want to use the transparency master at the end of this manual chapter to discuss students' perceptions of the effectiveness of these titles, pointing out the strategies used in various titles, such as:

Question Format:

"How Clean and Green Are Hydrogen Fuel-Cell Cars?" (Chapter 9)

Thesis Format:

"How Cigarette Advertisers Address the Stigma Against Smoking" (Chapter 11)
"The Myth of Violence in the Old West" (Chapter 22)
"Spare the Rod, Spoil the Parenting" (Chapter 14)

Purpose Statement Format:

"Mobile Phone Tracking Scrutinized" (Chapter 13)
"A Proposal to Provide Cruelty-Free Products on Campus" (Chapter 16)

Colon Format:

"Paintball: Promoter of Violence or Healthy Fun?" (Chapter 14)
"Sesame Street: Brought to You by the Letters M-A-L-E" (Chapter 15)
"The Hardest of the Hardcore: Let's Outlaw Hired Guns in Contemporary American Warfare" (Chapter 16)

Which of these titles do they most like? Why? Is there one format for titles that they like more than the others? Why? Is there one format they particularly dislike? Why? Would all of these titles be similarly appropriate and effective for all audiences? How should audience affect the writer's creation of a title?

Titles can also combine several of these four formats. Some examples of readings in *The Allyn & Bacon Guide to Writing* that combine formats are these: "The Hardest of the Hardcore: Let's Outlaw Hired Guns in Contemporary American Warfare" (Chapter 16), which uses both a colon and thesis format; and "Who Do You Want to Be?: Finding Heritage in Walker's 'Everyday Use'" (Chapter 12), which combines question, purpose statement, and colon formats. After the discussion of titles, ask students to apply what they've learned by choosing a writing project they wrote earlier in the course and revising its title. Have them share their revisions in groups or call on several students to share their revised titles with the class.

Similar activities can be done to motivate students to write stronger introductions and conclusions. Ask them to select several closed-form essays in *The Allyn & Bacon Guide to Writing* (perhaps ones they are interested in because of the class discussion about titles). They should read the essays in their entirety, but pay special attention to the essays' introductions and conclusions. How well does each satisfy the student as a reader? What piques or deters students' interest? Having read the body of the paper will help students identify which type of conclusion the writer has used. Again ask students about the role of audience in constructing an introduction and conclusion. Conclude the activity by having them revise the introduction and conclusion of an earlier assignment.

Skill 10: Effective Topic Sentences

Closed-form prose is structured so that points (main ideas) are placed before particulars (examples and supporting evidence). This order is preferable because readers' needs are different when reading closed-form prose than when reading open-form prose. In Chapter 1, Ramage, Bean, and Johnson explain that readers of closed-form prose are often busy and thus need texts that are clear, easy to summarize, and predictable enough in form that readers can glance at the beginning of each paragraph and understand the main ideas. This skill helps students learn how to meet the needs of busy readers for an easily understandable structure.

One example of closed-form prose that students frequently encounter is the type of informative writing used in most college textbooks. You might ask students to notice where they most often direct their attention when reading college textbooks. When they use a highlighter, take notes on their reading, or otherwise interact with a textbook, how often is their attention directed to the beginning of paragraphs or sections? How do students think their understanding and retention of the information would change if the particulars preceded the points? Ask students what other writings they encounter regularly in which they would expect to find points before particulars.

You may also want to comment upon how the points-to-particulars order corresponds with what their former writing teachers taught them about the function of topic sentences. A topic sentence is the "point" of the paragraph and generally begins the paragraph. The advice to put points before particulars in closed-form prose is consistent with the purpose of the topic sentence. "Points before particulars" is also sound advice, though, for larger portions of the text than single paragraphs. It is relevant for every level of the text: its overall thesis, its major sections (which may span several paragraphs or pages), as well as its individual paragraphs.

Knowing the structure of points to particulars can be generative. Students can check that they adequately develop both points and particulars as they compose; if either is sparse, students then know what they must add. The points alone form a summary or abstract of the text, while the particulars are what make the points believable. Tell students that if their "particulars"—their examples and support—are each referred to only briefly, the text needs more of them; if the particulars are extended examples, in most cases fewer will suffice.

Skill 11: Transitions and Signposts

Ramage, Bean, and Johnson allude to the concept of transitions in Skill 9, when they discuss the need for each part of a closed-form piece to link to the preceding material. The list of transitions provided in this lesson is very thorough and illustrates how important transitions are between and within sentences as well as between paragraphs.

If you would like to encourage the use of headings and subheadings as transitional devices, make sure students know that headings must be grammatically parallel. Parallel structure is explained in Handbook 4 of the textbook. If your class is using the brief edition of the textbook, without the Handbook, explain that all headings of the same level must have the same grammatical structure: if one is a noun, they all must be; if one begins with a verb, they all must; if the verb ends in "-ing," they all must; and so on.

If students are using headings in a long document and wish to include subheadings too, a tree diagram (explained in Skill 7) can help them identify appropriate places for the subheadings. Explain to students that the visual presentation of headings and subheadings must reflect the hierarchy of ideas in the text (see Chapter 4, Concept 12, on document design as well). Ideas that would be presented as major branches in a tree diagram must be identical in their font size and style, indentation, and use of capitalizations, boldface, and italics. Ideas that would be identified as minor branches of a tree diagram must be different in appearance from the ideas of the main branches, and identical in form to other minor subheadings. You might ask students to identify the styles of headings and subheadings in this chapter of *The Allyn & Bacon Guide to Writing*. Tell students there is no single format for distinguishing headings and subheadings, as long as the hierarchical and lateral relationships between ideas are clear.

For example, the largest headings in this chapter are for the ten skills. The skill titles are each in large bold fonts. Tell students to contrast this heading with the subheadings for this skill. The main subheadings are "Use Common Transition Words to Signal Relationships" (page 531), "Write Major Transitions Between Parts" and "Signal Transitions with Headings and Subheadings" (both on page 533). Visually, all have a font size smaller than that of the first lesson and only the first letter of key words is capitalized, rather than all letters being capitalized (as are the "For Writing and Discussion" sidenote titles). The next level of headings, identifying the "thought exercise" within each of these subsections, is even smaller in font size, although in all-capital letters, and is centered between the left and right margins (see one example on page 507). Prompt students to analyze the headings and subheadings throughout the remainder of this chapter too. They will discover another level of headings in Skill 7, where "Outlines" and other third-level subheads appear in a smaller and italicized font. Ask students to explain the rationale for this difference in size. Students may design their own heading and subheading styles for their texts but must be sure to apply the styles consistently.

Skill 12: The Old/New Contract

In closed-form prose, the sentences of most well-written paragraphs are so thoroughly governed by the old/new contract that the sequence of the sentences cannot be changed even slightly. An activity that impresses upon students this phenomenon is to give them separate slips of paper, each containing a single sentence from a closed-form paragraph, and ask them to reconstruct the paragraph. You can prepare for this activity with minimal effort. Copy or type the first full paragraph of this chapter, beginning every sentence on a new line, so that after you duplicate the sheet for each group of students, the sentences can be cut apart with scissors. In class, give each group a set of jumbled sentences and tell students to rearrange the sentences into their proper order.

When the groups are finished, have them compare their arrangements with one another and with the original version in the textbook. In all likelihood, all of the versions will be identical, which will surprise students who have never been aware of the old/new contract. Ask them to discuss the decision-making process they undertook when arranging sentences. If there is some variation of sentence order among groups, ask students to discuss the reasons for their differences.

You may also want to assign students to analyze a paragraph or two of their own past writing to determine how well they instinctively follow the terms of the old/new contract. Direct students to revise any places where the old/new contract is broken. Students should also determine the variety of ways they link back to old information. If necessary, they should revise the paragraphs to increase the variety. You may want to mention to students that deliberate attempts to adhere to the old/new contract as they write may stifle their ideas, causing writer's block. Therefore, it may be best to administer this principle when revising.

Skill 13: Organizational Moves

The organizational moves discussed in this lesson can be applied to small segments of a text (such as a few sentences or a single paragraph), large segments (numerous paragraphs or pages), as well as the entire text. Clarify for students that although Ramage, Bean, and

Johnson explain some moves using paragraphs as examples and explain others using tree diagrams as examples (representing the structure of the entire text), all of these organizational moves can be used for any amount of text. You can incorporate this lesson into peer review activities in order to help students see how these moves are used with different amounts of text.

To help students comprehend the structure of texts, you may want to have them analyze the organizational moves they made in a paper they wrote earlier this term or prior to this semester. What organizational moves did they make unknowingly? If the paper had organizational weaknesses, where were moves needed but absent? What moves would have corrected those weaknesses? If students don't have former papers of their own to analyze, you might ask them to bring to class a text they have read that could be improved with better organizational moves. Whether their work is their own or someone else's, students should come prepared for a group discussion of the text's existing structure and organizational moves that would improve it.

Skill 14: Conclusions

You may want to use this lesson in conjunction with Lesson 4 on introductions. Students often wonder how to distinguish introductions and conclusions, since both are often thought to summarize an essay. The questions embedded in this lesson will help students think about the type of conclusion best suited to their essay. As with the introduction, the conclusion is best written late in the process, when students are more clear on the meaning and significance of their text.

Using the "For Writing and Discussion" Activities

There are thought activities and/or "For Writing and Discussion" activities included with every skill in the chapter, and these are very helpful as in-class exercises. They work very well for promoting whole-class practice of skills that you may then ask students to do individually or in peer review groups. Doing the "For Writing and Discussion" activities allows students to practice skills with common materials.

For the activities that require tree diagrams, you may want to ask some students to copy their tree diagrams on the chalkboard for class discussion. This practice would be helpful for the activities on organization in Skill 13.

Chapter 19
Composing and Revising
Open-Form Prose

Understanding the Chapter's Goals

This chapter offers a fuller treatment of open-form writing, a rhetorical option that is discussed repeatedly throughout *The Allyn & Bacon Guide to Writing*. In Chapter 1, Ramage, Bean, and Johnson discuss the differences between closed and open forms. In Chapter 4, the authors offer guidelines about selecting style in any given piece. Chapter 7, about autobiographical narrative, gives students an opportunity to write a specific genre of open-form discourse. The exploratory essay assignment in Chapter 8 is also at least partially open form because of its emphasis on the writer's process toward a thesis.

This chapter explains rhetorical principles and techniques that are common to most genres of open-form discourse. Like Chapter 18, it is presented as a series of discrete skills that highlight different elements of open-form prose. The chapter can be taught at any time during the course, although it may be most helpful to teach it in conjunction with Chapter 7 on autobiographical narratives or with any other writing project that involves elements of open-form prose. You may teach the lessons in any order, and you may choose to assign some to the whole class and some to individual students.

Reinforcing the Chapter's Rhetorical Principles

Skill 15: Creating a Story

This lesson introduces the distinction between a story and an "and then" chronology. The contrast between the two student readings in this lesson (one in the running text of the chapter, and the other in the "For Writing and Discussion" activity) provides an accessible way for students to articulate for themselves stylistic differences that can affect readers. Students can usually discuss the student examples very well, but have trouble with the more theoretical components of this lesson. Working with the examples first, before the students read the rest of the lesson, usually works well. Although a story consists of depicting events in time, essays that depend purely on chronology to advance the plot often lack tension (the central problem in "The Stolen Watch").

Ramage, Bean, and Johnson identify four components of effective stories: depiction of events through time; connectivity; tension or conflict; and resolution. Of these four elements, students are most likely to need help understanding tension. To students without strong literary training, the words "tension" and "conflict" may have misleading

187

connotations. Students may think that to have narrative tension, a story has to be about a stressful situation, or that to have "conflict," the characters in the narrative need to have a combative relationship. It is likely, though, that some students in your class will understand these terms more accurately (particularly if they have taken introductory literature courses), so you may wish to begin your discussion by asking students what "tension" and "conflict" mean in this context.

Once all students understand that narrative tension/conflict denotes difference, but not necessarily negativity or aggression, you might ask students to create an analogy or metaphor (individually or in small groups) that conveys their understanding of these terms. This exercise is similar to the "For Writing and Discussion" activity in Chapter 1 that asks students to generate metaphors for closed and open forms. The section of this manual that accompanies that activity provides tips for helping students think of metaphors and would be relevant here as well.

To review all components of a story, you may wish to try the following activity, which could take most of a class session to complete. Ask students to think of one event that has happened to them in the last week that can be presented as a story; then give them a few minutes to freewrite about the event. Next, direct students to form groups of five. One student should begin the group activity by orally recounting his or her story. The remaining group members should try to identify the story components. To keep all group members involved, each can be assigned a certain analytical task. Whoever is sitting to the left of the storyteller can briefly identify the key events of the story; moving clockwise, the next student can explain the connectivity of the events; the next can discuss the tension or conflict; and the last can identify the resolution. Once one student's story has been analyzed, the next student in the circle, moving clockwise, can tell his or her story and the analytical assignments can similarly shift one person. In this manner, all students can gain experience creating and analyzing all aspects of the story. You may wish to analyze one or two students' stories together as a class before the groups convene to ensure that all students understand the components adequately. When the groups are finished, ask if any had trouble analyzing a story, or what component of the stories was most difficult to identify. You can discuss a particular story, or particular story elements, as a whole class.

Skill 16: Writing Low on the Ladder of Abstraction

Ramage, Bean, and Johnson devote considerable discussion to word choice for open-form prose. Whether the words are specific, revelatory, memory soaked, or figurative, students should realize that highly descriptive words greatly enhance open-form writing. You may wish to remind students at this point of the attention that advertisers give to minute details. Like advertisements, open-form prose strives to shape an image and create a mood, so care in details is similarly important. Advise students to be attuned to stylistic matters throughout their process of planning, drafting, and revising open-form prose.

Skill 17: Disrupting Readers' Desires

At first glance, descriptions such as "disrupting predictions," "making odd juxtapositions," "leaving gaps," and "employing unstable points of view" seem to depict the behaviors of weak writers. Yet often in open-form writing, these characteristics are effective when they are used deliberately and purposefully. Make sure students understand that open-form writing does not mean that anything goes, that the writer holds no obligations to the reader. Yet structural unconventionalities, used well, can significantly contribute to the reader's engagement with a text. Peer review workshops on drafts provide the ideal means for student writers to learn whether their texts' structural irregularities entice or unduly frustrate readers. This lesson helps students see that the structural considerations are rooted in their purpose and relationship with the reader.

Skill 18: Tapping the Power of Figurative Language

This lesson explores the differences between figurative and literal language, noting the ways figurative language is often a hallmark of more open-form prose. Metaphors and other forms of figurative language enable writers to compare or equate unlike things, and the juxtapositions inherent in this language can extend the work of Skill 17.

Skill 19: Expanding Styles

This lesson introduces the technique of creative imitation, in which you work with a passage from an expert writer, substituting your own content but imitating the style and organization of the original. Ramage, Bean, and Johnson note that creative imitation often helps writers attain new insights into their subject matter. Creative imitation is also useful because it must begin with careful stylistic analysis. This lesson contains a series of questions that will help students describe the style of an expert text. It can be helpful to introduce creative imitation first to the whole class, so that you can discuss the style of the original.

If you use stylistic imitation as a technique, make sure to connect your use of stylistic imitation to your discussion of source citation and plagiarism (using Chapter 23, Skill 28). Your expectations for documented research work may well be different from your expectations for creative imitation, and you need to be very clear with students about the differences you see between the two activities.

Skill 20: Creating Voice

It is important to discuss closed and open forms as a continuum so that students understand that characteristics of the open form are adaptable to many writing projects, not only autobiographical narratives. Humor is perhaps the most common example of an open-form technique that appears regularly in more closed-form prose. Still other elements of open-form prose appear in different genres. Ramage, Bean, and Johnson cite the exploratory essay assignment in Chapter 8 as one example of prose that has traits of the open form, yet is not fully so. When discussing this continuum, have students refer to Figure 1.1 on page 10 in the textbook. This visual can remind students of the variety of ways in which closed and open elements can be combined.

If you did not do so during your class discussion of Chapter 1, you may now wish to have students bring to class brief readings they have found that they would identify as having both closed and open elements. Popular magazines are a good source for such materials.

Using the "For Writing and Discussion" Activities

This chapter has many "For Writing and Discussion" activities to give students ample practice analyzing and composing open-form prose. Assign as many as you have time for because few college teachers give students a chance to gain experience with open-form texts. You can use these activities either to help students read and analyze others' open-form texts, or to help students revise their own open-form texts.

The activity on page 554 asks students to analyze the essay "The Stolen Watch" as an example of an "*and then*" narrative that fails to meet the criteria for a story. "The Stolen Watch" meets the first criterion of a story by depicting events. However, the criteria of connectivity, tension or conflict, and resolution are not met satisfactorily. The only connectivity throughout the narrative is the inclusion of the narrator and Karen as characters. Although there is potential for tension/conflict and resolution in two arenas—the narrator's relationship with Karen, and the theft and return of the narrator's watch—neither is adequately developed to gain the reader's involvement. Challenge your students to imagine how this narrative might be retold to constitute a story. What events would need to be omitted? What theme could be developed to better connect the story's events? How could the tension/conflict and resolution be developed so that they engage readers? The other questions in this activity bring students into discussing "Berkeley Blues." See the "Discussing the Readings" section of this chapter for some perspectives on the ways that essay functions as a story.

The "For Writing and Discussion" activity on page 557 directs students to use specific, revelatory words to describe particular people and settings. Students may feel uneasy with the stereotyping this activity makes them to engage in. Assure students that they can depict the people and settings listed in the exercise however they wish: the point is to understand how language conveys powerful images. This activity also offers students practice with choosing descriptive words for open-form prose. The memory-soaked words this activity elicits may vary depending on the age, gender, socioeconomic class, race, ethnicity, and cultural heritage of your students. Other differences will probably be reflected in the memory-soaked words as well, such as the region where the student grew up and even the student's unique family traditions. Writers need not over-explain the emotional connotations of word choice. It's best to let readers either discern the meaning from the context of the passage or simply overlook the emotional impact of the word choice with no crucial loss of the text's meaning.

The activity on page 560 invites students to examine figurative language that is successful and clichéd. You may bring in a reading for students to analyze, or you can use the text's suggestions of readings in Chapter 7. Achieving consensus can be difficult with this activity, and the lack of consensus offers the chance to explore why some people consider language trite that others find engaging.

On page 562, students are instructed to do creative imitations. You may need to help students understand that in creative imitation, it is perfectly acceptable—indeed, required—to adopt the structure and organization of the original. As Ramage, Bean, and Johnson note, this technique has centuries of history behind it. Students who are worried about plagiarizing might need some help getting started (and of course, you will need to be clear about the difference between this exercise and an exercise in incorporating sources effectively). You can do a creative imitation of a short passage as a whole class before moving into individual work. Allow students to share their imitations and then discuss which imitations seemed more or less successful.

The activity on page 563–564 asks students to evaluate the appropriateness and appeal of humor in instructional books. You may wish to expand on these questions by having students discuss the use of humor in texts other than instructional books. For what kinds of texts would humor be a strong asset? On what basis do students base their opinion: the text's purpose? the text's subject matter? the text's audience? Are there purposes, subject matter, or audiences for which humor would not be appropriate in open-form prose?

The final "For Writing and Discussion" activity on page 565 is especially important for prompting students to see the relationship between forms of writing and forms of thought. The exercise asks how changing a particular writer's stridently closed-form text to open form might change the writer's thinking. Adapt this question to allow students to assess their own experiences as well. How has learning to compose open-form texts changed their thinking?

Discussing the Readings

"Berkeley Blues" (pages 547–549)

In the first edition of *The Allyn & Bacon Guide to Writing*, Ramage and Bean included the following helpful discussion of this narrative's theme:

The theme of 'Berkeley Blues,' baldly stated, might be 'It is bad to stereotype people.' But the story resonates more deeply than this. The story looks at the source of stereotyping—superficial knowledge, social and economic difference, and the fear that results from ignorance—as well as its effects. Moreover, it juxtaposes [white] middle-class students' fearfulness to the black man's confounding message of love. Whereas the old man is an impenetrable mystery to the students, their thoughts are apparently transparent to him. It would be difficult to put all this into a one-sentence moral like the moral of a fable. And so it would be with most good stories, no matter how simple they appear. (499–500)

Writers must often quite carefully decide what to include and what to exclude from a narrative so that the desired theme is clear. You may wish to have students analyze how the effect of this narrative would change if the depiction of events were altered in even minor ways. For example, how would the impact of the essay have been different if the writer had omitted his suspicion, in paragraph 14, that the man was about to reveal a knife rather than a flask? How would the essay change if the writer omitted paragraph 17? What would be the effect of expanding the essay to include how the writer now responds to disadvantaged strangers as a result of this incident? This discussion should help students understand that the depiction of events is not automatically determined once the writer chooses his or her topic; it too requires decisions of craft.

"Living Like Weasels" (pages 566–569)

This essay is often lyrical in its wording, providing students with ample opportunity to analyze specific words, figurative language, and memory-soaked phrases. Students can work in pairs or small groups to identify examples of each; as a class, then, compare what wording different groups picked out as being particularly striking. Encourage students to not restrict their selections to nouns, but to also include verbs, adverbs, and adjectives. For example, in the first paragraph, unusually descriptive verbs are used in the phrases "his tail *draped* over his nose," "*crunching* the brain at the base of the skull," and "a weasel who was *socketed* into his hand."

You may also want to point out that in addition to using words that are memory soaked, Dillard sometimes associates a strong image with a particular word, then uses that word again later in the essay to recall the same image and emotions. In other words, through her descriptive powers, Dillard creates a memory for a particular word, then repeats the word later in the essay in order to recall that memory. For example, in paragraph 2, she offers a graphic description of a weasel's tenacity in remaining affixed to an eagle's throat even in death. The final word of the essay is "eagles," which conjures in the reader's mind the strong visual image from that second paragraph and the emotions that image evoked. Your students may want to try this strategy of creating specific, emotion-laden associations for words early in their texts, then judiciously repeating these now-memory-soaked words later in the text.

Chapter 20
Asking Questions, Finding Sources

Understanding the Chapter's Goals

This chapter provides an overview of the research process and gets students started with three basic research skills. It previews and complements the more detailed instruction in the other chapters in Part 4 of *The Allyn & Bacon Guide to Writing*. The overview of research presented here also complements the view of the composing process presented in Chapter 17 as well as Part 1 of the textbook. This overview of research presents a sensible introduction to research that explains why learning to research effectively can be difficult, and how thinking about research rhetorically benefits writers.

Ramage, Bean, and Johnson put research in the rhetorical framework the text has developed all along. Researched writing pursues interesting questions or important problems; it presents a "contestable thesis" (573) that allows readers to see how the writer has evaluated and synthesized sources to come to a position. Researched writing also uses appropriate documentation to display the research process in the text. As you begin to work with this section of the textbook, remind students that the principles introduced in many previous chapters are still at work. The informative writing project in Chapter 9, for example, can be easily connected to the rhetorical principles here, and the basic view of writing as a question-based and rhetorical activity (Chapters 1-4) is the foundation for this presentation of research.

Reinforcing the Chapter's Rhetorical Principles

Research as a Learned Skill

Ramage, Bean, and Johnson lay out research with a set of skills explained over three chapters. It is important to let students know that your class will support them, and instruct them, in how to do research. Many students experience research as a lonely endeavor. They may have cultivated independent abilities to locate information on the Internet and in libraries; they may have had experiences with note cards (sometimes faked after the fact!) or outlines or required summaries of sources; they may have experienced research as something negative. Other students, of course, may be skilled at locating information and may enjoy it. Remember that your students bring many prior experiences with them to your class; your instruction builds on what they have already done.

Skill 21: Arguing Your Own Thesis

This skill is fundamental to a writer being in control of a researched project. As Ramage, Bean, and Johnson note, a good question helps keep a writer focused and engaged. This first skill set involves two "For Writing and Discussion" activities, and it uses as an extended example James Gardiner's research (which was discussed in Chapter 8 and will be featured again in Chapter 23). It is very important to spend extended time with this skill, since the development and evaluation of a research question is very important. The better a research question students start with, the better their writing processes and projects will be.

Spend time on the distinction between a topic and a question. A question will help students see that they are pursing a purposeful project. A good question will help students focus attention on what they want to find out, and what their own role in the process will be. The bulleted list on page 608 will help students establish an active stance in the research process.

You can use the "For Writing and Discussion" activity on pages 576–577 to help students understand what this active stance feels like. Working together, they can develop questions that are appropriate to a variety of roles, and then they can do the same for their individual research projects. It can also be helpful to ask them to trace James Gardiner's research steps. Designing a set of recursive activities that ask students to generate and evaluate research questions will help students identify their interests. At the end of this lesson, you can collect students' own research questions and give them feedback. Even with in-class attention to questions, it is likely that some students will need to revise their questions further.

Skill 22: Understand the Different Kinds of Sources

This skill emphasizes the different kinds of sources students are likely to encounter in their research processes. Just as earlier chapters emphasized that different kinds of texts may require different reading processes (Chapter 6) and writing processes (Chapter 17), this skill reminds students that different kinds of texts may require different research processes. You may find it helpful to spend time on this lesson with connections back to Part 1 of the textbook, which emphasizes a general rhetorical framework. Table 20.1 graphically represents rhetorical differences among different kinds of sources.

It's a good idea to spend some time developing a shared vocabulary for discussing sources. While every student in your class will know what a book is, the term "periodical" (which is frequently used by librarians, and may appear in your library's catalog, signs, or handouts for students) is likely to be less familiar. Students will be familiar with various periodicals, of course, but they won't know the term. Use this lesson as an opportunity to acquaint your students with the vocabulary used by your campus library.

Table 20.1 distinguishes scholarly, trade, reference, public affairs, and niche magazines. If you have preferences about what kinds of sources students should concentrate on (or avoid), make that clear. It can be helpful to visit the library together, or invite a librarian to visit your class, in order to have some hands-on demonstrations with different types of sources. It can be helpful for students to see, for example, a discussion of eating disorders in an article in the *American Journal of Psychiatry* (a scholarly journal), a local and national newspaper, a public affairs magazine, and a niche magazine for young women. You can provide copies of a set of articles for your students and invite groups to compare pairs or groups of the articles, noticing differences in everything from document design to titles and types of evidence (this would be a good extension of the "For Writing and Discussion" activity in this section.

Skill 23: Purposeful Strategies for Finding Sources

This skill addresses what many students already consider to be the fundamental research skill: how to locate relevant sources. If you have worked with the previous skills in this chapter, students should have a good research question and a basic understanding of the kinds of sources they may encounter (or the kinds of sources you require) for their current project.

The skill begins by presenting how to find books in an online catalog after looking at a library homepage. You may find that it is more effective to start this skill at its third main section, on using licensed databases, since most projects in first-year composition courses do not permit students time to read a book in the course of a researched project. This section also introduces subject and key-word searches and basic skills for searching. Table 20.2 summarizes Boolean search commands for easy reference.

As you introduce students to licensed database searching, focus attention at first on one database to which your students have easy access. Even if your assignment permits students to do more wide-ranging research, starting with one database is a good way to have students practice accessing a database through your library's interface and reading the complicated information on the header. If you don't have an overhead projector in your classroom that can be connected to the database, use Figure 21.2 to help students work through the electronic headers together.

Web searching is a complicated matter. For some classroom activity ideas, see this manual's chapter on using *The Allyn & Bacon Guide to Writing* in an electronic environment. It is important that your activities help students understand the difference between different search engines and how to "read" a URL in order to determine the nature of the site (see the example on page 590). If students can identify the nature of the source, they can apply the information in Chapter 6 on reading rhetorically to begin their analysis.

Using the "For Writing and Discussion" Activities

If you can meet in a library classroom or a computer classroom, you will make it easy for students to try their hands at database searching. Forming a partnership with a librarian may extend your options. Consider scheduling time in the library more than once. Students will need some hands-on orientation to your local resources as research skills are introduced, and they will likely need another round of assistance once they get into their projects and begin running into problems. This is to be expected, and you will learn a lot if you are able to work with your students as they research (rather than hearing reports about problems after the fact).

It can be helpful to use mini-quizzes after library tours or research skill practice sessions, more to help you evaluate how much information students retained. A short quiz that asks students to identify the names of three good databases in your library, or to define what different Web site extensions mean, will help you see whether more presentation of search and evaluation strategies is necessary.

Chapter 21
Evaluating Sources

Understanding the Chapter's Goals

This chapter deals with the three essential skills for novice researchers. Students will learn a variety of strategies that will help them control the research process. As with the previous skill-based chapter, you will find that you have a great deal of flexibility in working with this material. Some skills you will want to assign to the whole class, and use as the basis for homework and in-class activities. Others you may assign only to individual students. You need not assign them in order, and you can come back to the skill sets as many times as needed during any researched writing projects.

Reinforcing the Chapter's Rhetorical Principles

Skill 24: Read Rhetorically

This lesson returns to a familiar theme: it is important to read rhetorically in order to make the best use of time and sources. The connections to Chapter 6 are myriad here; as the skill explains, reading strategies will depend on the writer's purpose, and the purpose varies with the stage of the writing assignment. Emphasize that students should read broadly and quickly in the early stages; they should look for sources that will help them get a good sense of their research question (connect back to Chapter 20's Skill 21 as well).

The questions in the table on pages 593–594 will help students read rhetorically.

A series of exercises that can be helpful here involves asking students to evaluate the nature of the bibliographies developed by the students whose work appears earlier in the textbook. To begin with, students can look at the sources mentioned in James Gardiner's exploratory essay and annotated bibliography for this project on school violence (presented at the end of Chapter 8) and at the bibliography on his final version of the essay (presented in Chapter 23, in Skill 32). Ask students to evaluate the bibliographies, examining the kinds of sources Gardiner used early and later in the process. Do his early sources serve the overarching purpose this skill calls for?

Once students have established their own preliminary bibliographies and gotten some general reading underway, it will be important to take effective notes. Ramage, Bean, and Johnson advise that writers should determine how a source might be used in a project in order to select a note-taking strategy. Sources will end up being used in ways the writer fails to predict, of course, but some early consideration of these questions will help prevent problems later. Encourage students to become familiar with the four purposes for taking notes outlined in this skill set; it will make it easy for them to talk with each other, with you, and with librarians about their emerging projects, and it will also focus their attention when taking notes.

Material from Chapter 8 on exploratory writing will be helpful here. Reviewing James Gardiner's first exploratory essay will help students understand how he reflected on the first sources he encountered. You will likely have to remind students that the form of Gardiner's exploratory essay is not to be reproduced in the opening section of their researched essays. Rather, the habits of mind Leigh displays should be reproduced by students as they take notes.

Skill 25: Evaluating Sources

A key element of note-taking and the early research process is the ability to evaluate sources and determine their usefulness for the project. Ramage, Bean, and Johnson advise evaluating sources in four ways: test the author's angle of vision, degree of advocacy, reliability, and credibility. Table 21.1 in this section represents the political bias of some popular magazines and commentators. The place of publication is often a good clue to an author's angle of vision, and it can also be connected to an author's degree of advocacy. The reliability of a source can be difficult for a novice writer to determine. If you connect this skill set with the lessons in Chapter 13 on synthesis, you will help students learn to cross-reference their reading.

You may find it helpful to assign an annotated bibliography as part of the research process. The bibliography can contain a short summary of each key source, as well as an evaluation of a source according to the criteria presented here. If you have your class work with common materials, you can assign annotations to different groups, which provides a good way for students to practice this complicated skill before having to do it independently.

Skill 26: The Rhetoric of Web Sites

This skill is an extension of Skill 25, but it involves some specialized evaluation of electronic sources. The chapter in this manual on using *The Allyn & Bacon Guide to Writing* in electronic classrooms contains useful information on activities involving searching for electronic information.

As the material in this skill makes clear, the World Wide Web is an incredible research tool. Both its possibilities and perils are under- and over-estimated by teachers and students alike, and it is important for you to work through your own assumptions about the Web and its function in your writing assignments. Web sites are wonderful resources for introducing students to issues of document design (see Concept 12 in Chapter 4), and they are also wonderful resources for getting recent scientific data, current news, and personal expression. Web sites are also wonderful resources for teaching about credibility and ethos, since it is all too easy to find examples of poorly designed Web sites or Web sites with erroneous information. The extended examples in this section of the chapter works with Web sites about women and gun control, and it helps students evaluate the visual display of the sites, and analyze the domain names and the site rhetoric. Ramage, Bean, and Johnson propose that students evaluate Web sites according to these criteria: authority; objectivity/disclosure of advocacy; scope of coverage; accuracy; currency. These evaluation criteria are presented with sample questions in Tables 21.2.

Using the "For Writing and Discussion" Activities

This chapter's activities are linked to Skill 26, on Web site evaluation. They are quite rich and could easily take multiple class periods or be turned into a slightly longer writing assignment. These activities will give students practice in working as writers with Web materials. You can connect this work to Chapter 15, on using criteria to evaluate arguments.

Chapter 22
Incorporating Sources into Your Own Writing

Understanding the Chapter's Goals

This chapter deals with the use of sources in students' own writing. The skills in Chapters 20 and 21 helped students locate and evaluate sources; this chapter will help them incorporate sources into their own writing in order to fulfill their own purposes. These discrete skills are best assigned one at a time. Because working with sources is a complicated business, this chapter is one to which you and your students will return at various points during the semester. It makes sense to have the whole class work with this chapter to start with, and then you can refer individuals and groups back to these skill presentations as needed. Chapters 20 and 21 are useful in getting students started with researched writing, and Chapter 22 is useful helping students wrap up their researched work.

This chapter will help students determine how best to make use of their sources, how to integrate others' ideas with their own, how to indicate to readers where different ideas originated, and how to use APA or MLA format for in-text citations. The work in this chapter assumes that students have already identified a research question and located important and relevant sources.

Reinforcing the Chapter's Rhetorical Principles

Skill 27: Focusing on the Argument

Ramage, Bean, and Johnson stress that "there is no one right way of using a source" (page 613). This skill reminds students that their own purpose in writing determines how they use sources. Several different examples, using the same source in very different ways, illustrate this skill in practice.

Skill 28: Working with Sources

Skill 24 in Chapter 21 introduces students to various note-taking strategies aligned with various purposes for using a source. Generally, most writing teachers expect researched writing to demonstrate students' abilities to summarize, paraphrase, and quote from sources; it's important to teach students how to decide when to use each of these skills. The table in this section of the chapter outlines when students may want to summarize, paraphrase, quote short passages, or quote long passages from a source.

Students can use James Gardiner's sample research paper in Chapter 23 to analyze how those guidelines worked for him. Assign students, either individually or in groups, to read through the essay, noting each instance of source use. Some sample questions you can use to follow up on students' reading:

- For each citation, why do you think Gardiner used the source as he did? In other words, why did he choose to summarize/paraphrase/quote that particular source? Although it may be difficult without the sources at hand, try to determine whether the use of the source is effective or ineffective for the point Leigh is making.

- For each citation, are attributive tags used to fully acknowledge the origin of ideas and to provide a transition between the voice of the student writer and the voice of the source writer? Do the attributive tags indicate that Gardiner has evaluated the credibility of each source?

- What is the proportion of summary to paraphrase to quotes in the essay? (These are listed in what would generally be descending order of frequency.) Are any of these used too much or too little?

- How does the parenthetical documentation reveal Gardiner's ability to integrate sources? For example, does each citation of a source truly contribute to the paper, or do some seem like padding? Are each of the sources dealt with in distinct sections of the paper, which can be indicative of a "cut and paste" paper that subsumes the writer's own voice, or are some interwoven throughout the essay, which can indicate that the writer, not the sources, is in control?

The section of this skill on using attributive tags should help students see how the active reading and critical evaluation skills presented in Chapters 6 and 21 are reflected in their formal writing. The activity on page 620 will give students practice in evaluating different uses of attributive tags, although they may find it easier to evaluate the examples in the student paper at the end of the chapter because they will have more context for each tag.

Skill 29: The Mechanics of Quoting

This skill helps students see how to work with the material they wish to quote. It builds on the previous skill, emphasizing how students actively work with source material as they draft. This skill builds on Skill 28, helping students see how attributive tags work in action, how to blend a quoted phrase or word into a sentence, and how to modify a quotation to make it fit the grammar and context of a sentence. It also looks at how to decide when to use a block quotation. This skill section abounds with examples, and you should direct students' attention to examples that are relevant for the drafts they are working on. A good workshop activity is to assign groups to use a particular strategy from this section, simply to give everyone practice with different techniques.

Skill 30: Avoiding Plagiarism

Issues of plagiarism are always important in researched assignments, and this skill introduces the ethical and conceptual dimension of plagiarism. Ramage, Bean, and Johnson note that plagiarism has two forms: failure to provide citation (that is, a reference to the source used) and failure to use the techniques of citation (quotation marks or block indentation to mark language borrowed from a source). The examples on page 625 provide an excellent illustration of the extent to which similarities in sentence or paragraph structure should be considered.

Using the "For Writing and Discussion" Activities

The activities in this chapter, like those in Chapter 21, offer hands-on practice associated with both skills presented here. The activities presented in Skill 30 are well used in class, where you can see the kinds of questions students have as they practice working with sources. It can be very helpful to ask groups to work together on the activities on pages 620, putting their answers on an overhead transparency, on the board, or in a computer file that can be shared with the rest of the class. When students have the opportunity to see the different ways these tasks can be approached, they will better understand the complexities involving source use.

In general, Ramage, Bean, and Johnson's discussion of plagiarism should be sufficient to ensure that students move in the right direction on source use. Remember that using sources is complicated, and not all students will learn all of this material at the same pace. Some students will take longer, and you will need to consider how to tell the difference between plagiarism as an issue of academic misconduct and improper use of sources as an issue of incomplete learning.

Set up your researched writing assignments so you have ample opportunity to interact with students as they proceed through the research, reading, and writing processes. If you collect work from students all through the research process, beginning with the development of research questions, you will be familiar with students' projects and able to help them throughout the process. As your researched assignment proceeds, consider collecting and responding to:

- Students' research questions

- A proposal for a researched project that provides more justification for the research question

- A preliminary bibliography (you might require a minimum number of sources, or a spread of sources from particular places, such as two from EBSCOHost, one from a newspaper, one from a book, one from an encyclopedia, one from before/after a particular date, etc.). Be prepared to be flexible if some students' topics don't lend themselves to particular kinds of sources.

- Initial reading notes (you might require a certain format, such as a double-entry journal, or you might require that certain evaluation questions be considered for a particular number or sources)

- A draft of the essay, with a bibliography page and in-text citation

- Selected sections with particular types of sources, or types of citations, used (you might require that peer review focus on sections of the essay that cite Web sites, or that summarize or use block quotations, for example)

You don't need to respond extensively to all this work. In some cases, you can quickly check through the work while students are doing an in-class activity. In other cases (such as with the drafts of the essay), you might want to take more time and care. But collecting work in stages will help you help students avoid plagiarism. You will see which students are having problems, and which are making errors in citation (conceptually or technically).

Chapter 23
Citing and Documenting Sources

Understanding the Chapter's Goals

This chapter deals with documenting sources, focusing more on the mechanics and less on the rhetorical strategies of citation. In this chapter, students will learn how to use parenthetical citation systems. This work allows students to show readers where different ideas originated, and how to use APA or MLA format. The work in this chapter assumes that students have already identified a research question and located important and relevant sources.

Reinforcing the Chapter's Rhetorical Principles

Skill 31: How Parenthetical Citations Work

This first skill explains how parenthetical citation work. Although this section is short compared to the other skills presented in this chapter, spend some time here. IF students understand the logic of in-text citations, they will have a much easier time determining which parts of Skills 32 and 33 they will need for the particular sources they cite.

Start by presenting the logic of in-text citation systems. Ramage, Bean, and Johnson point out that it is often difficult to construct in-text citations for downloaded sources. When material appears either on the Web or in a licensed database, citation requirements demand that students find the original print source to get complete information. (Most database headers supply the number of pages for an article, but don't give the full page range, which is required for a bibliographic reference.) Most students won't bother to get the original print source simply for what seems a minor technicality, and in some cases, the original source would be impossible to obtain in a timely fashion. You will need to work out how to compromise on citation systems with your class for exceptions like this. No matter how detailed your assignment sheet is in this regard, you will find that some students will discover a handy and relevant electronic source that doesn't quite fit anything in the text or on your assignment sheet. Simply use these exceptions as a chance to return to the section of the text on the logic of citation systems, and work out an appropriate solution.

Skills 32 and 33: MLA and APA Styles

These skills deal with the nuts and bolts of citation: the mechanics of MLA and APA styles. Although questions of punctuation loom large in the polishing of in-text citations and bibliographies, remind students that at heart, citation and documentation are ethical and rhetorical issues. Proper citation assures readers that writers have used well-researched and well-considered sources in the course of writing the project. In addition, the key differences between MLA and APA citation systems are driven by epistemological differences. For social scientists and scientists, the date of publication is crucial. That is why APA highlights the date, much more so than MLA, which focuses on the person who did the research. APA style highlights the main questions and conclusions of others' studies; MLA style is more discursive. These differences affect punctuation and layout, but they are rooted in disciplinary divisions between the humanities and the sciences.

That said, it is important that students learn the principle of following a style sheet. You might ask them to survey their other professors and find out what kind of citation systems are used in other departments on campus. You will likely find a range of answers. Some professors tell students that they can use any system they please, so long as they are consistent. Others will require APA, MLA, or other specialized disciplinary citation systems. Still others will model citation systems after a prominent journal in their field. While students will need to learn how to satisfy your expectations for effective citation in your course, they will also need to learn how to find out what other professors' expectations are.

Students should determine what kind of source they are reading, well in advance of the need to form citations and bibliographic entries so they can easily find the appropriate place in the textbook for guidance when it is needed. Some exercises that work well to supplement the text and help students learn to use whichever style you require are as follows:

- Provide a sample citation for a source the class has in common for students to use as a model. Constructing bibliographic entries can seem arbitrary, and a model that uses a source students are familiar with can make the textbook examples much more accessible.

- Construct bibliographies together in class, especially if the students have sources in common.

- Provide examples of researched writing with errors in documentation, and ask students to correct the errors (see transparency at the end of this chapter).

Practice Proofreading MLA-Style Documentation

Bibliography

Barr, Bob. Liberal Media Adored Gun-Control Marchers. *Insight in the News* 5 June 2000: 44. *ProQuest.* Lemieux Lib. Seattle U. 15 August 2001. http://proquest.umi.com.

Ferraraccio, M. "Metal Detectors in the Public Schools: Fourth Amendment Concerns." *Journal of Law and Education* 28: 209-29.

Stecklow, Steve. "Metal Detectors Find a Growing Market, But Not Many Guns." *Wall Street Journal* September 7, 1993: A1+

Stefkovich, Jacqueline and O'Brien, G.M. "Students' Fourth Amendment Rights and School Safety." *Education and Urban Society* 29 (1997): 149-159.

United States. Depart. Of Health and Human Services. Centers for Disease Control and Prevention. "Youth Risk Behavior Trends from CDC's 1991, 1993, 1995, 1997, and 1999 Youth Risk Behavior Surveys. *Adolescent and School Health,* 6 Aug. 2001. 11 Aug. 2002. http://www.cdc.gov/

Wilson, Joseph M., and Perry Zirkel. "When Guns Come to School." American School Board Journal 181.1 (1994): 32-34.

Yarbrough, Jonathan W. "Are metal detectors the Answer to Handguns in public Schools?" *Journal of Law and Education* 22 (1993): 584-87.

Errors on the Transparency

1. Should be works cited, not bibliography.
2. All entries should be typed double spaced.
3. In the first source, quotation marks missing around title.
4. In the second source, the author's first name should be written out.
5. In the second source, the year is missing after the volume number.
6. In the third source, the date should be in the format date/month abbreviation/year (7 Sept. 1993).
7. In the fourth source, the second author's name should be first name before last name, and there should be a comma after Jacqueline.
8. In the fifth source, the Web site provided is a very general one (the CDC's main home page). This will not get students to the particular report provided. (This error may be difficult to catch in this exercise, although sharp readers of the URL may notice it.)
9. In the sixth source, the name of the journal should be underlined.
10. In the final source, capitalization of the title should be regular.

Chapter 24
Essay Examinations:
Writing Well Under Pressure

Understanding the Chapter's Goals

This chapter challenges students to consider how to adapt the problem-posing strategies they've developed in other chapters to situations that don't allow the luxury of ongoing rethinking and revision. In addition to academic essay exams, students can use the strategies discussed in this chapter to respond to other situations that require the quick composition of a polished document, such as news articles, sales presentations, public information briefings, and business memos.

You can use this chapter in several ways: as a supplement to help students succeed in their other courses, as the basis for a timed writing assignment of your own, or in conjunction with one of the writing projects in Chapters 5–17. More discussion of each of these options is discussed below under the heading "Guiding Students through the Writing Project."

Reinforcing the Chapter's Rhetorical Principles

The Rhetorical Nature of Exams

As you begin this chapter, encourage students to discuss the exams they've taken or will be taking in their other courses. Suggest that they bring sample tests and responses to share with the class, and refer to these samples as you work through the chapter. If several students have a major exam coming up, ask the rest of the class to suggest preparation and composing strategies, then have the test takers follow up with an analysis of how well the recommendations worked. Even if few of your students are currently taking courses that incorporate essay exams, you can collect examples from your institution's test files or from colleagues' courses. Having a variety of models to examine helps students identify common rhetorical elements and reiterates the importance of this kind of writing task to their success as academic writers.

Students will most fully appreciate the differences between timed writing and out-of-class writing if they have plenty of opportunities to practice both. Throughout the course, offer students occasional opportunities to compose on the spot: at the beginning of class, give them ten or fifteen minutes to write a couple of paragraphs in response to a central question raised by that day's reading assignment; or have groups polish their response to one of the "For Writing and Discussion" activities to turn in. For longer essay assignments, see the exam option suggestions on page 676 of the textbook.

Preparation for an Exam

Pages 664–666 provide basic guidelines for learning and preparing material for an exam. If you will require students to take an essay exam, consider dividing the class into several study groups. Set aside some class time for groups to sort through the study techniques discussed in the chapter and devise a specific plan their group can follow to prepare for the test. You may even want to require groups to meet for a specified amount of study time (perhaps one to two hours) outside class. Talk with students about the benefits and drawbacks of studying collaboratively, and begin class each day with brief reports about how group work is progressing.

Exam Questions

When you introduce students to the question verbs in the table on pages 668–671, remind them that different professors may use terminology in different ways, and that disciplinary communities' ideas of what constitutes a "complete" or "logical" treatment of a topic vary somewhat. Some teachers look for coherent, independent arguments, while others may reward "all about" responses that rehash everything the student knows about the topic. Some value tightly organized essays, while others look primarily for relevant content, no matter how it's presented. Encourage students to see the terms and definitions in the chapter as general guidelines to be enriched by their own experiences. Compare the terminology on the "real" exams students bring to class with what is listed on the table here and invite students to create an appendix of additional terms, examples, and definitions.

Test Situations

Once students feel comfortable analyzing the kinds of writing tasks that commonly appear on exams, they are ready to grapple with the constraints a test setting imposes. As a prewriting technique, encourage students to arrange ideas in an idea map (explained in Chapter 2) or one of the organizational heuristics explained in Chapter 18, Skill 7: an informal outline, a tree diagram, or a flowchart. Draw students' attention to the sample outline on page 674 and point out how disorganized it looks initially: the writer has simply jotted down general ideas about each area of the question, then later added arrows to organize those ideas. Note also that the student's thesis doesn't materialize until the end of her "outline." Had she started writing without brainstorming, her thesis would likely have been less rich and her argument less complete.

Create opportunities for students to practice these prewriting techniques, especially if you'll have them write a timed essay in your course. Devise one or more sample questions, then give students five minutes to brainstorm and outline a response. As a class, compare and critique their outlines, discussing which of the approaches worked most successfully. If students want more help with invention, encourage them to review the writing strategies discussed in Chapters 2, 18, and 19.

Using the "For Writing and Discussion" Activities

The writing and discussion activities in this chapter have been sequenced to help students understand the requirements of an exam setting and to flourish within them. Try to set aside class time for these exercises, even if you don't plan to have students complete a full essay exam.

The section entitled "Analyzing Exam Questions," pages 666–673, lays out practical frameworks for understanding the rhetorical structure of exams that students can apply in almost any course. You can apply this material to essay exam questions that students collect in their other courses. Ask students to keep track of their essay exam questions, and at the appropriate time in the semester, invite volunteers to write their questions on the board, then have the class collaborate to identify key terms and decide how a successful response might be organized. Alternatively, if you plan to require students to take an essay exam at the end of the unit, let them try their hand at a question similar to the one you'll assign.

The exercise that begins on page 671 hones students' analytical abilities further by asking them to choose from a group of closely related questions the one that best matches a particular essay response. As groups discuss this task, encourage them to justify their responses by matching specific passages in each response to key terms and phrases in the question. You may want to raise one or more of the following points in your discussion.

Matching the essay with the appropriate question may prove tricky for your students. If confusion arises, observe that some instructors might consider this essay an adequate response to Question 1, but it probably wouldn't receive an "A." The essay focuses primarily on similarities between Swift's and Shelley's views and mentions only one, vaguely defined, difference (that Shelley "feels more optimistic" than Swift) in the final paragraph. An exemplary answer to Question 1 would identify several differences between Shelley's and Swift's views and illustrate these with textual examples. Although this response also touches on the concerns of Questions 2 and 3, neither scientific knowledge nor character analysis is central to the discussion. Because the essay revolves around the texts' exploration of human nature, most instructors would consider it an off-topic response to either question.

The essay is a successful treatment of Question 4, a lengthy question that requires sophisticated interpretation and analysis. Although the question begins with several generalizations and offers numerous topic options, note how this writer refines her response to fit the basic requirements: a discussion of two works on the list, geared to the key issue (how the texts suggest a pessimistic or optimistic view of human nature), and supported by specific textual examples. The discussion of *Frankenstein* is less fully developed than the section on *Gulliver's Travels*—perhaps because the writer ran out of time—but the overall strength and coherence of the argument earned it an A.

Guiding Students through the Writing Project

Students will learn the most from this chapter if you offer them concrete opportunities to apply their knowledge in one or more timed writing assignments. Depending upon your course plan and your pedagogical goals, you might integrate this chapter into a writing project in one of three ways:

One option is to teach this chapter as a separate unit, in which students prepare for and complete a timed essay exam using one of the three exam options in the "For Writing and Discussion" activity on page 676. Exam options one and two invite students to rethink and synthesize chapters they have already read in *The Allyn & Bacon Guide to Writing*; these topics will work particularly well if you don't want to build in the time it would take for students to master unfamiliar readings. The exam question for each of these options appears in the textbook, so students will know what to prepare beforehand. If you want to add an element of surprise, tell students that you will modify the question somewhat for the exam. Exam option three invites you to select your own exam topic. This option is best if you wish students to explore an issue not treated in the textbook, such as a local controversy, a current issue in language studies, or another appropriate topic. Distribute copies of the readings to students when you begin this chapter and gear class discussion to the upcoming exam topic as you work through the chapter. If you assign a timed essay exam, plan to spend at least two weeks on this chapter, so that students will have sufficient opportunities to prepare, and devote an entire class period to writing the exam.

If you don't want to devote a major writing project exclusively to exam writing, consider another option: pairing this chapter with one of the writing projects described in Chapters 5–17. For example, students studying Chapter 6 might prepare and write a "strong response" to a homework reading using the strategies discussed in this chapter. Sometimes doing timed writing in class offers a controlled way to see how students are thinking about their topics or research. This kind of pairing allows you to cover many skills in a single course unit. But if you decide to pair chapters in this way, be sure to allow enough time for students to study both chapters thoroughly. Also, if necessary, modify the writing assignment so that it is suitable for in-class writing (for example, eliminate requirements for outside research and streamline tasks too lengthy to be addressed in the allotted writing period). Assignments that might work particularly well in conjunction with this chapter include the projects in Chapters 5, 6, 10, 11, 12, and 15.

Finally, if you simply don't have the time or the desire to have students write a timed essay in your class, you can use this chapter as supplemental information geared to helping them improve their writing in other courses. In this case, you'll need to encourage students to bring in, and work with, as many samples as possible of exams and questions they've received in other courses. Even if you don't have students compose a full essay, provide plenty of opportunities for them to practice analyzing questions, brainstorming, outlining, and writing. At the very least, you can point out to students that the chapter is there for their independent use, and a few enterprising students may choose to work with some of the information on their own. In addition, the "For Writing and Discussion" activities offer a good starting point for practice.

Chapter 25
Assembling a Portfolio and
Writing a Reflective Essay

Understanding the Chapter's Goals

This chapter teaches students how to be reflective about their own writing. Two types of reflective self-evaluation are explained: single reflections, written to a nonjudgmental audience about one essay or draft; and comprehensive reflections, written to an instructor or portfolio reader to accompany a set of completed writing projects. The second part of the chapter explicitly associates comprehensive reflections with portfolios.

Rather than assigning a universal writing project, the chapter allows you to assign the type and number of self-reflective evaluations you consider most pertinent for your course. If you are using portfolios, consider assigning parts of this chapter early in the semester so that students understand your views on portfolio assessment. Portfolios function effectively if you work with students consistently to evaluate their own work. Students need to have practice reflecting on their work in order to assemble a good portfolio.

Reinforcing the Chapter's Rhetorical Principles

Portfolios

Portfolios are collections of work, selected by the author, including reflection or self-analysis. If you will be using portfolios to grade students' work, you will be giving them large stretches of time in which their work is not graded (you may be responding, of course, to the work, but not grading it). Make sure students understand how you will grade their portfolios when the time comes. Just as importantly, give students ample guidance about how to save their work and how to think about what to select for inclusion in the portfolio.

There are many reasons for portfolios. Some showcase a student's best work; others showcase growth over time; others showcase connections with an external theme (such as demonstrating learning in line with course goals or campus goals for general education). Be clear about the purpose of the portfolios you require, so that students can make informed choices about what work to include.

Reflection

Ramage, Bean, and Johnson explain that "to *reflect* is to turn or look back, to reconsider something thought or done in the past from the perspective of the present"

213

(page 679). This chapter focuses on reflecting about writing, and it connects well with Chapter 17 to show students how writing is a complicated and recursive process. The chapter provides a variety of structured invitations for students to think about their own writing, although it also points out some ways that reflection is used in other contexts to assess performance. This chapter is most useful as a means of helping students consider their own performance in the course or on a particular assignment. It is usually helpful to ask students to read this chapter in short segments in connection with an assignment they are completing. You will find it handy to return to this chapter at the end of every formal writing assignment so that students can reflect ever more thoroughly on their own work. It is also helpful to assign this chapter in conjunction with preparation for peer-reviewing activities. The more students reflect on their own work in advance of peer review, the better able they will be to participate in group or partner activities.

Using the "For Writing and Discussion" Activities

The activity on page 681 asks students to reflect upon a past experience and freewrite an evaluation of that experience from their present perspective. Some students may find it helpful to brainstorm ideas before they freewrite. Explain that they can generate ideas for this activity by constructing three columns: one labeled "Past View" (how they understood the experience at the time it occurred), one labeled "Present View" (how they perceive the experience now), and one labeled "Desired Changes" (how they would change the experience if they could). After filling in the columns that ask for their past and present perspectives on the experience, they can compare and contrast the columns to dialectically reach insights for the third column. In this "Desired Changes" column, they can record ways they wish the experience had been different, as well as what they would do differently if they had the experience today. This column can also help them identify ways they need to further reflect upon the experience: perhaps they are unsure of what could improve the experience; that uncertainty is itself something that needs to be changed, and they can record in this column what steps they could take to resolve their uncertainty. After this brainstorming, students should freewrite about the insights they have obtained to increase their understanding.

Guiding Students through the Writing Project

There is no prescribed writing project for this chapter. However, you may decide to assign students to write reflective self-evaluations at any time—even multiple times—during your course. To encourage an instructive dialogue between yourself and students, you may wish to have students submit a single reflection for every writing project. If so, the bulleted list of sample assignments on pages 682–683 will give you ample ideas. To keep students' interest, you may want to assign different forms of the single reflection for multiple assignments. You can also invite students to participate in creating reflective questions as the semester goes on. This will help students develop independent abilities to reflect on and assess their own work.

Even if your students are not having their work graded by a portfolio method, they can still benefit immensely from writing a comprehensive reflection on their work for the course. Consider having them write two: they can write the first one at midterm, to review the work they have completed for the course so far; they can then identify the skills they most want to improve in the remainder of the course; and finally you can help establish a plan to help them meet those goals. You may want to have students write such midterm comprehensive reflections and bring them to midterm conferences, so that you can compare students' assessments of their trouble spots with your own and together devise a detailed plan for their writing improvement. If you teach a long course session, you may opt to keep students goal oriented by having them write a reflection like this monthly. Students should also write a comprehensive reflection at the end of the term, to both articulate what they have learned and to plan how they intend to continue improving their writing skills beyond your course.

Some students may initially view reflective self-evaluations as busywork. There are several steps you can take to help them approach these assignments conscientiously. First, when you announce the assignment, set aside some time for students to frankly discuss the role they think writing plays in their lives. Some may not have much incentive to improve their writing skills because they think there will always be an available resource—a secretary, a computer software program, a skilled friend—to "fix" whatever mistakes they make. Others may value strong writing skills, but only see them as relevant to academic and career situations. Reflecting on their writing requires students to take writing seriously, so share with them some of the benefits you have experienced by being able to write well. In particular, share anecdotes of times when writing well gave you an unexpected advantage (e.g., you were able to resolve a consumer complaint easily because you could present yourself professionally and clearly in a letter; you were able to comfort a grieving friend because you could express your feelings compassionately in a sympathy card). Students will only be motivated to write thoughtful self-evaluations of their writing if they are motivated to be better writers.

Students will also be more likely to prepare their reflections conscientiously if they are given adequate time to write them. If a reflection is due at the same time as one or more major writing projects, they are likely to devote their time to the project itself and complete the reflection quickly. If possible, make the due date for comprehensive reflections one class session after the assignments themselves are due. That deadline will ensure that students remember the work well enough to discuss it specifically, but are not so rushed completing the writing project that they have little time to write a reflection.

Finally, students will approach reflective self-evaluation assignments more seriously if you treat them seriously. This means that you must either grade them or comment on them in some detail. If you simply check off that the assignment was done, many students will not put forth the effort that a sincere reflection requires. If you don't feel you have time to respond in writing to the reflections, do so orally, in conferences or by briefly calling students to your desk individually while the rest of the class works independently or in groups on a "For Writing and Discussion" activity in the chapter you are presently discussing. If you decide to grade the reflections, to ensure that students write their reflections honestly (rather than trying to guess what you want them to say), tell them that the reflections will be graded only on the basis of the four criteria for good reflections discussed in this chapter: they should be selective, specific, dialectical, and adequately detailed.

Answers to Handbook Exercises

Page 716-717

Another difference between a taxi driver and other occupations is the way that taxi drivers interact with people. Driving a taxi is one of the few jobs where you really get to "know the customer." In other service jobs, you rarely get to know the customer's name. As a waiter or bartender, you can wait on 100 people in a night or mix drinks for 200 without personally talking to 15 of them. In a taxi, however, each customer spends at least ten to fifteen minutes in a quiet car with nothing else to do but talk with the driver.

Page 719

1. I love to hear coffee perking in the pot on lazy Saturday mornings. Another of my favorite sounds is rain on a tin roof.
2. Correct.
3. Freud assumed that the unconscious was the basis for human behavior. Therefore, he believed that the pleasure audiences receive from art comes from art's embodiment of unconscious material.
4. Correct.
5. Although scientists don't know for sure how much dinosaurs actually ate, they know that the food intake of the great reptiles must have been enormous. A question they ask themselves, therefore, is what the dinosaurs actually ate.
6. The doctor told me that my MRI revealed nothing to be alarmed about; nevertheless, she wants me to come back in six months for another checkup.
7. Juan and Alicia began taking the engine apart. They worked diligently for four hours and then discovered that they didn't have the right tools to continue.
8. Correct.
9. In a home aquarium, fish will sometimes die from overeating. The instructions on fish-food boxes, therefore, stress that you feed fish a specified amount on a strict schedule.
10. Correct.

Page 726

1. Under a pile of old rags in the corner of the basement <u>are</u> a <u>mother mouse and a squirming family of baby mice.</u>
2. <u>Hard work,</u> together with intelligence, initiative, and a bit of good luck, <u>explains</u> the success of many wealthy businesspeople.
3. The first <u>thing</u> she emphasized <u>was</u> the differences between Pacific and Atlantic breeding patterns of these fish.
4. <u>The myth, legend, prayer, and ritual</u> of primitive religions <u>contain</u> many common themes.
5. Unfortunately, <u>neither of the interviewers</u> for the local TV station <u>has</u> read any of her works.

6. There <u>are</u> <u>a number of students</u> who <u>are</u> waiting to see the teacher.
7. <u>Does</u> <u>one</u> of the students still have my notebook?
8. <u>One</u> of the students who <u>is</u> trying out for the play <u>wants</u> to become a professional actor.
9. <u>He</u> is the only one of all the students in the theater arts class who really <u>has</u> professional ambitions.
10. <u>The committee</u> <u>is</u> writing individual letters to the judge.

Page 728-729

1. We improved our car's acceleration by resetting the spark-plug caps and boiling out the carburetor.
2. Race-car driving requires practical experience and quick reactions.
3. After reading the events calendar, we decided to go to a festival of Japanese anime and attend the symphony afterward.
4. I want to read a biography of a flamboyant figure living in the twentieth century who has altered history.
5. Sasha not only does volunteer work in the school but also coaches soccer every fall.
6. Either you must leave early or you must leave after the major rush hour.
7. The harvest moon shone brightly, pouring its light over the surrounding water and making the evening a special moment in their lives.
8. You can avoid a comma splice by joining main clauses with a comma and a coordinating conjunction, by inserting a semicolon in place of the comma, or by changing one of the main clauses to a subordinate clause.
9. Again and again psychologists explore the same questions: Are we shaped by our heredity, by our environment, or by our will?
10. To make friends you must first be a friend and then listen carefully.

Pages 730-731

1. Feeling cold, tired, and depressed, my friend cried, tears streaming from his eyes.
2. Their heads tilted back in awe, the children began trying to count the stars on this summer's night.
3. Correct.
4. By studying the light reflected by Jupiter, you will learn its clouds are a poisonous mixture of ammonia floating in hydrogen.
5. Correct.
6. While my flight was cruising at 10,000 feet 45 miles east of Albuquerque, New Mexico, on July 16, 1945, at approximately 5:30 a.m., a brilliant flash of light, brighter than the sun, blazed across the sky.
7. Correct.
8. When we reported by radio what we had seen, ground authorities could find no satisfactory explanation.

9. Although we were still plagued by the event the following morning, the newspapers reported only that an ammunition dump had exploded in the approximate area where we had seen the flash.
10. Listening to the radio on August 6, 1945, we learned a similar flash of light occurred over Hiroshima, Japan; then we realized what we had seen several weeks earlier—the first explosion of an atomic bomb.

Page 733

1. <u>We</u> girls want to bike to the store.
2. Natalie, <u>who</u> received the scholarship, will study microbiology.
3. If you and <u>he</u> can visit Tim and <u>me</u> next month, we will tour the national park.
4. Jessica and Lin-Ju will bring <u>their</u> skis.
5. <u>His</u> playing loud music annoyed the neighbors.
6. He is the racer <u>who</u> I believe fell at the finish line.
7. This vacation was necessary for you and <u>me</u>.
8. A burglar stole our computer, but no one saw <u>him</u> entering the house.
9. Stephen or Tom will do <u>his</u> practicing before school.
10. Emily and Amy do <u>their</u> practicing faithfully every day.

Pages 738

1. He seems to be an unusually quiet person who cares a lot about other people.
2. A person who hurries is apt to waste time and material.
3. Ilana was interested in answering this question: What is the difference between "mental illness" and a disease of the brain?
4. Unfortunately, before he settled the issue, the mayor fostered a bitter public debate. He erred in pitting some of his key subordinates against one another and inflaming many other people's emotions.

Page 739

1. The victor received the rewards.
2. Don't kill a goose that frequently lays golden eggs.
3. Training children to avoid risk often makes them timid adults.
4. Juanita realized that she preferred to change her major from history to mathematics.
5. The teacher examined the student's locker because the teacher suspected the student had hidden drugs.

Pages 743-744

1. The carpet layers installed the wrong carpets while the owners were away.
2. Unchanged (intransitive).
3. Hot liquid blackberry jelly was ladled into sterilized jars by Beth.

4. The sleeping man was slowly covered with piles of sand by his little daughter, who wore a green sunsuit.
5. Scientists have discovered some of the most important scientific principles accidentally.
6. The turbine bearing rusted out and ruined the motor.

Pages 754-755

1. Whenever I go home to Bismarck, North Dakota, for Christmas vacation, the dinner conversation turns to cross-country skiing.
2. On my last visit, during dessert, my dad, who is an expert skier, asked me if I wanted to try dogsled racing.
3. "I've wanted to try dogsledding for years," Dad said, "but we've never had the equipment or the dogs. Now, however, my friend Jake Johnson, the new agent for Smith Insurance, has just bought a team and wants his friend to give it a try."
4. Rock shrimp, unlike some other species, have hard shells that make them difficult to peel.
5. Hiking or biking through southern Germany, you will discover a rich mosaic of towns, regional foods, colors, sounds, and smells of the rural countryside and historic Black Forest region.
6. Instead of riding on busy boulevards, you can pedal on a network of narrow paved roads built for farm vehicles or on graveled paths through lush green forests.
7. According to historian Daniel T. Rodgers, a central question that divided workers and employers in the nineteenth and early twentieth centuries was how many hours a day the average worker should work.
8. Believing strongly in tradition, the early factory owners thought their workers should follow the old sunrise-to-sunset work schedule of agricultural laborers.
9. This schedule, which meant 14-hour workdays during the summer, could also be maintained during the winter, thanks to the invention of artificial light, which owners rapidly installed in their factories.
10. Spurred on by their desire to create a shorter working day, laborers began to organize into forerunners of today's labor unions and used their collective powers to strive for change.

Pages 755-756

1. The two men defended themselves before the justice of the peace in Bilford; across the river, a similar case was being tried with attorneys and a full jury.
2. She claimed that most teenage shoplifters are never caught; moreover, those who are caught are seldom punished.
3. I admit that I went to the party; I did not, however, enjoy it.
4. I admit that I went to the party, but I did not enjoy it.
5. Although I went to the party, I did not enjoy it.
6. When the party ended, our apartment was in chaos from one end of the living room to the other end of the bedroom; a fine layer of confetti blanketed everything like snow.

7. Within 20 minutes of leaving the trail, we saw an antelope; two elk, one of which had begun to shed the velvet on its antlers; an assortment of squirrels, gophers, and chipmunks; and most startling of all, a large black bear with two cubs.

8. An effective education does not consist of passive rote learning; rather, it consists of active problem solving.

9. Failure to introduce and to use calculators and computers in school creates needless barriers for teachers and learners; furthermore, computer literacy is rapidly becoming a basic skill for the new millennium.

10. We watched the slides of their vacation for what seemed like an eternity—Toledo, Ohio; Columbus, Missouri; Topeka, Kansas; Omaha, Nebraska; and on and on across the continent.

Page 762-763

1. My mother told me that she didn't want me to buy a car until I had a "permanent" part-time job.

2. Jake has his little "quirks," as Molly calls them, but he is still lovable.

3. My adviser recently remarked: "The nervous student who encounters a professor who states, 'Twenty percent of the class usually fails,' must learn to say, 'Not I,' instead of giving up."

4. Did your friend's teacher really say, "Attendance is necessary in this class"?

5. "We are guilty of gross misuse of language," continued the speaker, "whenever we use 'disinterested' to mean 'uninterested.'"

6. "I spent two hours worth of good homework time," complained Thomas' friend Karen, "trying to invent a tongue twister that would make people stand up and shout, 'That's a masterpiece.'"

Using The Allyn & Bacon Guide to Writing *with Non-Native Speakers of English*

Non-native speakers of U.S. English (NNS), also referred to as ESL students, present unique challenges to a composition instructor. At the same time, a class populated by students from diverse cultural backgrounds provides a rich resource for discussion due to the breadth of students' collective experience. This chapter will help you focus on some issues of culture, writing style, and grammar that may set non-native speakers apart from U.S.-raised students.

Characteristics of Non-Native Speakers of English

Although they may have similar problems and difficulties with English composition, non-native speakers are hardly a monolithic group. Students' purposes for living and studying in the U.S. vary greatly and affect their relationships to the English language and to English writing.

Immigrant students who intend to stay in the U.S. permanently are more likely to care about learning U.S. culture and history; they may be more eager to develop the skills involved in participating in public discourse. Foreign students who plan to stay in the U.S. only long enough to earn a degree at a U.S. college are less likely to be interested in many of the culture-saturated, U.S.-specific topics that often serve as the basis for discussion in composition courses. Between those two extremes lie dozens of variations—including students who would be interested in U.S. culture but whose total effort must go into their coursework, and students who perceive themselves to be culturally savvy but whose misinterpretations are mind boggling.

In addition to language issues, students' educational backgrounds will affect their performance in the composition class. Formal education in some educational systems places great priority on memorization of material and little on interpretation. Some students may have been carefully taught never to challenge authority (including a text). Students with such training may have a very difficult time with assignments that require critical reading or formulating their own response to a reading. Developing their own opinions is something they've never been asked to do; in fact, they may have been strongly discouraged from any kind of independent thinking. Moving slowly through the material and exercises in Part I of *The Allyn & Bacon Guide to Writing* is especially important for such students.

Some students are accomplished writers in their own language and may have particular difficulty adjusting their styles to U.S. preferences. Spanish and Russian speakers, for example, have literary traditions that favor long, complex, elegant sentences full of intricate description. These students may find U.S. writing abrupt and artless. Japanese or Vietnamese students may employ symbolism so subtle that you miss it altogether. One strategy for dealing with cultural differences in writing styles is to provide opportunities for students to talk and write about their intentions in their writing, either in class, in personal conferences with you, or in peer review groups with one another.

Cultural norms affect approaches to citation and documentation of sources. Helen Fox's book *Listening to the World* provides an engaging introduction to the frustrations faced by international graduate students struggling to learn American-researched writing conventions. Very often, successful writing strategies that led to praise in different contexts are treated as suspect in the U.S. Listen carefully to what your students tell you about their past experiences with reading and research. Be very clear about the cultural biases that inform disciplinary expectations about citations systems. In Chapter 23, Ramage, Bean, and Johnson explain the conceptual differences between MLA and APA citation systems. Help students understand those conceptual differences, and be open to learning about conceptual differences between you and your non-native students.

The four skills of language use—listening, speaking, reading, and writing—seldom develop at equal rates for language learners. You're likely to encounter students with well-developed oral skills and lower English literacy skills, and students with well-developed reading and writing skills but poorer speaking and listening skills. The disparities for a single student between sound-based and print-based language can be so great that you'll sometimes wonder if you're dealing with the same person. Such disparities, however, are fairly common and are normal during language acquisition. Remember that it can take years for adult students to become fluent in additional languages, and be realistic about the goals you and your students form. Just as spoken accents may never fully disappear, so too will written "accents" linger long after a non-native writer has achieved considerable sophistication in English.

Pedagogical Courtesies

Often, small courtesies can make a tremendous difference in the success of your class. Attention to these concerns takes little effort, yet students are likely to notice and appreciate your consideration in these matters much more than the lesson that you stayed up all night to prepare.

- Ask students what they'd like to be called in class. Give yourself a system for notating the correct pronunciation, whether formal phonetic notation used by linguists, or an informal system you create that uses a combination of rhyme, similar sounds, and creative spelling. You should, for example, be able to remember whether "Kai" is pronounced to rhyme with "hay" or with "high." Some names contain sounds that don't occur naturally in English and are difficult or impossible for monolingual English speakers to pronounce; most students will respect your effort, regardless of your degree of success in producing unfamiliar sounds.

- Give all important information like assignments both orally and in writing (using the board or handouts).

- Make sure that your writing on the board is very legible, and that students have enough time to copy information.

- Be aware that ESL students may require extra time to read in English, so be prepared to help students adjust to in-class reading assignments.

- Be aware of abbreviations; they're not always as transparent as we think.

Topic Selection

Careful topic selection is one of the keys to writing a successful paper. It is important to keep ESL students in mind if you assign the whole class a single paper topic or a short selection of several topics. Obviously, topics that require extensive prior knowledge of U.S. culture or politics are inappropriate when other options are available.

It's also unwise to universalize an assignment with the directive: "Write about X in your country." Such an assignment is problematic because the particular X that you're dealing with may not have a close enough equivalent in all your students' countries. Also, information that is fingertip close for U.S. students may require substantial research for others, creating an imbalance in the work required to complete the assignment. Further, many immigrant students came to the U.S. at an age old enough to have a firm cultural/national identity, but not quite old enough to have a sophisticated grasp of history or politics. Such students are often embarrassed by their inability to speak as knowledgeable adults about their home countries.

In addition, where topics of international relations are concerned, students from countries engaged in disputes or negotiations with the United States may feel that etiquette and diplomacy restrain them from writing candidly. Refugees from war or famine may find it terribly painful to write about their past. Finally, students' strong feelings about their nations of origin sometimes prevent them from hearing any correction or criticism of their work, however gentle, when they write about home. Students may choose to write about their experiences or their home countries, of course, but it should never be required of them.

Peer Reviews

While the first peer review can be daunting for any student, it can be especially discomfiting for those unaccustomed to the American style of blunt, direct speaking. The practice of critical analysis involved in peer reviewing may seem uncomfortably aggressive, rude, or forward. Good preparation, well-defined review questions, and careful selection of group members can all ease the way considerably.

In addition to covering Chapter 17, spend as much class time as possible writing and discussing practice reviews of student papers in the text, using the same questions and format that the actual reviews will have. Have students assess the helpfulness of one another's practice reviews. These preliminary exercises can be done in the same groupings that you will use for the peer reviews in order for group members to get to know one another's work style.

You may want to choose only some of the peer review questions that appear at the ends of every chapter with a writing project, rather than using the entire set each time. A possible in-class exercise could involve students in small groups discussing and choosing which questions might be most valuable to them as writers. Such an exercise would project them into the role of review recipients and help them to envision the usefulness of the review they are about to write.

Sometimes, when reading drafts aloud, students' pronunciation of English may make their writing sound choppy or awkward when it really isn't. Or students' ears for English may not be developed enough to allow them to catch all the problems that a native speaker could. Reading drafts aloud is still a worthwhile practice for such students; try to make sure, though, that students with strong accents are grouped with classmates less likely to make fun of non-native pronunciation.

Students who have studied English abroad are likely to be much more fluent with grammatical terms than their American counterparts, even if their grammatical performance is marked by systematic errors. You will find that many ESL students are able to have conversations about editing with more precision than some American students.

Textbook Comprehension

The following activity is useful for helping students to become more active readers and for developing an atmosphere of cooperation and collaboration among reticent students. It can be used for any section of the text. Try it early in the term and then repeat it for reading assignments that you anticipate will be difficult.

When the reading is assigned, distribute three to five index cards to each student. Assign them to write one question on each index card about anything in the reading that they don't understand or aren't sure about. The questions can be on any of three levels: words/phrases; sentences; paragraphs/concepts. At the next class meeting, bring three boxes or bags labeled with the above divisions and ask students to put their index cards in the appropriate container. Then have student volunteers copy the questions onto the blackboard. This elaborate procedure is worth the extra effort because it ensures anonymity and prevents the potential embarrassment someone may feel by asking a "stupid" question.

Next, explain that by working together, many of the questions can be answered, since each person knows different things. Ask a volunteer scribe to write student-supplied answers on the board. After you're sure that the procedure is working and you sense sufficient focus and momentum, you should leave the room. Explain that you'll check what they've written and answer whatever questions are left when you come back. Then do so. (You don't need to go far—just step into the hall so you can see how on track they stay, and come back as they start to finish.)

Leaving the room is a good way to enhance the student-centeredness of the exercise. When students answer each other's questions, they have an opportunity to notice that their efforts go toward helping one another rather than impressing the teacher. Without the teacher present, students gain a little more practice in collaborative problem solving (which may be helpful during peer reviews), and their discussions may be less inhibited.

Grammatical Correctness

It's clearly unreasonable to expect that an ESL student who begins the semester with serious problems in English grammar will be able to produce grammatically flawless prose by the end of the term. What, then, is a reasonable expectation? Unfortunately, there is no easy answer or tidy formula. What you can do is target one or two specific competencies for each student that can be addressed and improved in the limited time that you have.

When you evaluate the first set of writing assignments, identify the most serious grammatical or style problems for each student. There is an almost infinite set of possible trouble spots, but the most common patterns of grammatical problems for non-native speakers can usually be classified into one of these categories: nouns (and articles), verbs, prepositions, or subordinate phrases or clauses. It is possible to make perceptible progress in any of these areas during a course, and it's reasonable to expect a gradual reduction in targeted errors.

Once you've become acquainted with students' writing, ask them to identify what they think are their most serious grammar problems and what sections of the

Handbook address these problems. Have them hand this in so you can approve their choices or suggest something else. Then have students select one of their drafts—maybe a current rough draft in the revision stage—and follow the Handbook suggestions for making corrections. This will help students apply the grammar lessons provided in the Handbook to their own writing.

The style problems of non-native speakers are generally similar to those of other students and can be treated nearly the same. Note, though, that while native speakers usually can easily distinguish between formal and informal speech, non-native speakers may not yet have developed that distinction. They may need to go a little slower in order to accommodate a smaller repertoire of English style patterns. Also, you may encounter students whose phrasing is grammatically correct, but markedly foreign. Such phrasing, particularly if the grammar is sound, is not likely to change by any deliberate means. You may decide to correct or mark only the elements that are unusual enough to damage the writer's argument or credibility, explain the logic where feasible, and live with the rest. You may also decide to introduce a new phrase or idiom each week, to help students add to their English vocabulary.

The Handbook

Grammar Exercises

Non-native speakers may be more aware of grammatical terms and concepts than native speakers. They've had to consciously learn perfect tenses, gerunds, past participles, and all the things that native speakers never have to think about. If you use the Handbook, especially HB2, for whole-class exercises, you could provide an opportunity for those ESL students who are usually reticent to assume leadership roles to do a little showing off.

Grammar exercises can be tedious and rote. To make them more meaningful, use student-produced sentences and forms as much as possible when you need supplementary material. For example, for the description of basic sentence patterns in Handbook 2, have students take a page from one of their drafts and identify each sentence according to the five sentence types.

Nouns and Articles

Some of the most common ESL grammar error patterns involve incorrect articles or pluralizing of non-count nouns. The simple little English words "a," "an," and "the" are devilishly difficult for students whose native languages don't have equivalent forms (and many languages don't). The chart and explanation of articles at the end of this chapter in the instructor's manual is suitable for use as a transparency master; they can form the basis of a class activity. (Note: if you wish to use this page as a transparency or handout, be sure to cover the answer key at the bottom of the page before duplicating it.) The chart assumes familiarity with the concept of count and non-count nouns. If you're a native English speaker, you've probably never thought about the distinction, but it should be intuitively clear. Your students who received formal instruction in English are almost certainly familiar with the categories, even if they are not quite proficient in the application. Students who acquired English informally may need to begin with an explanation of count/non-count nouns; they can be referred to the books listed below or any good intermediate-level ESL grammar book.

Prepositions

Prepositions can be particularly troublesome for English learners. Because they are often used in very idiomatic or particular ways (why do we say "at the expense of..." but "to the credit of..."?), acquisition is accomplished mainly through lots of practice. The chart at the end of this manual chapter, also suitable as a transparency master or handout, works with one of the more logical patterns for the words "at," "on," and "in," showing gradations in preciseness of placement in space or time. The system works reasonably well, yet there are common exceptions that are difficult to explain, like "She's been at the university for seven years," but "She's been in the biology department for seven years." There is no good way to effectively convey this and the hundreds of other nuances and exceptions to students. Exercises help, but exercises alone will never be enough.

Certainly you should mark incorrect prepositions. Yet since fluency with prepositions is such an advanced stage in language acquisition, it may be unfair to subtract points for an incorrect preposition unless perhaps it is utterly logic defying and repeated often. Keep the emphasis on the positive development of vocabulary by providing regular opportunities for students to learn prepositions in phrases or idioms.

Additional Resources

There are literally hundreds of ESL grammar texts and workbooks currently in print. All have their strengths and weaknesses. Here are two that are very helpful for college-level students and will help you get a sense of how grammar is organized and presented:

Azar, Betty Schrampfer. *Understanding and Using English Grammar.*
Englewood Cliffs, NJ: Prentice Hall, 1989.
    This book has very clear (although terse) explanations and lots of good exercises.

Celce-Murcia, Marianne, and Diane Larsen-Freeman. *The Grammar Book: An ESL/EFL Teacher's Guide*. Rowley, MA: Newbury House, 1983.
    While intended for teachers, advanced students could find this book very helpful.

Fox, Helen. *Listening to the World: Cultural Issues in Academic Writing*. Urbana IL: NCTE, 1994.
    This study of international graduate students offers a nuanced analysis of the ways culture, gender, status, and academic expectations interact.

Articles with Count and Non-Count Nouns

	COUNT		NON-COUNT
	SINGULAR	PLURAL	
a/an	a river an onion	-----	-----
the	the river the onion	the rivers the onions	the traffic the rice
none	-----	rivers onions	traffic rice

Articles with Count and Non-Count Nouns

You'll notice that each category—singular count, plural count, and non-count—has two correct possibilities. This guide will help you choose the correct usage.

1. Do I use <u>a/an</u> or <u>the</u>?

Use <u>a</u> or <u>an</u> when you introduce a singular count noun for the first time to your conversation or writing. All other times you refer to the same object, use <u>the</u>.

Examples:
Nancy put <u>an</u> onion in the salad.
<u>The</u> onion is from her mother's garden.

2. Do I use <u>the</u> or leave out all articles?

Use <u>the</u> to refer to a specific item (or items) that your listeners or audience already know about. Leave out articles to refer generally to all items of that name, or to non-specific items.

Examples:

<u>The</u> rice is almost ready. (Specific rice that is cooking now)
Rice is very expensive. (All rice is expensive right now)

Molly is wearing <u>the</u> earrings you gave her. (Specific earrings)
Molly wears earrings every day. (Not specific earrings)

Using Articles with Count and Non-Count Nouns

Choose the correct way to complete the sentences below. Use a, an, the, or no article.

1. Bennie's roommate has _____ cold.

2. _____ students in Dr. Grahn's class have a lot of homework.

3. I showed her _____ photos in my wallet.

4. Do you like _____ tomatoes in your salad?

5. They agreed that _____ health is very important for _____ athlete.

Answer Key

1. a
2. the
3. the
4. no article
5. no article; an

Using Articles with Count and Non-Count Nouns

Find the incorrect articles (a, an, the, or no article) in the passage below, and correct them. HINT: There are ten errors.

The bus that I rode this afternoon was very crowded. A people were standing in the aisles, and all the seats were full. A woman got on with the large bag of the groceries, and she asked someone to hold it for her. A man put the bag on his lap. After a few blocks, bus turned a corner very fast, and the bag fell on a floor and split open. A bottle broke, and a milk spilled on someone's feet. There was rice on seats and rice on the floor. Oranges went rolling all over the bus, between a legs of all the people. It was so crowded that nobody had room to bend over and pick them up. The woman was yelling, and many people were laughing. No one knew what to do. Bus driver had to stop the bus, and some people got off in order to make room for others to pick up the oranges. I was very glad when I finally got off a bus!

Answer Key:
The bus that I rode this afternoon was very crowded. [No article] People were standing in the aisles, and all the seats were full. A woman got on with a large bag of [no article] groceries, and she asked someone to hold it for her. A man put the bag on his lap. After a few blocks, the bus turned a corner very fast, and the bag fell on the floor and split open. A bottle broke, and [no article] milk spilled on someone's feet. There was rice on the seats and rice on the floor. Oranges went rolling all over the bus, between the legs of all the people. It was so crowded that nobody had room to bend over and pick them up. The woman was yelling, and many people were laughing. No one knew what to do. The bus driver had to stop the bus, and some people got off in order to make room for others to pick up the oranges. I was very glad when I finally got off the bus!

The Logic of Three Prepositions

	SPACE	TIME
at · **(point)** PRECISE PLACEMENT	sitting at her desk staying at home	at 10:30 p.m. at the moment
on _____ **(line)** PLACEMENT ON A LINE	on Palmer Street on my way	on Tuesday on their anniversary
in O **(whole)** PLACEMENT WITHIN A WHOLE	in New Orleans in Guatemala	in October in the evening

Using The Allyn & Bacon Guide to Writing *in Electronic Environments*

Creating recommendations about how to teach *The Allyn & Bacon Guide to Writing* in an electronic environment is a daunting task. Each institution has different resources available. You may be teaching primarily with local network resources. You may have limited access to the Internet. You may have a course management system on your campus that you're very comfortable with, or you may still be exploring how it works. You may have both local network writing tools and full Internet access. You may have the ability to schedule a drop-in lab, or you may teach in a sophisticated networked classroom. You may have the ability to bring a networked station into a traditional classroom. The problem of addressing the range of resources is compounded by the rapid pace of technological change. The tools that are available now may be slightly dated (sometimes even outdated) by the time you read this. The most important thing you can do to prepare yourself and your students to use networked technologies in writing and research is cultivate rhetorical awareness of networked possibilities. If you help students see general possibilities for reading and writing with new technologies, they will be able to adapt to technological environments.

To counter these difficulties, this section of the manual will focus on possibilities that are at the forefront of teaching in electronic environments today, with the hope that as change progresses and institutions upgrade, these activities will be viable for most situations. For additional advice, read Chapter 21 in the textbook, "Evaluating Sources," which contains discussions of evaluating Web resources, and the corresponding discussion of the chapter in this manual. Also, you may wish to consult *An Introduction to Teaching Composition in an Electronic Environment* by Eric Hoffman and Carol Scheidenhelm, available from Allyn & Bacon as a complimentary supplement for instructors who adopt *The Allyn & Bacon Guide to Writing*.

Institutions and Teacher Authority

Institutional Relationships

Whatever your situation, strive to develop solid working relationships with the technical support staff and instructional technology specialists at your institution. Since technology is such an integral part of computer-assisted writing instruction, and most of us have yet to become, or may never want to become, experts with technology, it is crucial that you have institutional resources to provide advice and support. This doesn't mean that learning the technology is not an important part of teaching with computers; it simply means that your learning should be fostered by a healthy relationship with the people at your school who can help you the most and who will also benefit from understanding your goals and interests. Make sure you know what, if any, workshops are available for teachers and students, and make sure you know what number, if any, you can call for technical help when problems arise.

Issues of Authority

One of the largest issues that you will need to tackle as you work in a computer-assisted environment is the issue of teacher authority. Some teachers find that a breakdown of traditional authority takes place in computer classrooms (a shift which is more pleasing to some than others!) and you can use this to help support the textbook's emphasis on student activities and collaboration. Computer environments bring many more voices into classroom situations. The model of the instructor as the disseminator of knowledge is less viable in an electronic classroom; students are easily drawn into their own work with easy access to a network. Pedagogies that take advantage of computer networks, in fact, highlight student-student connections, and seek to actively shift the teacher's role. A networked classroom offers possibilities for making students' work public, and for allowing students easy access to one another during or between classes. This can allow a wider range of student concerns to be presented to the class as a whole.

Additionally, the nature of online environments shifts many pedagogical situations. For instance, in an electronic discussion, messages can be strangely disembodied from their speakers. Although a name is attached to each statement, when messages roll down a screen organized only by the order in which they are sent, there may appear to be little difference between a comment made by the instructor and one put forth by a student; they are equal voices in the conversation. Students who are hesitant to break into a class discussion may find it easier to enter a typed conversation; you may find that different weight is assigned to different contributions in online versus face-to-face discussions.

In many ways, this is a good thing. Not only are messages judged more on their own merits than on the basis of who sends them, but also the relatively egalitarian nature of these forums prompts more students to contribute. As you might guess, however, the shifting of authority can also be a cause for concern for some teachers and students who are accustomed to the traditional workings of traditional classrooms. Electronic conversations may erode into frivolous play, even name-calling and offensive speech. If you're an instructor who has been concerned with authority in a traditional classroom you may balk at the prospect of amplifying this concern by using computers. In any event, you should be aware of "netiquette" issues as students move online, and you should take the same care to orient students to your expectations, and to the rhetorical possibilities, as you would with any other activity.

Two recommendations may ease these potential problems somewhat. First, you will need to reassess your own position on instructor authority. The computer classroom is in many ways a decentered classroom. If you feel you need a strong presence in the classroom in order to teach successfully, you may wish to reconsider teaching with computers. The second recommendation qualifies the first. Although teaching with computers is a form of co-teaming, it isn't entirely divorced from traditional roles. You can work toward striking a balance between the environment that is developing in your class and your own sense of what is appropriate. You don't need to use computers simply because they are there; it's perfectly okay to use non-networked activities within a computer classroom. At the same time, this chapter of the manual encourages you to consider how some traditional activities can be extended and enhanced by access to computers. You will need to work within the uncertain confines of the decentered computer environment, but make that work coincide with your own goals and teaching style.

Local Opportunities

Although much attention has been given to the Internet in recent years, you can pursue a number of activities that will mesh with *The Allyn & Bacon Guide to Writing* in a local classroom setting. If you are teaching using local classroom writing software, or a commercial course management product like WebCT or Blackboard, you can practice important writing skills by having students use the software to archive work, conduct group meetings between class sessions, or post responses to a forum in advance of class meetings.

Real-Time Conversations

One of the greatest benefits of computer-assisted writing instruction is the opportunity to have conversations with classmates using the "chat," "discussion," or "InterChange" function of your local network. These electronic conversations provide your students with opportunities to explore problems and brainstorm ideas. Since messages are freely exchanged in these forums, students feel like equal participants in an evolving conversation. Additionally, messages are composed on the keyboard and sent as text, so not only are students presenting ideas in an ongoing dialogue, they are composing as they do so. Electronic conversations, then, give them a chance to converse within a community and practice their writing.

Note, however, that these forms are geared toward free-flowing exchanges of ideas. Students will be less likely to concern themselves with the sentence-level structure of their writing as they will with the way their thinking fits in with the others in the group. Because participation increases in electronic discussions, students are likely to be exposed to an array of perspectives about the topic. Since these conversations evolve as they take place, students can also see the way that a given position is complicated through the process of electronic dialogue. Statements are often challenged. Students are prompted to clarify their positions, refute those of others and synthesize multiple perspectives. All of these activities will benefit students using *The Allyn & Bacon Guide to Writing* as they work to clarify and articulate their own thinking about an issue.

If your system allows you to archive real-time conversations, you can take transcripts to class for later analysis. If an online discussion started off a unit, you will find that it raised many issues that can be further explored. You can highlight some interesting themes in the discussion and ask students to follow up with the next day's activity, for example.

Local Collaboration

Another possibility afforded by some local networks is the opportunity to collaborate with classmates on writing projects. Some programs offer an electronic whiteboard or other collaborative mechanism. These functions allow a group of students to work on the same page at the same time. Most of them have a text-editing feature and some allow students to draw or exchange graphics. Be aware that the logistics of these mechanisms make them most suitable for small group collaborative projects. Also, don't forget that the mediation of these collaboration tools offers the same benefits and potential pitfalls presented by electronic discussions. There may be an increase in participation and a more fruitful production of ideas, but at the same time students may more easily fall off task or forget the people on the other side of the machine. As with most activities, you should balance using these electronic tools with traditional face-to-face models.

The Allyn & Bacon Guide to Writing and the Internet

By this time, most people have been exposed to some hyperbole about the Internet. The resources on the Internet can be staggering, and the interpersonal connectivity that it affords is unprecedented. Both of these potentials—the ability to use the Net to gather resources and the possibility of joining active discourse communities—make using the Internet a natural fit for teaching with *The Allyn & Bacon Guide to Writing*.

Teaching with the Internet affords excellent opportunities to teach about source evaluation and analysis. Many of the resources that students come across will be hastily written, poorly researched, and extremely biased. On the other hand, the Internet is also a source for up-to-date scientific information, news accounts from a variety of perspectives, and other kinds of data that would be difficult to find in a library. You can use the criteria for evaluating sources in Chapter 21 to help students understand how issues of authority and credibility are important to consider on the Internet.

It is also important for you to guide students in the etiquette expected of them in electronic environments. Just as you would help students prepare for face-to-face interviews with community members, prepare students for their research forays on the Internet. Especially in its conversational forums, the Net can still be very much a place of anarchy. Students may enter contentious conversations about hot topics and be surprised or shocked at the passions evident online. Exposing students to discussions centering on sex, violence, and intolerance may not always be good idea — either from a pedagogical or an institutional perspective. Additionally, many of the participants on the Net are less than ideal conversants for students who are just joining discourse communities. Many "Netizens" have little patience for "newbies." Advise students to "lurk," or observe, any online forum to get a sense of how people contribute before they post themselves.

There are, then, beneficial and detrimental ways of adapting this technology to your writing instruction. Always explore Net territory yourself before assigning a task to students. Not only will it be important for you to map out the logistics of the assignment—logging on to a news server, for instance—but you will also be able to get a sense of how well the task will mesh with your teaching goals. You will also get a first-hand view of how difficult the task will be for students to accomplish, and you will see what directions will be needed. Only use that technology that will support your pedagogical goals. It is often a misconception that computers make tasks easier. They do considerably speed up operations like word processing, but at the same time they complicate activities. Because each technology brings costs in terms of the time requirements and learning investments, use only what you need.

Also, have a backup plan and steel yourself for when things go wrong. Invariably—and especially if you are working with technology that is new to you—a planned 15 minute e-mail tutorial will balloon into a whole class period, or the server will suddenly go down in the middle of your Web demonstration. When such things do happen, take it in stride and be ready to think fast or fall back on some other activities. Keep these general recommendations in mind as you read through the discussion of specific Internet media below.

Research and the World Wide Web

As you teach any of the research components of *The Allyn & Bacon Guide to Writing*, you benefit tremendously from sending students out onto the World Wide Web. The Web has been mushrooming for the past few years and shows no signs of stopping. When students search on the Web, they will be able to easily access files that previously required a fair amount of finger-work to obtain. So, if students have access to the Web, they will be able to bring back abundant information for their research topics. Chapter 21's lessons on learning the rhetoric of the Web will be important for students who need to sift through much irrelevant information.

There are essentially two ways of finding information on the Web. The first method involves browsing for resources. Students can spend some time exploring the available resources on the Web and developing their thinking about an issue. These browsing adventures often begin with an unfocused attitude and can be seen as a means of arriving at a more specific idea of what kind of information students are looking for and what they wish to write about. There is some benefit in randomly surfing the Web, but to make these initial forays more productive, try to steer students toward some of the sites that organize information under broad subject headings. Google is now so dominant that many students are unlikely to have experienced many other search engines. Search engines with large subject categories make useful starting points for students who are beginning the research process. Although things shift rapidly on the Net, here are two useful subject category sites where you can send students:

EINet Galaxy   Yahoo!
http://www.einet.net/   http://www.yahoo.com/

The second method for locating information is by using keyword searches. Just like a search of a library's electronic catalog, Web keyword searches allow you to look for information by combining different terms and querying large databases. This is probably the most useful way of finding specific information on the Net. However, since Web databases are so large, there are a few caveats. First, if your students use a search term that is too broad, their results will be overwhelming. Submitting a query for a term like "politics" will bring back far too many results that cover a broad range of topics. Therefore, when you ask students to articulate their projects as research questions, also point out the need to narrow their search queries. A student who has focused an interest in politics into a research question like "What will be the impact of welfare reform on urban children?" will be able to perform searches looking for terms like "welfare," "children," or "poverty" with appropriate qualifications and terms added to narrow the searches usefully.

You will also want to be sure that students learn the basic strategies for refining searches (connect to the lessons in Chapter 20 on this point). These include combining search terms, searching for specific people, events, or phrases, and excluding items from a search. A query for "children" will be no better than a search for "politics," but combining the terms and searching for information that is related to "children and poverty and welfare" will most likely bring back information relevant to the student's project. You might ask students to develop a list of potential search terms ahead of time as a way of focusing their projects and preparing them for their queries.

Here are some of the most useful keyword search engines:

Google   Lycos
http://www.google.com   http://www.lycos.com

Altavista   WebCrawler
http://www.altavista.com   http://www.webcrawler.com

Infoseek   Yahoo!
http://infoseek.go.com   http://www.yahoo.com

A useful class activity is to ask students to repeat the same Web search in three different search engines and report to the class about how easy it was to use the search engine and what kinds of results each generated. This activity will help students explore the Internet beyond their favorite portal (many students consistently use only one search engine), and it will help students see that repeated searches are useful.

Finally, whether students are browsing to open up ideas and focus their topics, or are looking for specific information, you should stress the importance of tracking their movements. Students should understand the navigational features of most software, including Bookmarks, Favorites, and Hotlists. They should also save and document their discoveries. If your campus has course management software in use, it probably contains a feature that allows students to save files and links in a central resource area; make sure students know how to use these features to create personalized resources accessible from anywhere. Internet services like http://del.icio.us help to create bookmarks that are accessible from anywhere, as well. The process of saving files and documenting their location, as well as the date they were accessed, is crucial because resources on the Net are often in a state of flux. Since sites are constantly being updated and servers go up and down, online information can be quite protean. The best way to be sure that students have access to the resources they need is to stress the importance of saving potential resources as they browse.

E-Mail for Your Class and on the Net

If your plans for implementing technology other than the Web are limited, using e-mail may be one of your most rewarding tools. With e-mail, you will be able to coordinate and tap into the resources provided by your institution. Most institutions now provide students with e-mail accounts; refer your classes to your campus computer consultants so that they can get e-mail accounts set up and receive information about logistics.

Early in the semester, establish the importance of e-mail and spend some time making sure that all students have gotten their accounts and mastered the basics (have a first week homework assignment to send you an e-mail introducing themselves—this ensures that they all know what your address is, and it gives you a way to save their contact information, which can be useful if students prefer to use a non-university address for their correspondence). Once students have e-mail accounts set up and are comfortable handling messages, there are a number of ways you can incorporate e-mail into your curriculum. The first involves simple day-to-day contacts. By using e-mail you can significantly expand the temporal and spatial boundaries of the classroom. Students can contact you whenever a problem or question pops up, but you will have the luxury of responding at your own convenience.

Additionally, you can use e-mail to facilitate the operation of the class. Your institution may have the capacity to set up a mailing list for your class. If so, you can easily send announcements about scheduling, reminders about assignments, or other important information to all the members of the class. If you don't have access to a class mailing list, you can use the "nickname" feature of mail readers to create an alias that will send mail to each member of your class.

A related activity involves using a mailing list to foster discussion of class topics. Students can exchange messages about class materials. and the class as a whole can engage in an ongoing e-mail conversation. If you don't have access to a mailing list for this purpose, again, you can use the nicknames function of mail readers. In this case, however, each member of the class will need to set up a nickname for the other class members, so you may want to copy all of the students' addresses into a file and distribute that for students to use in creating nicknames.

Finally, you can use e-mail to facilitate student-to-student contact. If students are working on collaborative projects, they can set up nicknames for the other members of their group. Again, since the constraints of time and space are mostly overcome by e-mail, coordinating things like project tasks and meetings can be greatly simplified. Students can also use e-mail when working with one another on peer-review exercises. By mailing their work to their reviewers, students not only simplify logistics but also begin an e-mail exchange. When a reviewer responds by pointing out a potential problem, the original student can write back, offering clarification or asking for an explanation. These exchanges can be kept up for the duration of student projects.

All these activities involve mastering some logistics. Getting accounts set up and getting students comfortable with e-mail takes some time. Some students may have trouble subscribing to mailing lists or setting up nicknames. In general, however, investing that time early in the term will be worth the effort.

Documentation of Electronic Sources

As you may imagine, keeping track of this wide variety of Internet resources is no easy task. When resources disappear over time and exist in a number of different forms in different places, developing a workable citation convention is no easy matter. This problem has been compounded by the early attempts of traditional citation guides like the MLA and the APA, which have come up short in accounting for the dynamic nature of the Internet. At the time of this writing, the standards for citing and documenting online sources do not cover all of the media the Internet offers.

In some ways, this grants you some added flexibility. You can settle on something yourself, or you may want to ask your class to develop a standard as a way of thinking about issues of documentation. You can also decide to use the MLA and the APA styles, which do cover some sources. You may also want to use one of the styles that is gaining favor among instructors who use the Internet, such as Janice Walker's adaptation of the MLA style (see site address below).

Whatever you decide, there are some minimum requirements that you should consider. Because resources change so much on the Net, citations should always include a date of access. This may be different from the date of publication, but it is likely to be more helpful to future researchers. Additionally, citations should indicate which of the Internet media the source is taken from. For example, if a source is taken from a newsgroup, the media "Usenet" and the name of the newsgroup should be included. Finally, if the resource can be found at a specific Internet address, for example the URL of a Web page, then that information should also be provided.

Here are some sites where you can get more information on documentation:

The Columbia Guide to Online Style
http://www.columbia.edu/cu/cup/cgos2006/basic.html

MLA and APA Information at Purdue
http://owl.english.purdue.edu/handouts/research/index.html

The International Federation of Library Associations citation guides
http://www.ifla.org/I/training/citation/citing.htm

Conclusion

The electronic classroom and *The Allyn & Bacon Guide to Writing* can enhance each other's use. Problem posing, composing with a purpose, and considering audience and genre are a natural part of most Internet activities. Thinking about various perspectives, focusing projects, and putting ideas through healthy dialectic processes are not just recommendations made in *The Allyn & Bacon Guide to Writing*; they are also the results of most Internet interactions. The Net has ample forums for students to practice exploratory writing as well as any other form of composition that might lie along the open/closed continuum. In short, the Internet, like *The Allyn & Bacon Guide to Writing*, offers your students a number of ways to strengthen their thinking and writing.

Finally, the Internet can invigorate many of your own ideas about teaching and writing. Here are some additional sites where you will find helpful advice:

Longman/Prentice Hall's MyCompLab
http://www.mycomplab.com/

The Allyn & Bacon Guide to Writing Web site
http://www.ablongman.com/ramage5e

The Computer Writing and Research Lab (at the University of Texas at Austin)
http://www.cwrl.utexas.edu

Mark Gellis' The Rhetoric Page at Kettering University
http://www.kettering.edu/~mgellis/GMI_Rhet.htm

An Introduction to
The Allyn & Bacon Guide to Writing
and
The WPA Outcomes Statement for First-Year Composition[1]

This portion of the manual addresses the Council of Writing Program Administrators' *Outcomes Statement for First-Year Writing*. This statement was developed over a four-year period. A core group of college writing teachers from across the country organized meetings, forums, conference presentations, and workshops to involve a wide range of teachers in discussions about what should be taught—and learned—in first-year writing sequences. From the start, the group recognized that standards for student achievement can be set at only the local level. Individual teachers, programs, and departments must work to set standards for their particular contexts. Whether you are planning one section or overseeing a program, this chapter of the manual should help you explore *The Allyn & Bacon Guide to Writing* in relation to the *Outcomes Statement* as you develop standards and expectations appropriate for your setting.

This chapter of the manual presents the full text of the *Outcomes Statement*, followed by commentary on *The Allyn & Bacon Guide to Writing*. Note that the *Outcomes Statement* also appears in the textbook itself, in a chart at the start of Part 2, with correlations to specific chapters in *The Allyn & Bacon Guide to Writing*.

---

1 The *Outcomes Statement* was published as "WPA Outcomes Statement for First-Year Composition," in *Writing Program Administration* 23.1/2 (Fall/Winter 1999): 59–63. It was officially endorsed by the Council of Writing Program Administrators in April 2000. It was also published in Harrington, Susanmarie, Rita Malenczyk, Irv Peckham, Keith Rhodes, and Kathleen Blake Yancey (Steering Committee of the Outcomes Group) "WPA Outcomes Statement for First-Year Composition." *College English* 63.3 (January 2001): 321-325.

The *Outcomes Statement* and additional background are available at the Outcomes Statement Archives, housed at http://comppile.tamucc.edu/WPAoutcomes/index.htm.

More information about the Council of Writing Program Administrators, a national association of college and university faculty with professional responsibilities or interests as directors of writing programs, is available online at http://www.wpacouncil.org.

WPA Outcomes Statement for First-Year Composition

Introduction

This statement describes the common knowledge, skills, and attitudes sought by first-year composition programs in American postsecondary education. To some extent, we seek to regularize what can be expected to be taught in first-year composition; to this end the document is not merely a compilation or summary of what currently takes place. Rather, the following statement articulates what composition teachers nationwide have learned from practice, research, and theory. This document intentionally defines only "outcomes," or types of results, and not "standards," or precise levels of achievement. The setting of standards should be left to specific institutions or specific groups of institutions.

Learning to write is a complex process, both individual and social, that takes place over time with continued practice and informed guidance. Therefore, it is important that teachers, administrators, and a concerned public do not imagine that these outcomes can be taught in reduced or simple ways. Helping students demonstrate these outcomes requires expert understanding of how students actually learn to write. For this reason we expect the primary audience for this document to be well-prepared college writing teachers and college writing program administrators. In some places, we have chosen to write in their professional language. Among such readers, terms such as "rhetorical" and "genre" convey a rich meaning that is not easily simplified. While we have also aimed at writing a document that the general public can understand, in limited cases we have aimed first at communicating effectively with expert writing teachers and writing program administrators.

These statements describe only what we expect to find at the end of first-year composition—at most schools a required general education course or sequence of courses. As writers move beyond first-year composition, their writing abilities do not merely improve. Rather, students' abilities not only diversify along disciplinary and professional lines but also move into whole new levels where expected outcomes expand, multiply, and diverge. For this reason, each statement of outcomes for first-year composition is followed by suggestions for further work that builds on these outcomes.

Rhetorical Knowledge

By the end of first year composition, students should

- ❖ Focus on a purpose
- ❖ Respond to the needs of different audiences
- ❖ Respond appropriately to different kinds of rhetorical situations
- ❖ Use conventions of format and structure appropriate to the rhetorical situation
- ❖ Adopt appropriate voice, tone, and level of formality
- ❖ Understand how genres shape reading and writing
- ❖ Write in several genres

Faculty in all programs and departments can build on this preparation by helping students learn

- ❖ The main features of writing in their fields
- ❖ The main uses of writing in their fields
- ❖ The expectations of readers in their fields

Critical Thinking, Reading, and Writing

By the end of first-year composition, students should

- ❖ Use writing and reading for inquiry, learning, thinking, and communicating
- ❖ Understand a writing assignment as a series of tasks, including finding, evaluating, analyzing, and synthesizing appropriate primary and secondary sources
- ❖ Integrate their own ideas with those of others
- ❖ Understand the relationships among language, knowledge, and power

Faculty in all programs and departments can build on this preparation by helping students learn

- ❖ The uses of writing as a critical thinking method
- ❖ The interactions among critical thinking, critical reading, and writing
- ❖ The relationships among language, knowledge, and power in their fields

Processes

By the end of first-year composition, students should

- ❖ Be aware that it usually takes multiple drafts to create and complete a successful text
- ❖ Develop flexible strategies for generating, revising, editing, and proofreading
- ❖ Understand writing as an open process that permits writers to use later invention and rethinking to revise their work
- ❖ Understand the collaborative and social aspects of writing processes
- ❖ Learn to critique their own and others' works
- ❖ Learn to balance the advantages of relying on others with the responsibility of doing their part
- ❖ Use a variety of technologies to address a range of audiences

Faculty in all programs and departments can build on this preparation by helping students learn

- ❖ To build final results in stages
- ❖ To review work-in-progress in collaborative peer groups for purposes other than editing
- ❖ To save extensive editing for later parts of the writing process
- ❖ To apply the technologies commonly used to research and communicate within their fields

Knowledge of Conventions

By the end of first-year composition, students should

- ❖ Learn common formats for different kinds of texts
- ❖ Develop knowledge of genre conventions ranging from structure and paragraphing to tone and mechanics
- ❖ Practice appropriate means of documenting their work
- ❖ Control such surface features as syntax, grammar, punctuation, and spelling

Faculty in all programs and departments can build on this preparation by helping students learn

- ❖ The conventions of usage, specialized vocabulary, format, and documentation in their fields
- ❖ Strategies through which better control of conventions can be achieved

Introduction to *The Allyn & Bacon Guide to Writing* in relation to *The Outcomes Statement*

The *Outcomes Statement* distinguishes *outcomes*—concepts and abilities that can be generalized across contexts—from *standards*—levels of achievement that need to be specified in relation to the particular curriculum sequence in a department. As you plan your course, you will be making many decisions about the standards that will drive your classroom (which are, in turn, influenced by your program and department standards). You will also make many decisions about the particular activities you and your students will undertake to explore the world of college rhetoric.

The Allyn & Bacon Guide to Writing offers a range of writing projects, many more than can be used in a single semester. The choices you make for your course and section(s) will be governed by your students' past writing experiences, the options open to them later in the curriculum, and your estimates of their needs and abilities. As you select assignments and modify them to fit your local situation, you have many decisions to make about how students complete the assignments. An easy example of this is the fact that most of the writing projects in *The Allyn & Bacon Guide to Writing* allow for, but do not require, outside research. As you select assignments, you will need to make choices about how you and your students will engage with the material. You will also be making choices about the genres available to students, the levels of formality involved in assignments, the relationship between reading and writing, and many other areas. This chapter of the instructor's manual outlines different approaches to those choices. It offers an overview of both *The Allyn & Bacon Guide to Writing* and the *Outcomes Statement* in the hopes that you will spend more time with each, working to build an effective curriculum for your local setting.

The Allyn & Bacon Guide to Writing and Rhetorical Knowledge

The *Outcomes Statement* asks that students address rhetorical knowledge in several dimensions: they should be able to address rhetorical situations by appropriately manipulating purpose and audience in relation to voice, tone, and format; they should write in several genres, and they should understand the relationship between reading and rhetorical knowledge.

Part 1 of *The Allyn & Bacon Guide to Writing*, "A Rhetoric for College Writers," introduces students to the basic elements of rhetoric, including the interaction of purpose, writer, audience, content, form, and meaning. The opening chapter sounds a theme that repeats throughout the text: writers are people who pose problems and ask questions, pursuing those problems and questions in a variety of ways. The kinds of choices that writers make are illustrated with the presentation of open- and closed-form prose, which *The Allyn & Bacon Guide to Writing* presents in the first chapter as a continuum, not a strict opposition. By illustrating forms of writing along a continuum, the text presents writers as active decision-makers. The writing projects embedded in Parts I and II (Chapters 5–16) offer students many chances to make decisions in writing projects as varied as an autobiography, an argument, and an academic research proposal, or a proposed solution to a local political problem. *The Allyn & Bacon Guide to Writing* thus presents the chance to work in varied genres within a consistent rhetorical framework. In each chapter, students are asked to think about audience, purpose, format, language, and structure and how those elements affect content and meaning.

The text's primary task is to help students think and act like writers. *The Allyn & Bacon Guide to Writing* takes students' writing and thinking seriously, and assumes that students can grapple with complexity. Rhetorical scaffolding helps students do this. Chapter 1 asks students to consider writing as problem posing, immediately involving students in activities that address subject-matter problems and rhetorical problems. Issues of audience, purpose, and genre come up from the start.

In Chapter 1, open-form and closed-form prose are depicted as occupying two ends of a continuum along which a variety of choices are possible—as writing moves along the continuum, issues of thesis identification and placement, language, and style are treated differently. Authors Ramage, Bean, and Johnson note that while students are often bothered by teachers' refusal to list simple rules for good writing, "the problem is that different kinds of writing have different criteria for effectiveness, leaving the writer with rhetorical choices rather than with hard-and-fast formulas for success" (page 6). From the start, they confront what students expect—a set of rules and guidelines—without sacrificing rhetorical concerns. *The Allyn & Bacon Guide to Writing* offers a highly structured approach to rhetorical situations, using structure to create spaces for students to wrestle with subject matter and rhetorical questions.

Chapter 1 most directly addresses rhetorical knowledge, arguing that both internal and external forces affect writing. This chapter brings together advice and practice about the writer's motivation, purpose, audience, genre, structure, and style. Like each of the opening chapters, Chapter 1 closes with a brief writing project; this one asks students to "translate" a piece from one writing situation to another. This exercise, which could be used quickly in class or as the basis for an extended assignment, offers students a chance to practice skills that will be valuable in any formal writing assignment. The chapter also contains a variety of "For Writing and Discussion" activities that ask students to engage in creative imitation, analysis, reading, and sharing activities. These short exercises will support class activities that extend students' engagement with the textbook chapters.

Chapter 1, Concept 3, focuses attention first on issues of purpose: *why am I writing this piece? The Allyn & Bacon Guide to Writing* treats purpose as falling into one of several categories: to express, to explore, to explain, to analyze, to persuade, or to entertain. The early focus on purpose invites students to firmly establish their position regarding their writing. Focusing first on purpose reminds students that successful writing demands engagement. However, successful engagement demands analysis of both purpose *and* audience, and *The Allyn & Bacon Guide to Writing* presentation of expressive writing (arguably the type of writing least sensitive to audience considerations) notes that an impulse to share in writing is an impulse to share *with an audience*. Chapter 1 presents audience and purpose as always intertwined—and also notes that purposes can be overlapping and fluid. Exploratory writing, which seeks a thesis, can become informative or analytical writing, and literary purposes can always overlap with other purposes. Chapters 2 and 3 explore the ways the writer's sense of purpose helps guide exploration of subject matter and document design.

The writing projects presented in Part 2 are too numerous to cover in a single semester. As you (and your students) choose among them, you will be making choices about which genres students will work in. The first chapter in this manual offers suggestions about how to pair various chapters in Part 2—for instance, the project on exploratory writing (Chapter 8) can be paired with any of the chapters on persuasion and argument or cause and consequence (Chapter 14–16). Whether the exploratory part of the project is a full-fledged essay, as Chapter 8 offers in the essay project, or developed informal writing that leads to the full essays offered in the later chapters (as is the case in Chapter 13), would depend on the nature of your course. Working with whatever chapters you choose, students will be guided through different structures for different situations, asked to specify their audience and purpose and to shape content appropriately.

The relationship of rhetorical knowledge to reading is addressed most explicitly in Chapter 6, "Reading Rhetorically." This chapter focuses on the ways reading processes, like writing processes, must match goals and situations. Reading strategies will vary based on the readers' own goals—looking for a particular detail? or a thorough understanding?—and the genre they are reading. Reports, for example, with sections and subheadings, lend themselves to previewing and selective reading. Other genres will lead readers to use other strategies. This chapter encourages students to read in multiple drafts, just as they will write in multiple drafts. Each writing project chapter further supports this approach to reading by including short reading selections followed by "Thinking Critically About…." sections, which help students go back into their reading to think again about how the rhetorical situation has affected both writer and reader.

The Allyn & Bacon Guide to Writing and Critical Thinking, Reading, and Writing

The *Outcomes Statement* section on critical thinking, reading, and writing approaches reading and writing as complex and flexible processes for learning as well as communicating. By thinking critically, students will see how writing is an opportunity for them to use their rhetorical activities to develop ideas, situate their own ideas in relationship to others', and understand how language use can confer power on speakers and writers.

A focus on critical thinking, reading, and writing runs throughout *The Allyn & Bacon Guide to Writing*, as the text's Part 1 makes clear. The focus on problem posing means every chapter asks students to begin writing by locating an area of uncertainty—an area of tension, a question without an answer, a problem to be solved. The chapter on exploratory writing (Chapter 8) will be useful for you, even if you don't ask students to complete the writing project there. Similarly, the Learning Log Tasks presented in Chapter 13 can be good models for preparatory tasks for any writing project. Chapter 8 illustrates how writers seek a thesis by considering multiple solutions to problems. The student samples in this chapter are good illustrations of how to approach this work at an introductory level. The samples (one on preventing violence in schools, the other on hospices) show students' processes as they begin to make sense of the issues involved in their projects. The activities built into the "Composing Your Exploratory Essay" section will inspire class activities for virtually any writing project.

The writing projects in Part 2 all use a consistent structure. The project assignment is presented at the start, and short readings by students and professionals are used to model the kind of writing assigned and to model the kinds of critical questions readers should ask about such writing. A section on composing the essay contains various strategies for invention, drafting, and revision; guidelines for peer reviewers close each chapter. This structure illustrates that there are many steps in any writing project, thus helping students to see the tasks involved when writing their essays. The chapters make clear that not all tasks require equal amounts of time and effort for each project or for each writer. *The Allyn & Bacon Guide to Writing* encourages students to reflect on the requirements of their assignment and their rhetorical situation in order to make good choices.

Part 2 opens with two chapters that build an effective bridge between the opening section's focus on rhetoric and *The Allyn & Bacon Guide to Writing*'s writing projects. Chapters 5 and 6 build on the foundation provided in Chapters 1 and 4 to help students understand that seeing and reading are acts of interpretation. Seeing and reading rhetorically involve assigning meaning to particulars, and using particulars to build larger points. These are key steps in the fulfillment of any writing project, and these two chapters will help students work with ways of using writing for inquiry, learning, and thinking. The writing projects embedded in these two chapters make links between writing to learn and writing to communicate.

Most of the writing projects leave open the possibility of research. The issue of finding, evaluating, analyzing, and synthesizing appropriate primary and secondary sources is highlighted in Chapter 13, which leads students through a project dealing with multiple sources in order to develop a strong and informed thesis. These skills are important in the chapters involving argument (Chapters 14–16), as well as Chapter 10, "Analyzing Field Research Data" and Chapter 9, "Writing an Informative Essay or Report." You will find many opportunities to bring readings and research into each chapter, whether you use the readings in the text, ask students to find their own, or make your own class assignments.

Whatever choices you make about the role of independent research in your curriculum, Part 4, "A Rhetorical Guide to Research", will be invaluable. This section offers a rhetorical view of research, inviting students to think about why research can be difficult, and it offers a list of seven essential rhetorical skills for researchers. In Chapter 20, Ramage, Bean, and Johnson stress that strategies for converting an interest into a good research question must take priority over strategies for locating sources. Without a good research *question*, writers will quickly be awash in sources that are difficult to synthesize. Before moving to lessons about how to find sources, the chapter spends considerable time helping students understand what kinds of sources they are likely to encounter. After writers are comfortable with framing research questions, they are ready to move to the lessons on finding information in libraries and databases, and the chapter closes with lessons on evaluating traditional and electronic information. In Chapter 22, "Incorporating Sources into Your Own Texts," students will learn how to incorporate sources into their texts. This chapter stresses the complexity of working with sources, and it highlights the rhetorical choices students make as they decide whether to summarize, quote, or paraphrase sources.

The Allyn & Bacon Guide to Writing does not explicitly address the connections between language, knowledge, and power, but it does build in numerous student and professional writing samples that illustrate how people use writing in many different settings. It thus emphasizes that writing rhetorically means writing effectively—and that leads to success. While *The Allyn & Bacon Guide to Writing* takes care to introduce students to college writing expectations, it also builds bridges between academic and non-academic writing. The writing examples, both student and professional, show writers debating and researching matters of local and national importance. The graphics that head each part of the textbook additionally emphasize that writing is a way to express political concerns and join in the process of creating social change. The text provides many opportunities for you to show students that writing is a means of action, that writing allows not only the successful completion of graded assignments but also successful involvement in public debates. Writing situations referred to throughout the book demonstrate professionals and students engaging with local political and campus issues. The opening discussion of writing as problem posing shows professional writers (both in and out of academe) using writing as a means of professional advancement. Furthermore, the chapter on essay examinations (Chapter 24) offers students another connection between writing and power: advice in their writing textbook about how to take tests in other classes (assuming that most writing classes don't use essay exams).

On the whole, *The Allyn & Bacon Guide to Writing*'s focus on posing questions, solving content problems, taking risks, and seeking to inform and surprise audiences well supports outcomes related to critical thinking, reading, and writing. Each chapter provides careful scaffolding for working through complex issues in a way that should make students more aware of the processes required to move through a series of complex tasks for any assignment.

The Allyn & Bacon Guide to Writing and Processes

The *Outcomes Statement* section on processes challenges students to develop flexible processes that encourage good development of ideas, balancing individual and collaborative work at all stages of essay development. *The Allyn & Bacon Guide to Writing* offers considerable and valuable guidance for the development of writing processes, from the start of the book to the end.

In the first chapter, on writing as problem posing, the text presents writing as an activity that usually occurs over time: writers wrestle with ideas, a process that involves many activities. Chapters 2 and 17 preview a range of exploratory techniques—both written and oral—that will help students pursue ideas and raise more questions. Writing processes are presented not simply as stand-alone activities, but as a vital part of intellectual exploration. Exploratory activities are valued not in themselves, but because of the thinking they encourage—what the text calls "wallowing in complexity." *The Allyn & Bacon Guide to Writing* links exploratory processes to the features of academic disciplines, college professors' expectations, and also individual development. Chapter 2 introduces techniques that will no doubt be familiar to many teachers—idea mapping, freewriting, dialectic discussion, journals, and reading notes. The text pushes students to consider these activities as flexible tools that will encourage invention. Chapter 17 and Chapter 2 are well paired at many points in the semester. Chapter 2 closes with attention to Peter Elbow's "Believing and Doubting Game," an activity that could spur a longer assignment or could be a quick class activity. Exploratory processes are the key to full engagement with writerly problems.

The focus on exploratory activities is supported in each chapter in the writing project section. A section on "Shaping and Drafting" appears in each chapter. The composing strategies suggested reinforce the text's basic theme that writing is about making good decisions. The text takes students seriously, and charges them with the responsibility for making good decisions—and the composing sections offer advice about how to do that. Composing strategies must be used in light of the assignment's purpose, the essay's context, and the readers' expectations. Making those decisions means considering all elements of the rhetorical situation.

Chapter 7, "Writing an Autobiographical Narrative," provides a good example of the presentation of flexible processes. The chapter presents the assignment and its fundamental characteristics, using freewriting techniques early in the chapter as an example of ways to develop early ideas. Structured, complete-the-sentence activities prompt students to consider some of the basic moves involved in this assignment (completing a sentence such as "You think that Maria has led a sheltered life until…" helps students see how a good narrative essay develops tension and contraries). Processes are used to engage students throughout the chapter. The "For Writing and Discussion" boxes offer processes that ask students to brainstorm and then discuss. The processes nurtured here move between individual and group work, and they encourage students to see the early stages of a project as a time to consider many possibilities.

Chapter 13, "Analyzing and Synthesizing Ideas," similarly introduces students to a range of processes, this time addressing reading and writing. A series of Learning Log Tasks are built into the chapter. These tasks move students through careful examination of sources, modeling good reading and note-taking habits.

As each writing project develops, students must make more definitive choices. Guidelines for peer reviewers, included at the end of every writing project chapter, are tailored to the particulars of each project. The structured conversations that result from students' use of the forms direct them to see that writing involves rethinking at later stages, that writers must sometimes go back to the beginning to rethink what's already on the page or screen. And the peer review guidelines urge students to take their roles as readers seriously—each form prods readers to identify potential revisions that would improve the text, but also prods them to explain their readings of the text. The peer review guidelines thus ask students to work with one another, while encouraging writers to take responsibility for their own texts.

Chapter 25, "Assembling a Portfolio and Writing a Reflective Essay," overviews the purpose of reflection (to evaluate, describe, and interpret past experience) and illustrates uses of formal and informal reflection both on the job and in the classroom. This chapter supports single reflection assignments (on one experience or essay) and comprehensive reflection assignments (on a sequence of assignments of a whole semester). This material will be particularly helpful to classes using portfolio assessment, but can be adapted to other assessment situations as well. Moving through Chapter 25 at various points in the semester will provide a forum for students to articulate their evolving notion of their writing processes.

For those looking for further support for peer review, Chapter 17, "Writing as a Problem-Solving Process," contains a thorough discussion of using peer reviews in the revision process. This chapter also stresses the ways that experienced writers revise. This chapter reinforces the support for writers' choices offered in each writing project chapter, noting that every writer makes unique choices that suits the rhetorical occasion. The focus here is on each writer coming to awareness of the kinds of strategies that work in particular situations. Yet the text's respect for each writer's decisions does not mean that it refrains from enforcing practice. Indeed, the chapter is highly structured, guiding students through a process of writing that focuses on exploring a problem, drafting, and returning to consider the problem. "For Writing and Discussion" boxes in this chapter offer various exercises that give students practice in different kinds of revising.

On the whole, the chapters on revising, group work, and each writing project nurture students' development of processes that should enhance students' abilities as problem posers and idea generators.

The Allyn & Bacon Guide to Writing and Conventions

The *Outcomes Statement* section on conventions links conventions (often thought of as surface issues of spelling or usage) to rhetorical concerns, illustrating that conventions are functions of genre, that documentation is a complex task learned over time, and that many issues of grammar and usage are relatively stable in formal writing situations. *The Allyn & Bacon Guide to Writing* supports these outcomes by illustrating how textual features are linked both to genre and audience expectation, and by offering a carefully sequenced Handbook (in the hardcover edition) on editing.

Formats for different kinds of texts are covered in each writing project chapter. While the more open-form projects (such as the autobiographical narrative in Chapter 7) offer students wide choices, the chapters explain that choices are governed by constraints of audience and purpose. The more closed-form projects give overt guidance about structure, helping students to practice different forms (for argument and analysis) while introducing the rhetorical underpinnings of the forms.

Chapter 18, "Composing and Revising Closed-Form Prose," based on reader expectation theory, shows students how to create coherence for readers by linking new information back to old information. By showing why readers comprehend texts more quickly when the introduction forecasts the whole or when points precede particulars, *The Allyn & Bacon Guide to Writing* grounds principles of coherence in the psychology of reading rather than in hardbound rules. In contrast, Chapter 19, "Composing and Revising Open-Form Prose," shows how open-form writers conscientiously violate reader expectations and thus break the conventions of closed-form prose. Together, these chapters invite students to combine conventions in accord with the rhetorical situation.

Documentation is treated extensively in Chapter 23, "Citing, and Documenting Sources," which covers both MLA and APA systems.

The handbook chapters here address the challenge of teaching how to improve conventions by offering exercises that could be assigned to individuals or the class. The material in Part 6, "A Guide to Editing," illustrate the importance of editing (while offering hands-on guidance in learning this key skill). Self-assessment starts off Handbook 1, "Improving Your Editing Skills," enabling students to identify areas to explore in the rest of the handbook. The focus here is on smart editing—looking for problems, understanding how problems are viewed by readers and how they interact with rhetorical concerns, and finding strategies to use in editing and revision. The handbook chapters on sentences, punctuation, usage, and style neatly separate out various editing elements and offer many chances to practice. In conjunction with Chapters 18 and 19, on composing and revising closed- and open-form prose, respectively, the handbook offers a comprehensive approach to revision and editing that address all levels of texts.

The Allyn & Bacon Guide to Writing and Composing in Electronic Environments

As this manual goes to press, the Council of Writing Program Administrators is considering adding a section to *The Outcomes Statement* that addresses writing in electronic environments. *The Allyn & Bacon Guide to Writing* assumes that students are working in electronic environments at least some of the time (and this instructor's manual assumes that teachers are working in electronic environments at least some of the time—see the manual's section on that subject). Chapters 20 and 21 address finding and evaluating electronic sources, and readings throughout the textbook are drawn from a variety of sources, including blogs and Web sites. The discussion of exploratory writing processes and research strategies assumes that students will be working online.